ECONOMIC INEQUALITY
AND HIGHER EDUCATION

ECONOMIC INEQUALITY AND HIGHER EDUCATION

ACCESS, PERSISTENCE, AND SUCCESS

STACY DICKERT-CONLIN AND ROSS RUBENSTEIN
Editors

Russell Sage Foundation • New York

Library of Congress Cataloging-in-Publication Data

Economic inequality and higher education : access, persistence, and success/edited by Stacy Dickert-Conlin and Ross Rubenstein.
   p. cm.
   ISBN 978-0-87154-320-2
   1. Education—Economic aspects—United States. 2. Education, Higher—United States. 3. Income distribution—United States. I. Dickert-Conlin, Stacy. II. Rubenstein, Ross H.
   LC67.62.E254 2007
   379.2'6—dc22

2006038667

RUSSELL SAGE FOUNDATION
112 East 64th Street, New York, New York 10021
10 9 8 7 6 5 4 3 2 1

— Contents —

═ About the Authors ═

Stacy Dickert-Conlin is associate professor in the Department of Economics at Michigan State University.

Ross Rubenstein is associate professor of public administration in the Maxwell School at Syracuse University and is senior research associate in the Center for Policy Research.

Eric P. Bettinger is assistant professor of economics at the Weatherhead School of Management at Case Western Reserve and faculty research fellow in the education program at the National Bureau of Economic Research.

Ronald G. Ehrenberg is Irving M. Ives Professor of Industrial and Labor Relations and Economics at Cornell University, research associate at the National Bureau of Economic Research, and director of the Cornell Higher Education Research Institute (CHERI), which is funded by The Andrew W. Mellon Foundation, the Atlantic Philanthropies (USA) Inc., and the TIAA-CREF Institute.

Dan Goldhaber is research associate professor at the University of Washington's Evans School of Public Affairs and affiliated scholar of the Urban Institute's Education Policy Center.

Robert Haveman is John Bascom Emeritus Professor, Department of Economics and Robert M. La Follette School of Public Affairs, and research affiliate at the Institute for Research on Poverty at the University of Wisconsin–Madison.

Michael Kirst is emeritus professor of education and business administration at Stanford University, is faculty affiliate with the Department of Political Science, and has a courtesy appointment with the Graduate School of Business.

Bridget Terry Long is associate professor of education and economics at Harvard Graduate School of Education.

Amanda Pallais is a graduate student in economics at the Massachusetts Institute of Technology.

Gretchen K. Peri is a consultant with MTG Management Consultants, LLC, a Seattle-based public sector consulting firm.

Amy Ellen Schwartz is professor of public policy, education, and economics at New York University and director of the Institute for Education and Social Policy at New York University's Steinhardt and Wagner Schools.

Sarah E. Turner is associate professor of education and economics at the University of Virginia and a faculty research associate at the National Bureau of Economic Research.

Kathryn Wilson is associate professor of economics at Kent State University.

Chapter 1

Introduction

STACY DICKERT-CONLIN
AND ROSS RUBINSTEIN

I T IS well known that students from less economically privileged families face considerable barriers to entering and completing college.
There is also little doubt that postsecondary education is one of the
most important indicators of future labor market success and therefore
one of the most critical avenues for reducing persistent societal income
inequalities. Estimates suggest that an additional year of education causes
an 8 to 10 percent increase in wages (Card 1999) and the Bureau of Labor
Statistics (2006) reports that a postsecondary degree is necessary for
twelve of the twenty fastest growing occupations. Postsecondary education may have broader social benefits by increasing overall productivity,
increasing civic participation and decreasing criminal activity (Moretti
2004; Haveman and Wolfe 1994). Without access and persistence, higher
education does not necessarily mean success for lower-income individuals and does not spur greater economic opportunity and mobility nor
reduce existing gaps between the "haves" and the "have-nots."

This volume addresses this premise directly. We begin by documenting new and existing evidence on the extent to which income inequality
persists before, during, and after higher education. In chapter 2, Haveman
and Wilson find an almost 50 percentage point gap in college attendance
between students in the top and bottom economic quartiles, measured
either as family income or wealth, with a 35 percentage point difference in
college graduation rates. Even after controlling for other factors that affect
college attendance and persistence, they find that a student from the top
economic quartile is four times more likely than a student from the lowest
quartile to graduate from college.

These dramatic statistics document the extent of inequality in access,
persistence and success in higher education, but in doing so raise a number of critical questions. What are the underlying causes of these economic

disparities? Does it matter only whether a student attends college or also where a student attends college—for example, public versus private, two-year versus four-year? What are the most effective policy levers available to promote access and success in college for students from economically disadvantaged families?

As with most critical and contested public policy issues, the answers to these questions are complex and multidimensional. This volume takes such a broad brush approach to answering them.

The Focus of the Book

This volume is about improving higher education opportunities for students from low-income and low-wealth families, regardless of their race, ethnicity or gender. We proceed under the premise that greater economic inequality results in significant education inequality. There is, of course, a strong link between economic inequality and membership in groups traditionally underrepresented in higher education, such as first-generation college-goers and black and Hispanic students, so indirectly we address these issues. We focus more broadly on economic inequality, however, because it encompasses many students from these groups yet includes other underrepresented groups.

Why does income matter? Affordability may be the most obvious response and may receive the most policy attention. However, though the costs associated with higher education undoubtedly present a serious barrier to college attendance and completion for low-income students, financial aid and college costs cannot and do not account for most of the inequality in higher education processes or outcomes. For instance, income and socioeconomic status are also highly correlated with levels of preparation for college. Preparation comes in the form of information about the higher education process and academic training. Of course, preparation influences the decision to attend college, but also where to attend and the probability of success. Where students attend college is highly segregated by income, with low-income students overrepresented in two-year community colleges and dramatically underrepresented in the selective four-year universities. Unequal opportunities in high school may thus divert low-income students onto less productive paths than those of their higher-income, better-prepared counterparts.

What institutional structures cause inequality and how can they contribute to reducing inequality? The underlying causes of economic inequality in higher education are multifaceted and require a wide-ranging and diverse policy approach. Although higher education institutions are key actors in reducing inequality, they cannot effectively eliminate inequality on their own. Higher education institutions, particularly in the public sector, work in a decentralized and fragmented educational system that includes early childhood, elementary and secondary schools, and an array of executive branch governing boards and legislative committees. Both public and private institutions face additional pressures from multiple external forces, including ranking publications (such as *U.S. News and World Report*), testing companies, alumni, and the media. All these actors have helped to create current cycles of inequality and must play a role in reducing inequality in the future.

Within the higher education sector, reducing inequality will require a concerted effort among all types of institutions. Elite institutions, detailed in chapter 6, often receive the most attention for their efforts, but both space and resource constraints prevent them from significantly reducing inequality on their own. The substantial resource commitment by the elites may play an important role in setting an agenda for higher education institutions, but public and private, two-year and four-year institutions at all levels of selectivity are key if large numbers of traditionally underserved students are to be reached.

Under this framework, we convened a conference in September 2005 to focus on the current state of our knowledge about economic inequalities in higher education and the policy levers to address them. The goal was not to assign blame but to examine the extent and causes of these inequalities, and to identify promising solutions to address them. Toward that end, we brought together many of the country's top experts to discuss ways to improve access, persistence, and success for all students, regardless of economic circumstances. We sought to focus on issues often overlooked in current policy debates. The authors each examined a specific topic affecting access and success in higher education for students from low-income families. They have succeeded in producing a series of thought-provoking and insightful chapters that shed considerable light on the past, present, and future conditions of inequality in higher education. The authors document the extent of current problems and future prospects objectively, but the chapters also provide considerable hope that we can reduce these persistent gaps.

Overview of Chapters

In chapter 2, Robert Haveman and Kathryn Wilson set the stage for the discussion by documenting the extent to which growing income and wealth disparities in society widen disparities in higher education attainment. Their approach is novel because it follows families over more than twenty years of data to consistently show that, conditional on individual, family, and neighborhood characteristics, family income and wealth remain highly correlated with educational attainment, particularly college attendance and graduation. They estimate that the increase in U.S. income inequality over the past three decades has decreased the level—and increased the inequality—in educational attainment between those with high and low incomes. Widening disparities in higher education attainment, in turn, exacerbate income and wealth disparities, perpetuating a vicious and difficult-to-break cycle. They conclude boldly, that "contrary to the oft-stated belief in the leveling effect of higher education, because lower-income individuals are much less likely to secure higher education, the nation's colleges and universities appear to be an integral part of the process whereby family economic status is passed along from generation to generation."

In chapter 3, Michael Kirst begins to zero in on the causes of economic inequality within higher education. Specifically, he sheds light on how students' elementary and secondary school experiences allow them to arrive at the gates of higher education with dramatic inequalities. He introduces two themes that emerge throughout the volume: academic preparation for college and the role of broad-access postsecondary institutions, either nonselective four-year schools or open enrollment community colleges. Kirst challenges us to focus on the large group of lower-income students who attend broad-access postsecondary institutions and for whom the most relevant issue is not gaining admission to college, but succeeding once they have enrolled. He demonstrates that students at such institutions often arrive at college academically ill-prepared to complete college-level work and with little knowledge of college requirements, procedures, or expectations. Kirst argues that "the better high school students are becoming more closely aligned with higher education, but the weaker students are more disconnected." The increasing K–12 emphasis on standards and testing has revealed this disjuncture in stark relief because there is typically little alignment between the content of state-mandated secondary school assessments and the content of postsecondary placement exams. After documenting the causes and extent of the disjuncture, Kirst offers constructive recommendations for bringing K–12 and higher education into greater alignment to create a more seamless K–16 education system and improve opportunities for postsecondary success for students from low-income families.

Chapter 4, by Eric Bettinger and Bridget Long, and chapter 5, by Dan Goldhaber and Gretchen K. Peri, follow and continue to highlight the themes of preparation and the role of broad-access colleges. Bettinger and Long present important new evidence on one of the most common—and controversial—ways that higher education institutions, particularly in the public sector, address the needs of underprepared students: required enrollment in remedial or developmental coursework. They report that nationally in 2001 nearly one in three first-year students enrolled in remedial courses in mathematics, reading, and writing. Not surprisingly, remediation is more likely for black and Hispanic students and for students who report family incomes in the lowest income groups. Policies regarding remediation vary considerably within and across state educational systems, though, and only a few convincing studies identify their causal effects. Measuring causal effects of remediation is, of course, extremely challenging because students placed in remediation are relatively ill prepared for college and, therefore, have lower success rates than their counterparts.

Bettinger and Long, however, provide promising evidence from a unique Ohio data set that, for a subset of students, remediation improves outcomes such as college retention and graduation. At the same time, more systematic knowledge regarding the effectiveness of different methods of remediation and developmental coursework is needed. Noting the burden that remediation policies often place on community colleges, Bettinger and Long reiterate Kirst's sentiment that "the need for remediation is rooted in the K–12 system, and that reform efforts may therefore be better served by focusing on this level of education."

Dan Goldhaber and Gretchen K. Peri follow in chapter 5 with a more in-depth examination of community colleges—the institutions that have traditionally served as the gateway to higher education for most low-income students. They report that in 2002 almost 45 percent of postsecondary undergraduates students were enrolled in community colleges, with low-income students disproportionately represented. Goldhaber and Peri conclude that though academic performance, parental involvement, and policy[1] play a role in the decision to attend community colleges rather than four-year institutions, cost is the paramount factor. Because the choice of community college rather than four-year college attendance is highly correlated with income, assessing the role of community colleges in exacerbating or reducing inequality in higher education is not straightforward. On one hand, the authors point out that the lower cost of community college may provide opportunities that students would not otherwise have due to the high costs of four-year institutions—a democratization effect. However, choosing a community college may divert students from their ultimate goal of completing a four-year college by slowing their educational process down. Goldhaber and K. Peri point to at least two sets of studies that conclude that community colleges both divert and democratize, but that democratization dominates, suggesting that community colleges play a role in decreasing inequality. They conclude by calling for more research on how the links between community colleges and public four-year institutions influence the transition between the two.

At the other end of the higher education landscape are elite institutions. Amanda Pallais and Sarah Turner argue in chapter 6 that because these institutions are "perceived to be important stepping stones to professional and leadership positions, the representation of students from a broad range of socioeconomic backgrounds at these institutions is a significant demonstration of commitment to opportunity and intergenerational mobility." They examine recent efforts by the nation's elite institutions to recruit and retain more lower-income students, who have historically been vastly underrepresented in the nation's most prestigious colleges and universities. After identifying a number of barriers that lower-income students face—costs, lower academic achievement levels, inadequate information—they review recent initiatives intended to help students overcome them.

The initiatives at elite private universities have, for the most part, focused on financial aid, stressing transparency, reduced reliance on loans, and an emphasis on financial need rather than merit. Given the lower sticker and net prices of public flagship universities and the greater financial constraints they have faced in recent years, it is not surprising that their efforts have often stressed outreach, mentoring, and counseling efforts more than financial aid. Initial evidence from these initiatives is promising: a number of participating universities have seen substantial increases in the matriculation of students from lower-income families. Pallais and Turner argue, however, that it is too early to declare these programs unequivocal successes. Evaluations of the mechanisms by which these programs increase matriculation and longer-term study of student success after enrollment are critical. At the same time, such evaluation is not straightforward. Pallais and Turner note both the difficulty of isolating the impact of specific components within a multipronged initiative and the danger that evaluations of individual programs might fail to recognize potential reshuffling (rather than enlarging) of the pool of lower-income students at selective institutions. They conclude that, given the high costs and high stakes of such programs, rigorous evaluation is essential.

Examination of inequality in higher education is incomplete without a discussion of perhaps the most oft-cited factor potentially exacerbating higher education inequalities–the cost of attendance. The notion that high and rapidly escalating tuition is a primary factor reducing opportunities for lower-income and, increasingly, middle-income students, has gained considerable attention in recent years. Amy Ellen Schwartz brings data to bear on this issue in chapter 7 by examining trends in college costs, focusing not only on sticker prices (published tuition and fees) but on also on net prices (tuition and fees less financial aid). Surprisingly, perhaps, she concludes that "the news about college costs is not all bad." As most casual observers would suspect, she finds fairly dramatic increases in sticker prices between 1991 and 2005, even accounting for inflation. For lower-income students, however, the net price may be a more important indicator of affordability than sticker price. Using College Board data, Schwartz reports that as net prices rose among private institutions, they fell among public two-year and four-year schools. In recent years, two-year colleges have actually reported negative average net prices, reflecting average financial aid awards higher than average tuition and fees (not including room and board and, more important, opportunity costs associated with college attendance). Schwartz then takes this analysis one step further by also examining college prices adjusted for aid and changes in quality measures (such as faculty and student characteristics and campus life indicators). Although data are available only for the 1990s, the analyses suggest that quality improvements somewhat mitigated price increases during the period, particularly in the public sector. To the extent that students are sensitive to these price changes, recent trends may serve to sort lower-income students increasingly into public and, especially, two-year institutions. Borrowing a concept from elementary and secondary education finance, Schwartz discusses the importance, then, of ensuring adequate educational opportunities at higher education institutions, particularly those public four-year and two-year institutions that lower-income students are most likely to attend.

The concluding chapter, by Ron Ehrenberg, provides an overview of the barriers facing low-income students, the competing pressures buffeting higher education institutions, and thoughts on what future efforts to reduce inequality in higher education may hold. His review starts with a number of negative trends and their potential impact on students from low-income families, particularly those affecting public universities. Echoing Amy Schwartz's analysis, he points to stagnant public financial support and smaller tuition increases (in real dollars) relative to private sector institutions. These trends have left public institutions further behind private institutions on a number of important input measures, such as faculty salaries, average class sizes and use of full-time faculty. At the same time, financial aid policy in both public and private universities has increasingly moved away from the need-based aid (both internal and external) most likely to benefit economically disadvantaged students toward the merit-based aid more likely to benefit middle and upper income students. The jury is still out on the effectiveness of the initiatives Pallais and Turner describe in chapter 6, but Ehrenberg suggests considerable potential for improving opportunities for low-income students, particularly at some of the more selective public and private institutions. He aptly concludes with both a look to the future and thoughts on what can be done to improve access and success for lower-income students. Much like the other authors in this volume, he focuses on ways to align institutional incentives with the goal of improving the representation of lower-income students.

Policy Agenda and Recommendations

The high level of private and social benefits associated with higher education justifies strong policy interventions. The chapters in this volume contain a wealth of advice, recommendations and action items focused on improving opportunities for students from low-income families to enroll and succeed in higher education. Below we draw on the collective expertise of the contributors to set out a policy agenda for reducing inequality in higher education.

Improving Student Preparation

The chapters in this volume are consistent in demonstrating that inequalities in higher education reflect inequalities in family resources and educational opportunities that begin long before students reach the transition from high school to college. As Haveman and Wilson show, low-income students are less likely to graduate from high school, to attend college (even contingent on graduating high school), and to graduate from college (even contingent on attending college). The Kirst and the Bettinger and Long chapters describe the disconnect between expectations for students in high school and in college. If students are not prepared for college, no amount of financial aid will help them succeed. Inadequate preparation may be especially prevalent among low-income students who are more likely to attend schools with too few resources. Improving student preparation will not be easy and requires breaking down the traditional barriers that have separated elementary and secondary education from higher education. A multipronged effort could include:

Reducing the Disjuncture Between High School and College Assessments Although testing is prevalent at both college and secondary school, there is rarely alignment between the content and standards of the tests given at each level. This allows students to pass high school exit exams yet find themselves unprepared for basic college work (as defined by the colleges) and required to begin their college careers in noncredit remedial courses. Reducing this disjuncture would entail two major components. First would be greater cooperation between secondary and higher education officials in the development of the tests used for diagnostic and accountability purposes, and efforts to align both content and standards. Second, though we are reluctant to call for even more high school testing, students should be allowed and encouraged to take college placement exams before enrolling in college. Such early testing, for diagnostic purposes only, could allow schools and students to focus on problem areas well before students begin their college careers. The advanced placement (AP) program is an existing model of links between high schools and colleges that might effectively be extended to a broader base.

Improving Governance Linkages Between K–12 and Higher Education   Addressing disjunctures between education sectors is made more difficult by the "silos" in which each typically operates. Without unified statewide leadership and governance structures there may be little hope of getting all of the many moving parts of state educational systems working together. At the very least, each state must have structures and forums in place that enable leaders of each sector to communicate and plan collectively. More formal coordination, such as a statewide governing board with responsibility for elementary and secondary schools, community colleges, and four-year institutions, is a promising model.

Improving Linkages Between Two-Year and Four-Year Institutions   The Goldhaber and Peri chapter highlights wide variations in state policies to promote smooth transitions between community colleges and four-year institutions, despite the role community colleges often play as a critical starting point for students from low-income families. State efforts should focus on providing incentives for greater coordination and improved articulation between two-year and four-year public institutions. Some improvements, such as common course numberings and the governance changes just recommended, can be implemented directly by state policy makers. In other cases, incentives for greater cooperation may be the most effective policy levers. For example, state funding systems could provide financial incentives for four-year institutions to enroll and graduate transfers from two-year institutions. These incentives could also be tied to process improvements, such as the co-admission agreements that Goldhaber and Peri describe. Although financial incentives are not without cost, policies that improve the efficiency of transfers and help more students to eventually graduate from four-year institutions could easily recoup this investment.

Improving Resources in Secondary Schools   Students from low-income and first-generation college-going households need better information on the pathways to college, including college opportunities, standards, requirements and culture. Such information is now largely the responsibility of high school guidance counselors. Resources, however, are increasingly stretched thin, particularly in rural and urban districts. Because testing requirements are at the same time taking up an increasingly large share of teachers' and administrators' time, accurate and timely guidance services for students often become a low priority. Student preparation for college includes knowing which courses to take in high school, selecting schools to which to apply, and navigating the complex application and financial aid mazes. It is unrealistic to expect guidance counselors—who may be responsible for up to 700 students, as Bettinger and Long note—to provide the kind of high-quality counseling services that students from low-income families often need. A federal commitment to funding and training guidance counselors may be required, perhaps through generous matching grants for hiring and training counselors, targeted at poorer school districts. The call for higher resources need not stop in secondary schools, of course. As Haveman and Wilson show, income inequality over an entire childhood has long-term consequences. A commitment to early childhood education and enhanced resources for elementary school students could also help to reduce inequalities in preparation for higher education.

Providing Better Financial Aid Information

Researchers, policy makers, and the public have focused considerable attention on college costs, including both the rising sticker price of higher education and the distribution of financial aid. Several of the chapters in this volume address these issues. We conclude that creating a more stream-lined and transparent system of distributing financial aid is necessary if need-based aid is to effectively increase opportunities for students from low-income families. As Pallais and Turner demonstrate in chapter 6 and Schwartz in chapter 7, the net price of college often approaches zero for low-income students, particularly at community colleges and a small num-ber of elite institutions. Students and their families, though, may be largely unaware of the true cost of attending college during the critical years of preparation for and application to college. Providing better information can include several components:

Simplify Financial Aid Forms and Processes   Applying for financial aid requires filing the lengthy and complex Free Application for Federal Stu-dent Aid (FAFSA) and, potentially, providing additional information and documentation required by individual schools. Simplifying this process, perhaps by relying primarily on existing tax data (Dynarski and Scott-Clayton 2006) or providing a short version of the FAFSA for families with limited income and assets, could help demystify the financial aid process.

Provide Financial Aid Information Earlier   Many able students may not even apply to college, discouraged by the perceived high cost of attendance and the assumption that college is unaffordable. Even with a simplified finan-cial aid process, students and their families need information on the actual costs of college attendance early in the process. Families should be permit-ted and encouraged to fill out financial aid forms while students are in the middle or early high school grades. Although changes in financial aid poli-cies or family economic status may change actual aid awards when a stu-dent reaches college age, it is critical that students and families learn that college is affordable while they are still able to respond to the incentive of college attendance.

Reduce the Uncertainty of Financial Aid Awards   The growth of state merit aid programs over the past decade has largely benefited students from middle- and upper-income families, who are more likely to attend college and to meet merit-based eligibility requirements (Rubenstein and Scafidi 2002). A strength of these programs, however, is that eligi-bility requirements are simple, clear and well-known, and evidence suggests that students respond to the incentive of free college tuition (Henry and Rubenstein 2002). Although eligibility tied to grades or standardized test scores may do little to improve opportunities for low-income students, aid tied to other criteria, such as family income and high school course-taking, could provide simple and clear incentives to increase the pool of well-prepared low-income students interested in college. Such programs would likely need to offer guaranteed benefit levels—for example, full-tuition at public universities—along with clear eligibility criteria.

Improving Quality and Incentives in Higher Education

Much of our discussion thus far has focused on whether students go to college, but an equally important concern is where they go to college. As Kirst, Goldhaber and Peri, and Schwartz all note, the majority of students do not begin their higher education careers at selective four-year institutions but rather at less selective, often open enrollment institutions, many of which are two-year community colleges. The efforts of the selective universities, as described by Pallais and Turner, are important in setting agendas and focusing attention on the underrepresentation of lower-income students in higher education, but these institutions would hardly dent the underrepresentation even if they were to enroll only students from low-income families. Clearly, efforts to ensure that all students in higher education receive a quality education must look beyond the small set of elite schools and toward the institutions that most students will attend. Proposals to enhance quality and opportunities in these institutions include:

A Renewed Commitment to Funding Public Higher Education   The Ehrenberg chapter documents the declining state support for public higher education, with financial aid increasingly focused on merit rather than need. Schwartz's chapter, though, offers some cause for hope, finding net price decreases in the public sector, as well as quality increases during the 1990s. It is critical that students from lower-income families not simply have access to higher education per se, but have access to a high quality education and the services they require. Experience in K–12 education suggests that these students may require not only comparable but also additional resources if they are to have an equal opportunity for success (Duncombe and Yinger 2005). Such resources could include improved remedial courses, smaller classes, and help with study skills and time management. Policy makers at the state and federal levels must commit to ensuring that public comprehensive and broad-access institutions have the operating and capital resources needed to provide high quality education and services for students from low-income families.

Changing Institutional Incentives   As Ehrenberg notes, there is little doubt that higher education institutions respond to incentives, such as those embedded in the *U.S. News and World Report*'s rankings, among others. These rankings though, which place a high premium on factors such as student SAT scores and admission rates, tend to disadvantage schools seeking to serve a diverse student body. The policy lever here is unclear; policy makers have no control over rankings produced by private companies. Pressure for reform from within and outside the higher education community, though, has led *U.S. News* to report data on Pell Grant recipients, though not in the rankings themselves. States, which have been quite active in promoting accountability in K–12 education, could play a key role. At one end of the spectrum, states could simply collect data and report on the enrollment and success of lower-income students through widely disseminated institutional report cards similar to the school report cards begun in the 1990s. At the other end, states could offer rewards—such as increased funding and freedom from some regulations and oversight—or impose sanctions, based on institutions' success at enrolling and graduating increasing numbers of students from low-income families.

The authors in this volume add significantly to our understanding of the dynamics of economic inequality in higher education. At the same time, they—like all good researchers—also set out an ambitious research agenda to further our knowledge of causes, effects, and ways to reduce inequality. For example, what policies work best to mitigate the intergenerational transmission of inequality? How do college costs and perceptions of college costs affect enrollment decisions across income groups? What types of developmental courses are most effective for promoting success among lower-income students? What are the long-range effects of recent initiatives and programs aimed at reducing inequalities? What are the costs and benefits of these and other programs? As a practical matter, can we improve the available data on students that would allow us to identify causal links between policies and outcomes? These are but a few of the many questions raised in the chapters that follow. It is imperative that we expand efforts to rigorously study the effects of higher education policies and programs to better understand whether and how they work, what unintended negative consequences they may produce, and how to get the incentives right. The chapters in this volume provide much evidence and cause for hope, but also show that there is much work left to be done.

Acknowledgments

This book is the product of many people's long hours and efforts. We thank the discussants for the Syracuse University conference: Tim Smeeding of Syracuse University, Charles Clotfelter of Duke University, Michael McPherson of the Spencer Foundation, Ann Marcus of New York University, Vincent Tinto of Syracuse University, and Debbie Sydow of Onondaga Community College. We also thank the participants in the conference's practitioner roundtable: David C. Smith and Donald Saleh of Syracuse University and Myra Smith of the College Board. The chapters in this volume have benefited greatly from their keen insights and generous comments. We would particularly like to acknowledge Tim Smeeding, who first proposed the idea for this conference, helped us to conceptualize it and frame the issues, and was instrumental in keeping us on task and on time.

The Russell Sage Foundation provided generous support for the conference and preparation of this volume. We benefited tremendously not only from their financial assistance but also Eric Wanner, Akasemi Newsome, and an anonymous referee's insightful suggestions and patience in helping to plan the conference. Two anonymous referees provided detailed feedback on an early version of the volume that greatly improved the outcome. We also thank the Center for Policy Research in Syracuse University's Maxwell School and Syracuse University's Office of Enrollment Management for financial support.

The conference and volume would not have become a reality without the hard work of the staff in the Center for Policy Research. Seth Racine provided excellent research assistance. Martha Bonney, Mary Santy, Karen Cimilluca, and Peggy Austin provided invaluable logistical support. We are especially indebted to Kelly Bogart, whose organizational skills, hard work, and good humor made the conference and volume possible.

Endnote

1. This includes states that require developmental coursework and remediation training to be provided by community colleges rather than four-year colleges.

References

Card, David. 1999. "The Causal Effect of Education on Earnings." In *Handbook of Labor Economics*, edited by Orley Ashenfelder and David Card. New York: Elsevier Science.

Duncombe, William, and John Yinger. 2005. "How Much More Does a Disadvantaged Student Cost?" *Economics of Education Review* 24(5)(October): 513–32.

Dynarski, Susan, and Judith Scott-Clayton. 2006. "The Cost of Complexity in Federal Student Aid: Lessons from Optimal Tax Theory and Behavioral Economics." *National Tax Journal* LIX(2): 319–56.

Haveman, Robert, and Barbara Wolfe. 1994. *Succeeding Generations: On the Effects of Investments in Children*. New York: Russell Sage Foundation.

Henry, Gary T., and Ross Rubenstein. 2002. "Paying for Grades: Impacts of Merit-Based Financial Aid on Educational Quality." *Journal of Policy Analysis and Management* 21(1): 93–109.

Moretti, Enrico. 2004. "Estimating the Social Return to Higher Education: Evidence From Longitudinal and Repeated Cross-Sectional Data." *Journal of Econometrics* 121(1–2): 175–212.

Rubenstein, Ross, and Benjamin Scafidi. 2002. "Who Pays and Who Benefits? Examining the Distributional Consequences of the Georgia Lottery for Education." *National Tax Journal* 55(2): 223–38.

U.S. Bureau of Labor Statistics. 2006. *2006/07 Occupational Outlook Handbook*. Washington: U.S. Bureau of Labor Statistics. http://www.bls.gov/oco/oco2003.htm.

— Part I —

External Factors

Chapter 2

Access, Matriculation, and Graduation

ROBERT HAVEMAN AND KATHRYN WILSON

T HE NATION'S higher education system—its colleges and universities—serve several functions. They house the nation's most highly trained research teams in the nation's most advanced facilities. They are the source of much of the nation's technological advance, regardless of field or discipline. They offer training and education to the nation's youth. In this last role, colleges and universities create a skilled and knowledgeable work force—human capital—and thereby advance the nation's productivity.

Were these institutions an integral part of the market economy, they would sell their educational services to those families with young people who are willing to pay the most for them. And, as with boats, cars, and houses, the families with the greatest economic resources and the strongest tastes for advanced schooling for their children would purchase these services. Young people whose parents have high income and wealth and who (for whatever reason) value education highly would tend to populate the nation's colleges and universities. The gains from education—higher incomes, prestigious occupations, economic, social, and political status—would flow to those whose families already have these characteristics. Colleges and universities would become instruments for the intergenerational perpetuation of riches, prestige, and power.

However, historically, American universities and colleges have sought to avoid this market-oriented niche. Because of the unmarketed, external, and public goods effects of college-trained youth,[1] third parties have also been given a stake in who is educated. As a result, collective action—often in the form of public policies—supplements private demands and choices. Moreover, higher education leaders view their institutions as more than the producers of services to be purchased by the highest bidder. Indeed, historically these leaders have seen the role of colleges and universities to identify the highest potential and most able of the nation's youth, and to advance their knowledge and training. In this view, colleges and universities are institutions that produce educational services to be allocated according to merit and not to market. An extreme form of this view sees colleges and universities as merit-oriented filters, working to counter the effects of the market and to promote intergenerational mobility.

Hence, though colleges and universities charge tuitions, how their services are allocated is also influenced by a variety of public interventions. Some institutions are public: they receive public subsidies and set prices and ration services to meet collective goals, often expressed through the political system. These, and private ones as well, gain from publicly supported student subsidies, some of which are targeted to families with low incomes and limited ability to pay, and others are allocated to the students with the highest chances of success. Publicly subsidized loans are also available directly to students, their terms sometimes based on family economic resources.

One important question concerns the extent to which colleges and universities have succeeded in their desire to promote merit, foster economic mobility, and serve youth from less advantaged families.

Whence Cometh College Students?

A number of scholars and government researchers have attempted to characterize the economic backgrounds of the population of young people with various levels of education—the population to whom the educational services of colleges and universities have been allocated.

A National View

Table 2.1 presents a good overview of the trends over time in terms of who goes to college (Ellwood and Kane 2000). It says little, however, about total years of completed schooling or college graduation. For the earlier cohort (the classes of 1980 through 1982), the overall rate of college-going is 80 percent for youths from the top quartile of families (ranked by income), versus 57 percent for their bottom quartile counterparts.[2] Youths from the poorest families were concentrated in vocational and technical institutions, and those from the richest tended to enroll in four-year colleges. Over the ten years shown in the table, the overall enrollment rate rose by 7 percentage points. Whereas youths from the highest income families saw an increase of 10 percentage points, those from the lowest income families saw one of only 3 percentage points. In terms of attendance at four-year colleges, the gap between the highest and the lowest income youths increased far more than the overall gap in college going. The percentage of youths from the bottom quartile of families who enrolled in four-year colleges fell slightly (from 29 to 28 percent). That for youths

Table 2.1   Students Who Enroll in Colleges and Universities within
Twenty Months after Graduation from High School

	Total	Vocational-Technical	Two-Year College	Four-Year College
Class of 1980–1982				
Bottom quartile	57	12	16	29
Top quartile	80	6	19	55
Total	68	10	19	39
Class of 1992				
Bottom quartile	60	10	22	28
Top quartile	90	5	19	66
Total	75	7	23	45

Source: Ellwood and Kane (2000).

Table 2.2   Socioeconomic Status of Entering Classes by College Selectivity

	SES Quartiles		Total
	Bottom	Top	
Tier 1	3	74	100
Tier 2	7	46	100
Tier 3	10	35	100
Tier 4	16	35	100
Community colleges	21	22	100

Source: Carnevale and Rose (2004).

from the highest income families rose substantially (from 55 to 66 percent). The gap between the two groups increased markedly (from 26 percentage points to 38 percentage points).[3]

These patterns are consistent with tabulations by Anthony Carnevale and Stephen Rose (2004), who analyzed detailed data from the High School and Beyond study and the National Education Longitudinal Study of 1988. They divided all colleges and universities into four quality categories based on the Barron index, and all families into four socioeconomic status (SES) categories based on their income, parental education, and occupation. Their results are summarized in table 2.2. For the 146 top tier colleges and universities, which account for about 10 percent of all college students, 74 percent of the entering class is from the highest SES quartile and only 3 percent from the lowest. For the 253 colleges in the second tier, accounting for about 18 percent of all college students, the percentages are 46 (highest SES) and 7 (lowest SES). Only for community colleges is the composition of entering students by family socioeconomic status similar to that of all youths of college age.

Table 2.3   Percent of Students from the 1988 Eighth Grade Cohort

	Bottom Quartile	Top Quartile	Gap
Graduated high school	80	97	17
Took the SAT	32	68	36
SAT score > 1200	2	15	13
Given SAT = 5-600, go to college	87	97	10
Given SAT = 5-600, attended most expensive colleges	20	52	32
Given starting a four-year college, graduation from college	44	78	34

Source: Bowen, Kurzweil, and Tobin (2005).

Table 2.3 contains estimates found in the recent volume by William Bowen, Martin Kurzweil, and Eugene Tobin (2005) based on the class of eighth graders in 1988, that is, those who would have graduated high school by 1993. These statistics suggest that the concentration of youths from high-income families in America's colleges and universities directly reflects patterns in the preparedness of youths for the college education experience. The gaps in precollege preparedness—graduated from high school, SAT taking, and performance—are very large, and are reflected in college enrollment, enrollment in expensive colleges, and ultimately graduation from a four-year college. Perhaps the most arresting of these gaps is that in the propensity to even take the SAT exam, the test most indicative of plans to proceed to some college or university with a merit-based selection standard.

Although colleges and universities may seek to weaken the link between socioeconomic class and future life prospects, the effects of their efforts appear both muted and less effective over time. This is particularly true for four-year colleges and universities, the traditional heart of the higher education system, and the producers of what many judge to be the highest quality educational services. In sum, the allocation of higher education services, especially the highest quality of these services, is rather highly concentrated among youths from families with the highest economic status, and this concentration appears to be increasing over time.[4]

The Perspective of Selective Colleges

Consistent with their focus on inequalities and practices in most selective institutions, Bowen, Kurzweil, and Tobin also present statistics on 180,000 students who entered nineteen selective colleges in 1995. These statistics are summarized in table 2.4. The pattern of applications to these colleges and universities is predominantly from youths from high-income families. For high school graduates from the bottom income quar-

Table 2.4   **Patterns for Students Entering Nineteen Selective Colleges and Universities in 1995**

	Bottom Quartile	Top Quartile	Gap
Percentage of applicants from (compared to 25 percent of all students in each quartile)	11	50	39
Percentage of applicants admitted	34	43	9
Average SAT (public/private)	1169/1229	1259/1309	90/80
Percentage of admittees who enrolled	44	39	−5
Percentage of entrants who graduated	84	88	4
Earnings of 1976 full-time worker entrants after fifteen years*	$68,000	$86,000	$18,000

Source: Bowen, Kurzweil, and Tobin (2005).
*For the 1976 entering class, for eleven of the nineteen schools with 1976 data.

tile, who have taken the SAT and who presumably have some hope of being accepted by one of these schools, the likelihood of submitting an application to one of these colleges is only about one-fifth of that of their counterparts from the highest income quartile. Among those who do apply, the admission rate for the high-income students is nearly 10 percentage points greater than that of the low-income students. Among the students at these institutions, the SAT score of those in the bottom quartile ranges is about 80 to 90 points below that of their counterparts from the top income quartile. Having been admitted, however, the enrollment rate is higher for the low-income students, and the graduation rates are about the same.

The most revealing statistic is in the bottom row: Among the students entering and graduating from these selective schools, earnings (after fifteen years) of the students from the highest income families are more than 25 percent greater than those of the students from the lowest income families. Clearly, family economic status persists, even through the filter of the nation's most selective colleges and universities.

Inequality Patterns in Educational Attainment

These gaps in higher education attainment by family income rely on estimates of income that are both somewhat difficult to interpret and in some cases suspect. First, among the national data collected, income values are sometimes for the households in which students live and thus do not apply to the children's parents.[5] Second, for some data sources, including that used by Bowen, Kurzweil, and Tobin in their analysis of selective colleges, the parental income values are those supplied by the students in response to surveys, administered when the SAT or other achievement exam is administered. Substantial concerns with the reliability of this information have been expressed because student impressions of their parents' resources may not be accurate.[6] Third, in no studies thus far has allowance been made for the income needs of the families of the youths being studied. It clearly matters if a student from a family with an annual income of $50,000 has no or several siblings also competing for family resources. Finally, and most important, the values for parental or family income are one-year, snapshot (or transitory) values, and hence fail to reflect the long-term (or permanent) economic position of the family of the students.[7]

To gain a different, and more reliable, picture of inequalities in educational attainment, we have proceeded in a somewhat different way. We selected a sample of children from the Michigan Panel Survey of Income Dynamics (PSID) who were born from 1966 to 1970, and followed them from 1968, the first year of the PSID (or their year of birth, if later) until 1999. This cohort would be expected to graduate from high school in the mid- to late 1980s, and from college in the late 1980s and early 1990s. Educational outcomes were measured at age twenty-five, though to limit missing data, some respondents' outcomes were measured as late as age twenty-nine. After omitting observations for which information on core variables is missing, we have a sample of 1,202.[8] Survey weights are applied to yield a nationally representative sample of this cohort of American youths.

These data contain extensive longitudinal information on the status, characteristics, and choices of family members, family income, living arrangements, neighborhood characteristics, and background characteristics such as race, education, and location for each individual. To make comparisons of individuals with different birth years, we index the time-varying data elements in each data set by age.[9] All monetary values are expressed in 1993 dollars, using the consumer price index for all items. We merged census tract (that is, neighborhood) information describing the percentages of residents who are high school dropouts and who have low incomes from the 1970 and 1980 censuses with our PSID data. The census data are matched to the specific location of the children in our sample for each year from 1968 to 1985.[10]

We then tabulated a variety of measures of educational attainment for each member of this sample, measured at age twenty-five, including graduate from high school (0–1), attend college (0–1), graduate from college (0–1), and years of completed schooling.[11] For each youth, we also calculated a value of the permanent income-needs of the family in which he or she grew up—the average real value of the family's income when the youth is between ages two and fifteen, divided by the national poverty line for a

Table 2.5   Unweighted and Weighted Sample Means

Variable	Weighted Mean	Unweighted Mean
Education variables		
Years of education	13.06	12.51
High school graduate = 1	0.848	0.760
Attend college = 1	0.460	0.347
College graduate = 1	0.213	0.138
Income and control variables		
Family income-needs	3.053	2.416
Log of family income-needs	0.943	0.679
Family wealth, 1984	158,483	110,132
Log of positive wealth, 1984	9.680	7.621
African American	0.153	0.441
Female	0.473	0.469
Average number of siblings	1.755	2.101
At least one parent graduated high school	0.769	0.633
At least one parent attended college	0.395	0.269
Proportion years with single parent	0.153	0.270
Number of location moves	2.518	2.831
Percent neighborhood dropouts	14.43	16.71
Negative wealth, 1984	0.039	0.052
Tuition and fees per FTE Public 87	1.631	1.592
Education data missing for parents	0.037	0.072
Wealth data missing, 1984	0.006	0.108

Source: Authors' calculations.

family of that size.[12] Similarly, we calculated the average wealth (net worth) of the family in 1984, when the youths ranged in age from fourteen to eighteen years.

Table 2.5 provides weighted and unweighted means for all variables included in our models averaged over the 1,202 observations in our sample. Eighty-five percent of our (weighted) sample of youths graduated from high school and 46 percent attended college. They have an average of 13.06 years of completed schooling. The weighted average family income-needs over children's ages two to fifteen is 3.05, whereas the average family net worth in 1984 is $158,483.

Consider, first, the extent of educational attainment of youths from families of various levels of economic resources. Table 2.6 presents summary statistics for youths from the bottom and the top family permanent income-needs quartiles and the gaps between them. Table 2.7 presents similar results by quartiles of family wealth, measured in 1984. Both tables also show attainment statistics for the top and bottom deciles of the

Table 2.6   Percentage of Youths in 1966 to 1970 Birth Cohort by Educational Attainment and Family Average Income-Needs

	Bottom Decile	Top Decile	Bottom Quartile	Top Quartile	Gap
Graduate high school	56.8	97.7	64.1	96.1	32
Attend college	19.5	78.2	21.6	71.2	49.6
Attend college, conditional on high school graduation	34.3	80.0	33.8	74.1	40.3
Graduate college	6.3	49.1	5.6	42.1	36.5
Graduate college, conditional on attending college	32.3	62.8	25.9	59.1	33.2
Years of schooling	11.2	14.6	11.8	14.2	2.4

Source: Authors' calculations.

Table 2.7   Percentage of Youths in 1966 to 1970 Birth Cohort by Educational Attainment and Family Wealth in 1984

	Bottom Decile	Top Decile	Bottom Quartile	Top Quartile	Gap
Graduate high school	49.7	98.5	63.9	97.9	34.0
Attend college	12.6	74.9	24.2	73.7	49.5
Attend college, conditional on high school graduation	25.4	76.1	37.8	75.3	37.5
Graduate college	3.0	47.8	8.6	44.1	35.5
Graduate college, conditional on attending college	23.8	63.7	35.7	59.9	24.2
Years of schooling	11.4	14.5	11.9	13.5	1.6

Source: Authors' calculations.

respective distributions. The estimates are similar between the two measures of family resources—income-needs and wealth.

Whereas only about 22 percent of youths from the bottom quartile of families by income or wealth attended college, 71 percent of youths from families in the top quartile at least entered a college or university. The gap is nearly 50 percentage points. Between 42 and 44 percent of the youths from the top quartile of income-needs or wealth graduated from college, but only 6 to 9 percent of their bottom quartile counterparts did, a gap of more than 35 percentage points. Transitions from attending college if a high school graduate and from graduating having attended college are also shown. Again, substantial gaps between youths from the highest and lowest quartiles of family income-needs and wealth in the probability of making these transitions are evident. The gaps between the attainment levels of youths from the top and bottom deciles of the respective dis-

Table 2.8   Youths in 1966 to 1970 Birth Cohort by Educational Attainment and Average Income-Needs

	Bottom Decile	Top Decile	Bottom Quartile	Third Quartile	Second Quartile	Top Quartile	Total
High school graduates	6.6	11.6	19.0	25.2	27.1	28.7	100
College attendees	4.2	17.1	11.8	20.6	28.3	39.2	100
College graduates	2.9	23.2	6.6	17.4	25.9	50.1	100

Source: Authors' calculations.

Table 2.9   Youths in 1966 to 1970 Birth Cohort by Educational Attainment and Family Wealth

	Bottom Decile	Top Decile	Bottom Quartile	Third Quartile	Second Quartile	Top Quartile	Total
High school graduates	5.6	11.8	18.9	26.0	26.5	28.7	100
College attendees	2.7	16.5	13.2	18.8	28.3	39.8	100
College graduates	1.4	22.7	10.2	11.6	26.7	51.5	100

Source: Authors' calculations.

tributions are even greater, suggesting a rather continuous relationship between economic status and educational attainment.

A similar pattern of extreme inequality and gaps between youths from the top and bottom quartiles of family income-needs and wealth are observed when the allocation of educational services to youths from various economic backgrounds is measured. Tables 2.8 and 2.9 show the composition of all high school graduates, college attendees, and college graduates in our cohort of youths, by family income-needs and wealth quartiles. Again, the patterns for the top and bottom deciles of the distributions are also reported.

Among high school graduates, nearly 30 percent are from the top income quartile and about 19 percent from the bottom quartile. In terms of attainment—though not necessarily in terms of quality-adjusted attainment given differences in the resources and quality of schools attended—the distribution of high school educational services is relatively evenly distributed among children from various economic backgrounds. The pattern for college graduates, however, is quite different. Among all college graduates in this cohort, half are from families with the income-needs in the top quarter of the nation, but only 7 percent are from the one-quarter with the lowest permanent income-needs position. Similarly, the 10 percent of families in the lowest income-needs decile yield less than 3 percent of college grads. Although the patterns by wealth are similar, the concentration of college graduates among the nation's wealthiest quartile of families is even more extreme than the concentration by income-needs—only 22 percent of college graduates come from the bottom half of families in terms of the level of assets (net worth). Put another way, the nearly 80 percent of higher educational services sufficient to attain a college degree are allocated to youths from the most wealthy 50 percent of the nation's families, only 10 percent to the least wealthy 25 percent, and only 1 percent to the least wealthy 10 percent.

The Independent Effect of Family Income

Although these tabulations reveal substantial disparities in higher education attainments among high- and low-income youths, they do not indicate the effect of parental economic resources on attainments controlling for a variety of other factors. These—such as race, parental education, and family structure—might be correlated with both higher education attainment and parental income; if they are, the relationship of parental income to attainments seen in the simple cross tabulations would be exaggerated.

To obtain the independent effects of parental income on schooling attainment, we estimated a series of multivariate statistical relationships that include both parental income-needs and a variety of other factors expected to be related to youth's educational attainments. We focus on family economic resources (income relative to need and wealth) and control variables found to have persistent, robust, and statistically significant relationships with educational attainment in prior research studies (see Haveman et al. 2001).[13] These variables include race, gender, number of siblings, parental schooling, family structure, geographic moves, the percentage of neighborhood or census tract individuals who dropped out of high school, and public state university tuition and fees. Those variables with values that change over time are averages over the individual's ages from two to fifteen.

Table 2.10 presents our estimates. Consider, first, the relationship of the family economic variables (family income-needs and wealth) to educational attainments.[14] Average family income-needs over the two to fifteen age span is significantly and positively associated with all of the indicators of educational attainment, though only at the 10 percent level for high school graduation. These results support other research indicating that permanent parental income is an important determinant of educational attainment. Family wealth is also significantly related to all four education measures.[15]

The final two rows of the table show the elasticity of the education variables with respect to the family economic variables. The elasticity value is the percent change in education associated with a 1 percent change in income-needs (wealth). The elasticity of educational attainment with respect to family wealth is greater than the elasticity with respect to income-needs, and is particularly large for the college graduation outcome. A 1 percent increase in wealth is associated with a nearly equivalent (.92) percentage increase in the probability of graduating college, and a 1 percent increase in family income-needs is associated with a .69 percent increase in the college graduation probability. Part of this high wealth elasticity is due to the cumulative nature of the effect of wealth on education. Having higher wealth increases the probability of graduating high school and the probability of attending college, both conditions necessary to graduate from college.

The incremental elasticity for any level of attainment can be found by comparing elasticities across the education levels. For example, of the .92 elasticity of college graduation with respect to wealth, .337 (= .917–.581) is that of college graduation conditional on attending college, .406 (.581–.175) is that of attending college conditional on graduating high school, and .175 is that of graduating from high school. The elasticities show that the financial variables have a larger effect on attending and graduating college than on graduating high school. A 1 percent increase in income increases the probability of graduating high school by only .04 percent but of attending college by .55 percent.

The coefficient estimates on individual, family, and neighborhood characteristics in table 2.9 are generally as expected, though some are not statistically significant. Being African American or female increases educational attainment, but moving often during childhood, having more siblings in the home, or living in a neighborhood with a high percentage of high school dropouts tend to reduce education and are usually statistically significant. Parental education generally increases the educational attainment of the children, and the effect is significant for years of schooling and college graduation.[16] Controlling for these factors, the proportion of years in a single-parent family is positively related to attainment and generally statistically significant. This result is unexpected. The state public institution tuition in 1987 is negatively associated with the indicators of educational attainment, and is statistically significant for both years of completed schooling and college attendance.

To illustrate the effect of family income-needs and wealth on education, we use the estimates from the regressions in table 2.10 to calculate the mean predicted value of the education variables for a youth in the top and the bottom income-asset quartile, holding the other variables in the model at their actual values.[17] These estimates are presented in table 2.11. Even after controlling for race, gender, parental education, family size and

Table 2.10   Regression Results[a]

| | Years of Education | | High School Graduate | | |
Variable	Parameter Estimate	Pr > |t|	Parameter Estimate	Pr > ChiSq	Marginal Effect
Intercept	**11.540**	<.0001	−0.001	0.998	0.000
Log of family income-needs 2-15	**0.654**	<.0001	*0.190*	0.092	0.041
Log of positive wealth, 1984	**0.090**	<.0001	**0.081**	<.0001	0.017
Negative wealth, 1984	0.396	0.148	*0.411*	0.052	0.089
African American	**0.313**	0.014	**0.293**	0.008	0.063
Female	**0.416**	<.0001	**0.230**	0.010	0.050
Average number of siblings 2-15	−0.066	0.103	−0.033	0.328	−0.007
At least one parent grad high school	**0.567**	<.0001	**0.522**	<.0001	0.112
At least one parent attend college	**0.340**	0.012	0.122	0.355	0.026
Proportion years w/ single parent 2-15	**0.478**	0.008	−0.058	0.702	−0.013
Number of location moves 2-15	**−0.082**	<.0001	**−0.060**	0.001	−0.013
Percent neighborhood dropouts 2-15	**−0.026**	<.0001	**−0.016**	0.005	−0.003
Tuition & fees per FTE Public 87	*−0.179*	0.052	0.005	0.950	0.001
Education info missing for parents	**0.511**	0.017	*0.324*	0.063	0.070
Wealth missing, 1984	*−0.430*	0.063	−0.144	0.420	−0.031

Elasticity of education variables with respect to financial resource variables

Elasticity for family income[b]		0.048		0.042
Elasticity for wealth, 1984[b]		0.067		0.175

Source: Authors' calculations.

[a] Bold indicates the coefficient estimate is significant at the 5 percent level; italics indicates significant at the 10 percent level.

[b] The first number is the total elasticity and the number in parentheses is the marginal elasticity. For example, the elasticity of family income on attend college is 0.549, of this .042 is the effect on high school graduation and .507 is the marginal elasticity on attending college conditional on high school graduation.

Attend College			College Graduate		
Parameter Estimate	Pr > ChiSq	Marginal Effect	Parameter Estimate	Pr > ChiSq	Marginal Effect
−0.968	0.002	−0.362	**−1.922**	<.0001	−0.251
0.617	<.0001	0.231	**0.457**	0.001	0.060
0.064	0.000	0.024	**0.060**	0.028	0.008
0.152	0.546	0.057	0.310	0.402	0.040
0.274	0.010	0.103	−0.012	0.931	−0.002
0.235	0.004	0.088	**0.314**	0.002	0.041
−0.072	0.043	−0.027	−0.068	0.162	−0.009
0.206	0.069	0.077	*0.318*	0.057	0.042
0.027	0.798	0.010	**0.298**	0.015	0.039
0.311	0.040	0.116	**0.590**	0.003	0.077
−0.042	0.019	−0.016	**−0.059**	0.016	−0.008
−0.019	0.000	−0.007	**−0.017**	0.017	−0.002
−0.193	0.012	−0.072	−0.123	0.202	−0.016
0.466	0.010	0.175	0.166	0.547	0.022
−0.360	0.128	−0.135	*−0.838*	0.088	−0.109
	0.549 (0.507)			0.685 (.136)	
	0.581 (0.406)			0.917 (.337)	

Table 2.11   Predicted Education Values by Income and Assets

Predicted Education	Bottom Quartile	Top Quartile
Years of education	12.192	13.607
Probability of high school graduate	0.759	0.916
Probability of attending college	0.208	0.637
Probability of graduating college	0.077	0.299

Source: Authors' calculations.
Note: The predicted education values are calculated from the regressions in table 2.10. Bottom and top quartile refer to the weighted median value of income/assets within the lowest and highest quartile; all other variables are kept at their actual value.

structure, and neighborhood characteristics, family income-needs and assets profoundly affect a youth's educational chances. The predicted value of years of education for someone in the top quartile of income and assets is nearly 1.5 years higher than for someone in the lowest quartile (13.6 versus 12.2 years). Such differences are seen at all education levels; the probability of graduating from high school is .92 for youths in the top quartile compared with .76 for those in the bottom quartile, the probability of attending college is .64 compared with .21, and the probability of graduating from college is .30 compared with .08. Holding all of these other characteristics constant, a youth from the bottom quartile of the parental income-wealth distribution has only about one-fourth the chance of graduating college as a youth from the top quartile.

The Implications of Growing Family Income Inequality

Income inequality has increased substantially among U.S. households over the last thirty years, as is well known. For example, from 1973 to 1998, the Gini coefficient on family income—a standard measure of family income inequality—increased from .356 to .430, or by 21 percent (see Haveman et al. 2001). This uneven growth is likely to have important implications for both the overall level and the distribution of educational attainments. In particular, more rapid income growth at the top of the distribution relative to the bottom suggests that the related gains in educational attainment may also be concentrated among youths from high income families.

We are able to use our estimates of the response of changes in educational attainments to changes in income and wealth to explore the implications of the increase in income inequality from 1970 to 2000 for both the level and the inequality in educational attainments. To isolate the independent effect of increased income inequality from the effect of changes in the level of income over time, we simulate the family income distribution

Table 2.12   Predicted Values of Educational Attainment

	All	Bottom 25%	Lower 25%	Upper 25%	Top 25%	Top 5%
Years of education						
Simulated 1970	12.916	11.674	12.657	13.298	14.028	14.547
Simulated 2000	12.849	11.531	12.547	13.240	14.074	14.686
Change	−0.066	−0.143	−0.110	−0.058	0.045	0.139
Change	−0.51%	−1.23%	−0.87%	−0.44%	0.32%	0.96%
Graduating high school						
Simulated 1970	0.833	0.653	0.829	0.901	0.949	0.972
Simulated 2000	0.827	0.640	0.821	0.898	0.949	0.974
Change	−0.006	−0.013	−0.008	−0.003	0.001	0.002
Change	−0.70%	−2.02%	−0.94%	−0.34%	0.07%	0.22%
Attending college						
Simulated 1970	0.430	0.153	0.346	0.516	0.704	0.823
Simulated 2000	0.412	0.127	0.311	0.494	0.714	0.851
Change	−0.018	−0.027	−0.035	−0.021	0.010	0.028
Change	−4.16%	−17.30%	−10.03%	−4.08%	1.46%	3.45%
Graduating from college						
Simulated 1970	0.205	0.046	0.129	0.235	0.409	0.544
Simulated 2000	0.200	0.039	0.115	0.224	0.421	0.580
Change	−0.005	−0.008	−0.014	−0.011	0.012	0.036
Change	−2.50%	−16.76%	−10.66%	−4.81%	2.92%	6.60%

Source: Authors' calculations.
Note: Weighted, based on coefficient estimates in table 2.10. For this simulation, average family income was held constant and the percent of income held by each income quintile was adjusted to match the percent of income held by income quintile from 1970 and 2000. Thus, this simulation reflects the change in inequality from 1970 to 2000 holding constant overall level of income.

of our sample so as to match the distributions in 1970 and 2000, holding constant the average level of income of the sample. This simulation reveals the implication of a hypothesized increase in economic inequality, holding constant the overall level of income and all of the other characteristics of the population. Essentially, we hold constant the size of the income pie, and then measure the size of the slices (for seven percentile ranges) so as to match the actual distributions in both 1970 and 2000. Then, using the regression coefficients from table 2.10, we calculate the individual change in predicted educational attainment by predicting each person's level given an income value simulated to match the income distribution of first 1970 and then 2000 (see the appendix for a detailed discussion of the simulation procedure). The results are presented in table 2.12.

We estimate that the increase in family income inequality from 1970 to 2000 reduces predicted educational attainments for the bottom three quartiles of the family income distribution, particularly the bottom quartile. The probability of an individual in the bottom quartile graduating from high school falls from .653 to .640, a 2 percent reduction. Much greater negative effects for youths from the lowest family income quartile are observed for the probability of attending college and graduating from college, both of which fall by 17 percent. For youths from the top family income quartile, increases in predicted educational attainment range from a 1 percent increase in the probability of attending college to a 3 percent increase in the already high probability of graduating from college. Table 2.12 also shows estimates of the change in family income inequality for those in the top 5 percent of the distribution. The predicted gains in educational attainment are very large for this already high achieving group—increases in the probability of attending and graduating from college of 3 percent and 7 percent, respectively.[18]

The overall societal effect on educational attainment of the 1970 to 2000 increase in income inequality is decidedly negative. Although the effect on mean years of education and the probability of graduating from high school is quite small (.5 and .7 percent reductions, respectively), this masks the larger effects that occur at important education transitions. When measured over the entire population, the percentage of youths who attend college falls from 43 to 41 (by more than 4 percent), whereas the percentage who graduate from college falls from 21 to 20 (by 2.5 percent). We conclude that the growth of income inequality over the past three decades both decreased the overall level of educational attainment and increased the level of inequality in educational attainments between youth from high- and low-income families.[19]

These estimates suggest that the increase in income inequality of the magnitude that has been experienced in the United States over the past few decades has intergenerational effects with broad social implications. In particular, our results provide evidence that such a change results in greater dispersion of educational outcomes. The increased dispersion is primarily because those at the bottom of the educational distribution fall further from the mean; it implies a relative loss of human capital among those who have the least of it. Given the linkage between schooling attainments and labor market success, the increase in inequality in educational attainments is also likely to be reflected in increased earnings inequality. Furthermore, the continuing cycle of increased earnings inequality reflected in greater education inequality implies a pattern of persistently growing income and schooling gaps over subsequent generations.

Discussion and Policy Implications

We have documented the important role parental income plays in the educational attainment of children and the way in which increased income

Figure 2.1   **Median Annual Family Income, by Educational Attainment of Householder, 2001**

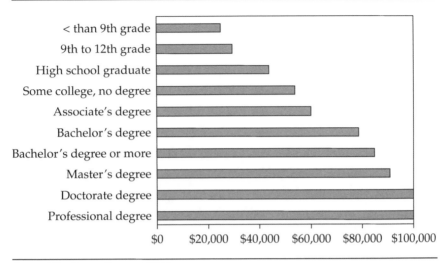

Source: U.S. Census Bureau (2001).

inequality has fueled increased educational inequality. If the inequality in terms of education attainment had no implications beyond this, there would be basis for concern. However, higher education attainment carries important implications for future economic and other attainments later in life.

The most prominent effect of incremental higher education relates to the market earnings and income impacts of schooling. Recently, Orley Ashenfelter and his colleagues Colm Harmon and Hessel Oosterbeek (2000) presented a meta-analysis of earlier studies and concluded that investments in higher education in the United States yielded 6 to 8 percent market returns for recipients. This compares favorably with returns on most other investments. Other analysts suggest an even higher return.[20]

These market returns in the form of earnings and income are reflected in figures 2.1 and 2.2. Figure 2.1 shows median household income for families headed by people with various levels of attained schooling. Where the median for families headed by an individual with only a high school degree was about $43,870 per year, for those headed by a college graduate it was $78,518. The earnings effects of higher education are also striking. Figure 2.2 shows much the same differential, but in this case for individual earnings. Moreover, it indicates that the earnings of college graduates relative to high school graduates has increased substantially over the years since the mid-1970s.

Figure 2.2   Mean Annual Earnings by Educational Attainment for Persons Eighteen Years Old and Older, 1975 to 2003 (Inflation-Adjusted to 2003 Dollars)

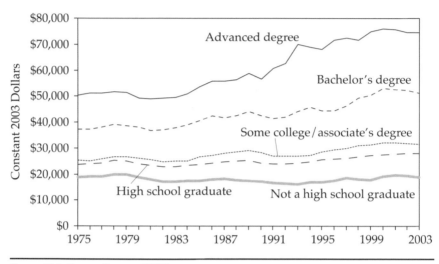

Source: U.S. Census Bureau (2003).

But, the full well-being that people gain from their schooling is only partially reflected in even the most reliable of the studies of labor market returns that Ashenfelter and his colleagues analyzed. These studies ignore a set of important and potentially dominant effects of additional investments in higher education. Table 2.13 provides a bird's-eye summary of the private and public benefits of education. The social and nonmarket effects of additional schooling are large, perhaps as large as the market-based effects of education to which economists pay so much attention. If we are correct, it is misleading at best and dangerous at worst to ignore these effects in debates over the optimal level of social (and public-sector) investment in schooling. A full assessment of the benefits and costs of additional investments in education must account for all of the effects of schooling, and not simply those recorded in a single market.[21]

The private and public benefits to education, and greater inequality in sharing in these benefits, provides a justification for why governments, colleges, and universities, and the secondary school system need to develop financing structures that will both maintain quality and increase access for students from lower-income families. Here we suggest a few policy approaches, reflecting the view that, by and large, students from high-income families will fare well, regardless of ability, and that more of the resources available to secure college admission and matriculation should

Table 2.13   The Effects of Additional Schooling

CATEGORY	ECONOMIC NATURE
Individual market productivity	Private; market effects.
Nonwage labor market remuneration	Private; market and nonmarket effects, e.g., fringe benefits and working conditions.
Intrafamily productivity	Private; some external effects; market and nonmarket effects, e.g., relationship between wife's schooling and husband's earnings.
Child quality: level of education and cognitive development	Private; some external effects; market and nonmarket effects, e.g., child education level and cognitive development are positively related to mother's and father's education.
Child quality: health and fertility	Private; some external effects, e.g., child health and reduced chances that daughters will give birth out of wedlock as teenagers are positively related to parents' education.
Own health	Private; modest external effects, e.g., own schooling positively affects one's health status, increases life expectancy, lowers prevalence of sever mental illness (including depression), and improves ability to deal with stressful events.
Consumer, marital and labor market efficiency	Private; some external effects; nonmarket effects, e.g., schooling leads to more efficient consumer activities; reduced costs of job search, increased regional mobility, and improved sorting in marriage market.
Attainment of desired family size	Private; e.g., contraceptive efficiency is positively related to schooling.
Charitable giving	Private and public; nonmarket effects, e.g., schooling increases donations of both time and money.
Savings	Private; some external effects, e.g., more schooling is associated with higher savings rates.
Technological change	Public; e.g., schooling is positively associated with research, development and diffusion of technology.
Social cohesion	Public; e.g., schooling is associated with increased voting, reduced alienation and social inequalities, opposition to government repression, reduced support for use of violence in protests, increased trust of others and membership in community organizations.
Self-reliance or economic independence	Private and public; e.g., more education associated with reduced dependence on transfers during prime working years.
Crime reduction	Public; e.g., schooling is associated with reduced criminal activity and a reduction in recidivism.

Source: Wolfe and Haveman (2003).

go to students from lower-income families. These suggestions are bold and deliberately designed to increase educational opportunities for low- and middle-income students; they take as given a pool of high school graduates who want more education, even if they are not fully and equally well prepared for it.

Strengthen Student Preparation

Our first policy recommendation is unexceptional, but costly and difficult to attain. For American higher education to thrive, it is essential that the links between K–12 education and postsecondary education be strengthened, and that a greater emphasis be placed on college preparatory coursework in the former. These two sectors do not communicate well with each other and increasing this interaction is a first step to rectifying that. Increasing equity in schooling attainments also requires that all students begin school on a more equal footing—universal high-quality preschool for all children may be a first step toward that goal.

Pricing and Performance

As now, in the future the bulk of low-income students will be educated by public universities. Although tuition at public institutions has been rising, it still falls well short of reflecting the real resource cost of the educational services provided. As a result, students who pay the full tuition—largely students from more affluent families—are receiving an implicit subsidy. One somewhat dramatic approach would be for institutions to simultaneously price tuition close to real costs and use the bulk of additional revenue to provide direct student aid targeted at students from low-income families. In addition to addressing the current inequity in the allocation of educational services, such an approach would tend to ration the limited supply of educational services (student slots) to those who value these services the most. Such a solution would also require a heavy advertising plan to make sure that lower-income families understood the net price of college was far below the sticker price, which is often the only information to which they have to react.

Pay-for-performance is another innovation for public universities to consider. Today state government financial support to public institutions typically comes in the form of a lump-sum appropriation. As an alternative arrangement, a scale for determining institutional support could be tied to the performance of institutions, such as retention rates, graduation rates, the ability to limit cost and tuition increases, or increases in their share of students from families with below-median incomes. Such an arrangement would have desirable incentive effects and would redistribute resources from low- to high-performing schools. Although a number of states have begun to set performance benchmarks for state universities, so far they have been reluctant to tie state appropriations to performance. But why should postsecondary education be excluded from pay-for-performance when elementary and secondary education are feeling these same pressures?

Limiting Public Subsidies to Private Schools

At present, a substantial amount of federal subsidization (guaranteed student loans, Pell Grants, tax subsidies) is made available to students who attend very wealthy institutions. These subsidies could be capped for wealthy universities that are able to increase their available student assistance. The reduced subsidy costs of this policy could be redirected to students attending less well-endowed schools, both public and private.

Student Assistance for Institutional Support

As four-year colleges and universities have become increasingly selective in student recruitment, students with the highest qualifications—most often those from the highest-income families—have been the targets of recruitment efforts and the recipients of increased merit-based assistance. This trend reflects a variety of forces, including the desire to increase institutional rankings in prominent publications (such as *U.S. News and World Report*), the tastes of faculty and other institutional stakeholders, and the pursuit of financial gains associated with the rapid increases in federal merit-based assistance that have been targeted on higher-income families. These forces are at play in both public and private higher education.

In response to this trend, both state and federal governments could redirect to students the financial support they now provide to colleges and universities, such as in the form of higher education vouchers. The direct student assistance could be targeted toward students from lower-income families. Such an arrangement would not only enhance equity but also require schools to compete for students and redirect their attention toward the tastes and demands of their student constituents and away from those of other institutional stakeholders, such as faculties.

One promising variant of this approach—income contingent student loans—is being experimented with by several countries. In this system, former students repay debt contingent on the incomes they earn after completing their schooling. This means that the ultimate capacity to pay is given weight in determining the repayment amount for which former students are liable. In other words, loans are repaid by taxing postschool earnings to recover only the costs incurred, plus a small interest rate. Australia and New Zealand, in particular, are in the forefront of these policies. The especially successful Australian program is being adopted in Asian nations as well (Chapman and Ryan 2005).

Conclusion

These results confirm and extend the findings of previous literature that economic inequality results in significant education inequality. The gaps in education by income level are striking, even after controlling for other family and neighborhood effects, with someone in the top quartile of income more than three times as likely to graduate from college as someone in the bottom quartile of income. In addition, the increase in inequality the past few decades has increased the inequality in education as well as lowering the overall education level. These results are more striking against the backdrop of other work presented here, that lower-income youths are more likely to attend community colleges or vocational schools and those that attend four-year colleges are likely to attend lower quality schools.

When the large and growing longer-run earnings gains and other benefits associated with a college education are taken together with the gaps in college going and college graduation between youths from high-income and low-income families, it is clear that the higher education inequalities become translated into lifetime earnings, income, and overall well-being inequalities. Contrary to the oft-stated belief in the leveling effect of higher education, because lower-income individuals are much less likely to secure higher education, the nation's colleges and universities appear to be an integral part of the process whereby family economic status is passed along from generation to generation.

Appendix: Simulation Procedure

To simulate the change in income inequality from 1970 to 2000, we adjust the income distribution of our sample to match that of the United States in 1970 and in 2000. The first two columns of table 2.14 show the share of aggregate income held by each percentile range in 1970 and 2000. The 20 percent of families in the bottom quintile had 5.4 percent of total income in 1970 but only 4.3 percent in 2000; the 5 percent of families in the 95 to 100 percentile range had 15.6 percent of income in 1970 but 21.1 percent in 2000.

We simulate the family income distribution of our sample to match the percentage of income held by each of seven income percentile ranges for 1970 and for 2000, holding constant the average income for the sample. The middle two columns of the table show what average income would have to be in each income range to have each percentile range have the appropriate percentage of income and to have average income for the sample remain at $44,500. For example, average income for those in the bottom quartile would be $12,000 to simulate 1970 and $9,600 to simulate 2000.[22] Based on the actual average income for sample members whose income puts them in this bottom income quartile, an adjustment factor is calculated that makes the sample average income match the simulated average.

Table 2.14   Simulation of Income Distribution 1970 and 2000

Income Percentile	U.S. Actual % of Income		Simulated Average Income		Simulated Income as % of Actual		Average Simulated Income/Needs	
	1970	2000	1970	2000	1970	2000	1970	2000
0 to 20	5.40	4.30	12,000	9,600	67.4	53.9	0.820	0.656
20 to 40	12.20	9.80	27,200	21,900	90.5	72.9	1.839	1.481
40 to 60	17.60	15.40	39,200	34,300	101.6	88.9	2.780	2.433
60 to 80	23.80	22.70	53,000	50,500	106.2	101.2	3.695	3.520
80 to 90	15.30	15.80	68,000	70,500	103.5	107.3	4.686	4.859
90 to 95	10.00	10.70	88,600	95,500	106.6	114.9	6.014	6.482
95 to 100	15.60	21.10	139,000	188,200	107.5	145.5	9.067	12.277
Total			$44,500	$44,500				

Source: Authors' calculations.

Following the same procedure, an adjustment factor is calculated for the other six income percentile ranges and then each sample member's income is multiplied by the appropriate adjustment factor for their income range to get simulated income. The adjustment factor used is labeled "Simulated Income as % of Actual" in the table.

We then calculate the income-needs ratio using this simulated income. Average simulated income-needs ratio for each percentile range is shown in the final two columns of table 2.14.

Endnotes

1. Although the individual receiving additional education gains increased income and a variety of other benefits, a number of other gains accrue to others and to society as a whole. Examples include technological breakthroughs, greater participation in a democratic government, and reduced criminal activity (see Haveman and Wolfe 1984; Wolfe and Haveman 2003).
2. The values shown in tables 2.1 through 2.4 (and 2.5 through 2.8) are unconditional means or percentages, and therefore show overall patterns by position in the income distribution, without controlling for other variables that may also influence attainment.
3. David Ellwood and Thomas Kane (2000) also report these gaps for students with similar mathematics test scores. For example, where 59 percent of high-income youths with test scores in the middle tertile attend a four-year college, only 33 percent of youths from the lowest income quartile (and with test scores in this range) do.
4. Over recent decades, the earnings return to college going increased substantially. It appears that youths from low-income families responded less strongly to these increased returns from higher schooling, and (of more concern) will not reap the gains of these returns in their future careers.

5. The estimates in table 2.1 reflect the efforts of these authors to measure parental family income in a consistent way across data sources (see Ellwood and Kane 2000, 320).

6. The level of family income reported on student aid application forms, and hence supplied by parents, is substantially greater than the income levels reported by the students themselves in response to survey questions.

7. This distinction is also important if one wishes to infer more than correlation between family income and higher education attainment. A number of recent studies have found that permanent household income is a significant determinant of both college attendance decisions by youths and the level of family investments in children, whereas transitory income is not (see Keane and Wolpin 2001; Cameron and Heckman 1998; Blau 1999; Carneiro and Heckman 2002).

8. Some of those observed did not respond in an intervening year but reentered the sample the following year. Such individuals are included in our analysis, and the missing information filled in by averaging the data for the two years contiguous to the year of missing data. For the first and last years of the sample, this is clearly not possible, and we assign the contiguous year's value, adjusted if appropriate using other information that is reported. Studies of the PSID find little reason for concern that attrition has reduced the representativeness of the sample. A recent study by John Fitzgerald, Peter Gottschalk, and Robert Moffitt (1998) finds that, although dropouts from the PSID panel do differ systematically from those observations retained, estimates of the determinants of choices such as schooling and teen nonmarital childbearing generated from the data do not appear to be significantly affected. They conclude, "Despite the large amount of attrition, we find no strong evidence that attrition has seriously distorted the representativeness of the PSID through 1989, and considerable evidence that its cross sectional representativeness has remained roughly intact" (251). Other studies that suggest that attrition in the PSID is not a cause of concern include Robert Haveman and Barbara Wolfe (1994) and Sean Becketti and colleagues (1988).

9. Rather than have the information defined by the year of its occurrence (say, 1968 or 1974), this time-varying information is assigned to the child by the child's age, allowing us to compare the process of attainment across individuals with different birth years.

10. The links between the neighborhood in which each family in the PSID lives and small-area (census tract) information collected in the 1970 and 1980 censuses have been (painfully and painstakingly) constructed by Michigan Survey Research Center (SRC) analysts. For the years 1968 to 1970, the 1970 census data are used in this matching; for the years 1980 to 1985, the 1980 census data are used. In most cases, this link is based on a match of the location of our observations to the relevant census tract or block numbering area (67.8 percent for 1970 and 71.5 percent for 1980). For years 1971 to 1979, a weighted combination of the 1970 and 1980 census data are used. The weights linearly reflect the distance from 1970 and 1980. For example, the matched value for 1972 equals $[(.8 \times 1970 \text{ value}) + (.2 \times 1980 \text{ value})]$.

11. We define a high school graduate as a person who has either completed twelve years of schooling, or who has received a general educational develop-

ment (GED) degree. A college graduate is a person who has completed sixteen or more years of schooling, and thus excludes those with a two-year college degree. A person is identified as attending college only if they have completed at least one year of college. All of these values are computed using information reported at age twenty-five.

12. Measuring income over a number of years minimizes the effect of temporary fluctuations in income from one year to the next, as well as measurement error. Hence, this value is an accurate measure of the "permanent" or normal income of the family (see Wolfe et al. 1996). Dividing the income level by the poverty line adjusts for differences in family size to provide a more accurate measure of the family's standard of living. For example, a family with one child and $30,000 in income will have a higher ratio of income to needs than a family with the same income but with six children.

13. The family income variable is measured as the logarithm of the ratio of family income each year from age two to age fifteen to that year's poverty line, averaged over the period. The family assets variable is the logarithm of positive family net worth in 1984; variables indicating negative or missing wealth information are also included. State public tuition and fees per full-time student is measured in 1987, when the individuals were between seventeen and twenty-one years old, and divided by 1,000.

14. In our analysis of the effects of changing economic inequality in the next section, we focus on the effects of these family economic variables.

15. The interpretation of the coefficient estimate on the wealth variable is complicated by the permanent measure of income included in the regression. The family income-needs ratio is measured from age two to fifteen, and thus the wealth variable captures a combination of wealth from other sources, such as inheritance, and the savings behavior of parents. Consider two families with identical initial wealth and income-needs each year, with one family saving a percentage of their income and the other spending all of it; the coefficient on the wealth variable may be capturing not only the additional resources available for education, but also unobservable parental characteristics such as a low discount rate or high educational attainment that may affect both the savings behavior of the parents and the child's education.

16. Parental education may have a less significant effect in our specification because a permanent measure of income-needs and wealth are also included in the regression. To understand the potential overlap in the parental education, wealth and income-needs, we estimated the correlation coefficients between pairs of these variables. They are as follows: wealth and income-needs (.568); wealth and parental high school (.381); wealth and parental college (.312); income-needs and parental high school (.468); income-needs and parental college (.485).

17. We calculate these predicted values by replacing actual income and wealth variables with the median income within the quartile for the financial variables, keeping all other variables at their actual level. Thus the numbers tell the weighted average of predicted education for the sample when the financial variables are at the bottom and top quartile level holding constant the other characteristics of the sample.

18. Although the regression contains both income and wealth variables, our simulation reflects only the increase in income inequality. Because the increase in

wealth inequality from 1970 to 2000 was in part independent from the growth in income inequality, our simulation understates the total effect of the greater inequality in financial resources.

19. We also simulated the differential effects on educational attainment of the actual change in the level and distribution of income in the nation from 1970 to 2000. The results of this analysis show that the positive effect on educational attainment from the increase in the level of income was greater than the negative effect of the growth in income inequality. Increases were recorded in all measures of educational attainment for all of the quartiles, but the gains for those from the top quartile were substantially greater than the gains for those in the bottom quartile. For example, the actual change in income over this three-decade period resulted in an estimated increase in the likelihood of graduating college for youths from the bottom quartile from .059 to .063, or by 0.4 percentage points (5.8 percent). However, this same overall economic change is estimated to have increased the probability of graduating college for youths in the top quartile from .400 to .556, or by 15.6 percentage points (39.1 percent). In other words, the positive effect on this measure of educational attainment for those in the top quartile of the income distribution was nearly forty times that for those in the bottom quartile.

20. The authors find rates of return about 1.3 percentage points greater in the United States than in other countries (primarily the United Kingdom, the other country with several such studies). They attribute that to the large relative increase in education-related earnings in the United States in recent decades. Orley Ashenfelter and Cecilia Rouse (1998), for example, find that in the United States the return to an additional year of schooling had grown from 6.2 percent in 1979 to about 10 percent in 1993.

21. See note 1. Estimates in Haveman and Wolfe (1984) suggest that these spillover effects may be equal in size to the private financial returns.

22. By contrast, the average income for families in the top 5 percent of the income distribution increased from $139,000 in 1970 to $188,200 in 2000.

References

Ashenfelter, Orley, and Cecilia Rouse. 1998. "Income, Schooling, and Ability: Evidence from a New Sample of Twins." *The Quarterly Journal of Economics* 113(1): 253–84.

Ashenfelter, Orley, Colm Harmon, and Hessel Oosterbeek. 2000. "A Review of Estimates of the Schooling/Earnings Relationship, with Tests for Publication Bias." *NBER* Working Paper 7457. Cambridge, Mass.: National Bureau of Economic Research. http://www.nber.org/papers/w7457.

Becketti, Sean, William Gould, Lee Lillard, and Finis Welch. 1988. "The PSID after Fourteen Years: An Evaluation." *Journal of Labor Economics* 6(4): 472–92.

Blau, David. 1999. "The Effect of Income on Child Development." *Review of Economics and Statistics* 81(2): 261–76.

Bowen, William G., Martin A. Kurzweil, and Eugene M. Tobin. 2005. *Equity and Excellence in American Higher Education.* Charlottesville: University of Virginia Press.

Cameron, Steven, and James Heckman. 1998. "Life Cycle Schooling and Dynamic Selection Bias: Models and Evidence for Five Cohorts of American Males." *Journal of Political Economy* 106: 262–333.

Carneiro, Pedro, and James Heckman. 2002. "The Evidence on Credit Constraints in Post-Secondary Schooling." *Economic Journal* 112: 705–34.

Carnevale, Anthony P., and Stephen J. Rose. 2004. "Socioeconomic Status, Race/ Ethnicity, and Selective College Admissions." In *America's Untapped Resource: Low-Income Students in Higher Education,* edited by Richard D. Kahlenberg. New York: The Century Foundation Press.

Chapman, Bruce, and Chris Ryan. 2005. "The Access Implications of Income Contingent Charges for Higher Education: Lessons from Australia." *Economics of Education Review* 24(5): 491–512.

Ellwood, David, and Thomas J. Kane. 2000. "Who is Getting a College Education: Family Background and the Growing Gaps in Enrollment." In *Securing the Future,* edited by Sheldon Danziger and Jane Waldfogel. New York: Russell Sage Foundation.

Fitzgerald, John, Peter Gottschalk, and Robert Moffitt. 1998. "An Analysis of the Impact of Sample Attrition on the Second Generation of Respondents in the Michigan Panel Study of Income Dynamics." *Journal of Human Resources* 33(2): 300–34.

Haveman, Robert, and Barbara Wolfe. 1984. "Schooling and Economic Well-Being: The Role of Non-Market Effects." *Journal of Human Resources* 19 (3)(Summer): 377–407.

———. 1994. *Succeeding Generations: On the Effects of Investments in Children.* New York: Russell Sage Foundation.

Haveman, Robert, Gary Sandefur, Barbara Wolfe, and Andrea Voyer. 2001. "Inequality of Family and Community Characteristics in Relation to Children's Attainments." Russell Sage Foundation. http://www.russellsage.org/programs/ proj_reviews/si/papers.htm#papers.

Keane, Michael P., and Kenneth I. Wolpin. 2001. "The Effect of Parental Transfers and Borrowing Constraints on Educational Attainment." *International Economic Review* 42(4)(November): 1051–1103.

U.S. Census Bureau. 2001. *Historical Income Tables, Families.* Table F-18. Washington: U.S. Census Bureau. http://www.census.gov/hhes/income/histinc/f18.html.

———. 2003. *Current Population Study.* Table A-3. Washington: U.S. Census Bureau. http://www.census.gov/population/socdemo/education/tabA-3.xls.

Wolfe, Barbara, and Robert Haveman. 2003. "Social and Nonmarket Benefits from Education in an Advanced Economy." In *Education in the 21st Century: Meeting the Challenges of a Changing World,* edited by Yolanda Kodrzycki. Boston, Mass.: Federal Reserve Bank of Boston.

Wolfe, Barbara, Robert Haveman, Donna Ginther, and C. B. An. 1996. "The 'Window Problem' in Studies of Children's Attainments: A Methodological Exploration." *Journal of the American Statistical Association* 91: 970–82.

Chapter 3

Secondary and Postsecondary Linkages

MICHAEL KIRST

INTERSPERSED WITH end-of-school-year and graduation news items, a spate of stories appear in national and local newspapers each year about stressed-out students and parents, competitive college admissions, a high school wall filled with college-rejection letters, the so-called new SAT, expensive tuition and onerous high school course loads. One gets the impression that this is the typical experience for college-bound high school students nationwide. Nothing could be further from the truth, because more than 70 percent of high-school graduates go on to postsecondary education within two years of graduation—although many are not prepared and do not succeed once they get there. ACT found that 51 percent were prepared in reading, 41 percent in math, and 26 percent in science (ACT 2005). This chapter focuses on the students who do not drop out of high school and who enroll at colleges that are either open enrollment or accept all qualified applicants. The 146 most selective colleges in the United States enroll only 11 percent of their students from below the median income (Kahlenberg 2004). If one includes high school dropouts as well as enrollees, just 10 percent of students from the bottom quartile of family income earn a bachelor's by age twenty-four versus 81 percent from the top income quartile (William Symonds, "America the Uneducated." *Business Week,* November 21, 2005, pp. 120–22).

Eighty percent of U.S. students attend postsecondary institutions that either accept all qualified applicants or are open enrollment.[1] Among undergraduates, about 40 percent attend an open enrollment community college (Marcus 2005). Low-income students primarily attend nonselective four-year schools or open enrollment community colleges. For example, nearly 66 percent of Latinos—compared with fewer than 45 percent of white students with similar academic backgrounds, which includes completion of core high school courses—initially enroll at open door institutions

(Bensimon 2003). In 2003, the median income for white families with children under eighteen years old was $61,970, $32,073 for Hispanic families, and $30,547 for African American families. About 25 percent of African Americans enroll at nonselective black colleges and universities (Bowen et al. 2005).[2] Two of every three high school graduates from the wealthiest quartile enroll in a four-year institution, compared with one in five from the lowest socioeconomic quartile (Bowen et al. 2005).

The initial problem many of these students face is having failed a place-ment exam, and having to enroll in remedial courses to start their higher education experience. Public policy has focused more on postsecondary access than on success or completion. For example, the California State Uni-versity remediation rate is nearly 60 percent for incoming freshmen, and most community college remediation rates in the state are even higher. Only 39 percent of college students who completed remedial reading courses completed a bachelor's degree, versus 69 percent of students who needed no remediation (Committee for Economic Development 2005). California State universities admit more than 90 percent of students with-out looking at SAT scores because adequate grades qualify the student for admission. Many four-year institutions around the United States are much easier to get into than California State University system.

When the University of California cut a few thousand admitted students in 2004 because of state budget cuts, I was besieged with media phone calls asking for comment. The same week, California community colleges cut between 50,000 to 100,000 students, but no one called—no one seemed to care. Community colleges receive much less media coverage than presti-gious universities (Adelman 2001). Many of these students at broad access postsecondary institutions have family responsibilities, attend only part-time, and "stop out" to earn more money for their education.

Postsecondary completion rates vary enormously depending on the type of student and the institution the student attends (Adelman 2005). The reasons for not completing college degrees or certificates are complex and involve finances, parental resources, family issues, and social integration at a campus. Estimates vary, but approximately the top 15 percent of U.S. students are well prepared and more than 80 percent of students at highly selective colleges and universities graduate (Adelman 2005). Because only six in ten college students graduate with a four-year degree, completion rates for broad-access institutions are much lower (CED 2005).

Only 7 percent of the students at highly selective institutions do not return for their sophomore year, but 37 percent do not at open enrollment higher education institutions (ACT 2005). Nationally, less than one-half of black and Hispanic students enrolled in college ever graduate (CED 2005). Of the students who begin at community college, 72 percent expect to get a four-year degree but only 23 percent end up with one (American Council on Education 2002). Bowen found that between 1970 and 1999, college enrollment rose substantially. Degree completion results have stalled, however, and the time taken to complete a degree has unquestionably increased over the past three decades (Bowen et al. 2005). But 88 percent of eighth graders want a college degree, because they think college will help them in a competitive job market (Schneider 2003).

Numerous studies reveal that students at broad-access colleges do not receive clear signals about college readiness (Kirst and Venezia 2004). They believe community colleges must accept anyone, and view it as a "souped-up high school." They do not realize community colleges design many of their courses to qualify for transfer to universities. High school students think their high school course and graduation requirements are enough to prepare them for four-year broad-access schools. These requirements, however, are minimal. They were not designed to help students be ready for college.

Students at minimally selective four-year colleges usually do not take math in their senior year of high school, and think that Cs and Bs in high school are adequate for freshman work in college. Most high school seniors do not complete much challenging academic work. UCLA surveys a national sample of incoming freshmen at four-year colleges each year (Young 2004). Nearly every year, the hours of study by high school seniors go down and grades go up. Sixty-five percent report doing five hours or less homework per week. In 1983, 47 percent did six hours of homework per week, versus only 28.4 percent in 2004. High school students do in fact significant work, but much of it is in off-campus jobs—fifteen hours or more per week.

Even broad access postsecondary education students who take the recommended college preparation courses in high school discover in their freshman year that college academic work is much different and more challenging than anything they encountered in high school (Conley 2005). So the problem goes beyond signals and information to include a fundamental misalignment of course content and expectations between secondary school and college (Schmidt 2002). For example, a recent ACT study found that college instructors believe grammar and usage skills are the most important writing skills needed by incoming students. ACT had found in 2003, however, that high school teachers consider them among the least important.

Opportunity to Learn

High school graduates who enter postsecondary education may never have had the opportunity to learn (OTL) what is necessary for college success. OTL means that the curriculum content necessary to reach particular academic standards must be presented to students (for example high school exit exam). According to the federal Goals 2000: Educate America Act, an OTL standard "means the criteria for, and the basis of, assessing the sufficiency or quality of the resources, practices, and conditions necessary at each level of the education system (schools, local educational agencies, and States) to provide all students with an opportunity to learn the material in voluntary national content standards or State content standards" (U.S. Code 1994, section 3).

Opportunity to learn standards are a relatively contentious issue. For some, they have the potential to remedy inequities in public education. For others, they represent federal or state intrusion over the power of localities to govern their schools (Porter 1995). OTL proponents emphasize that all students must be taught by well-prepared teachers the curriculum content necessary for college readiness. State academic standards require specific educational resources and conditions for children to reach proficiency, including certain instructional materials, technologies, teacher qualities, and facilities (Koski 2004). A missing ingredient in the recipe of high standards and college preparation is the assurance that all children will receive the classroom instructional opportunities to achieve to the level of college readiness (Conley 2005). African American and Latino twelfth graders across the United States read and do math at the same levels as white eighth graders on average (Kahlenberg 2004).

Data studies have documented that the conditions in the schools attended by high-risk children are so inadequate that they do not provide an equal opportunity for a quality education. Those conditions include

- lack of qualified teachers,
- high teacher turnover rates,
- poor working conditions for teachers,
- shortages of educational materials, including textbooks,
- poor physical facilities, and
- ineffective programs that involve parents.

OTL issues vary by state and locality with low spending per pupil as an important factor in determining OTL. For example, in California, which ranks forty-fourth in the nation in spending per pupil, the Rand Corporation documented the following (Carroll et al. 2005):

- Teachers in the schools with the highest proportion of underrepresented minorities are eleven times more likely to be in schools in which more than 20 percent of the teachers are undercredentialed and more than three times as likely to state that teacher turnover is a serious problem.

- Fifty-four percent of the teachers surveyed who teach science stated that they do not have enough materials and equipment necessary to do science lab work.

- Fifty percent of teachers surveyed who teach social sciences reported that they do not have enough atlases, maps, and reference materials.

- Thirty-two percent of teachers surveyed who use textbooks stated that there are not enough textbooks for each student to take one home.

When developing OTL standards and measuring students' OTL, the following elements are analyzed:

> One dimension is the content of instruction (including degree and depth of coverage of academic material and curricular emphasis for different groups of students). Delivery of this content [including instruction] . . . is another. A third area incorporates instructional resources that facilitate the delivery of instruction, including: materials and technology, safe and secure school facilities, and time. These categories overlap to some extent and different dimensions have more or less importance according to the perspectives of various constituencies: attorneys, academics, or education practitioners. Nonetheless, taken together, they constitute the fundamental resources comprising Opportunity to Learn. (Venezia 2007)

As stated, the academic content presented to students is a critical component of OTL. Clifford Adelman (1999) determined that the best predictor of students' success after high school is the rigor of their high school math curricula, particularly completing Algebra 2 and beyond. Tracking students into honors and nonhonors courses affects OTL by focusing low track instruction on low-level topics, whereas higher track instruction focuses on concepts, processes, and higher order skills. Tracking is intensified by placing the most experienced and highest status teachers in the highest tracks. Low income and students of color are disproportionately represented in nonhonors courses nationally. These courses also tend to be less challenging and to be taught by the least prepared teachers. Tracking starts early and can affect students' throughout much of their K–12 lives (Oakes 1985).

There is less consensus, however, about the OTL role of other resources (for example, books, laboratory supplies and space, libraries, computers, safe and clean facilities, time), than there is about the role of teachers and academic content. Some studies found that access to materials and appropriate school facilities are linked to students' OTL (see, for example, Greenwald, Hedges, and Laine 1996), but others did not find the same links (see, for example, Hanushek 1997). Evidence is well documented, though, that there are large disparities in available resources between and within schools and districts (Roza 2005).

The students who attend broad-access postsecondary institutions face many obstacles. High school counseling resources are minimal, parents know little about higher education, and high school teachers in the middle and lower ability groups do not provide much information about college (Tierney 2004). Because admission is virtually certain, the initial hurdle and de facto key academic standard for these students is a placement test after they enroll at postsecondary education. But high school students, teachers, and parents are largely unaware that a placement test exists, much less what it covers (Kirst and Venezia 2004).

Baltimore City Community Colleges (BCCC) provides an extreme example of the problems (Abell Foundation 2002). Of 1,350 first-time students who entered BCCC in the fall of 1996, only thirteen had received a vocational certificate, a two-year associate's degree, or transferred to a bachelor's degree granting college four years later. Ninety-five percent needed remediation and 45 percent required three math courses to reach the credit level. Their math placement test, Accuplacer™, was not matched to Maryland state high school math standards that emphasized "authentic problem solving" (for example, word problems with applications to real life scenarios). The BCCC placement exam included content beyond Algebra 2. Improvements in the K–16 system require simultaneously looking down from higher education to secondary schools as well up the pipeline. For example, the most relevant four-year schools for Baltimore high schools are Coppin State, Morgan State, and the University of Baltimore, not the selective schools that receive most of the media attention.

Better College Preparation

Although there are many causes of inadequate college readiness and failure to complete degrees and certificates, this chapter focuses on improving signals and the alignment of policies and curriculum, finance, data, and accountability between secondary and postsecondary education. Signaling theory suggests that streamlined and aligned high quality and appropriate content messages have a positive impact on students' learning and achievement, and that mixed signals—the current state of affairs— have the opposite effect (Bishop 2003; Rosenbaum 2001). Critical aspects of appropriate signals and incentives are simplicity, clarity, and consistency (Henry and Rubenstein 2002). Consistency is enhanced when signals, incentives, and institutional policies are aligned—for example, the alignment of format and content of state and local student assessments with SAT I. Incoherent and vague signals and incentives sent to secondary school students contribute to inadequate student preparation for postsecondary. Minority students are often placed in lower level academic high school courses and tracks that lead to decreases in motivation and preparation (Oakes 1985).

Rosenbaum found that in the Chicago area, because they do not want to give low-achieving students negative information about their future prospects, the counselors advocate college for all without stressing necessary academic preparation (Rosenbaum 2001). Because it is easy to enter so many four-year and two-year schools, there are few incentives to work hard in high school (Conley 1996).

A key issue is whether K–12 exit-level and postsecondary entrance-level signals and incentives are delivered to students in isolation from one another, or through interaction and reinforcement. Three possible scenarios for signal delivery to secondary school pupils are postsecondary education drives policy (Option A), K–12 drives policy (Option C), and combined efforts of K–12 and postsecondary education drive policy (Option B). The preferred delivery is Option B.

Combined efforts by postsecondary education and K–12 to send better signals can improve the college knowledge that is essential for K–12 student aspiration and preparation. College knowledge is acquired and possessed unequally among K–12 students and families of different social classes and racial-ethnic backgrounds. College knowledge by secondary school students and parents needs to include knowledge of tuition, curricular requirements, placement tests, admission procedures, and selection criteria. A particular high school's collegiate preparation culture cannot be fully measured with simple, visible, or discrete indices such as standardized test scores, honors, and advanced course offerings. Collegiate culture also encompasses the less tangible, more elusive qualities that can best be described through narratives that reveal the sustaining values or ethos of college readiness within a particular high school.

Signals and incentives transmitted through either a separate post-secondary education or a K–12 system, not in combination, will result in less student preparation, college knowledge, and postsecondary outcomes. Combined efforts between K–12 and postsecondary especially help disadvantaged students. AP students can succeed with less K–16 cooperation. The courses AP students take have college standards embedded. Teachers can be a critical resource, but students in nonhonors courses are given less information about college by their teachers than those in honors (Venezia, Kirst, and Antonio 2003). Clear and consistent K–16 signals are related to positive outcomes, such as less remediation and higher completion rates (Henry and Rubenstein 2002).

Stanford's Bridge Project and other research document major differences among students in the amount, clarity, and depth of signals they receive about what they must know and be able to do to succeed in college (Kirst and Venezia 2004). Five findings are particularly significant:

- *Inequalities Exist Across Education Systems.*   Many students in middle- and lower-level high school courses are not reached by postsecondary education outreach efforts, or by college counseling staff in their high schools. Many economically disadvantaged parents often lack experience and information concerning college preparation. There is also an unequal distribution of such resources as college information centers on high school campuses, opportunities to make college visits, and visits from college recruiters on high school campuses.

- *Student Knowledge of Curricular Requirements Is Uneven and Vague.* Students appear to have considerable partial knowledge of curricular requirements; slightly more than half knew three or more course requirements, but critical gaps in coursework make many students ineligible for colleges they want to attend (Kirst and Venezia 2004).

- *Teachers Play a Major Role in Helping Students Prepare for College but Do Not Have the Resources They Need to Give Students Accurate Information.* Teachers often take a greater role in helping students prepare for college than counselors, but do not have the same or adequate connections or knowledge of standards in broad-access postsecondary institutions and up-to-date admission and placement information.

- *Students are Generally Unaware of the Content of Postsecondary Course Placement Exams.* Across all the states studied, fewer than half the sampled students knew the placement testing policies for the institutions in the study. Failing placement exams, of course, is one reason that students start in remedial courses. As one California high school student commented, for example (Venezia, Kirst, and Antonio 2003, 35), "I think they should prepare us better for the placement tests so that we don't get stuck in basic classes. I think we should have the opportunity to know, not necessarily what's on the test, but have a good idea of it so that we know what to expect."

- *The Distribution of College Preparation Information to Parents Is Inequitable.* Among economically disadvantaged parents in Illinois, Maryland, and Oregon, 42 percent, 44 percent, and 47 percent respectively, said that they had received college information, versus 74 percent, 71 percent, and 66 percent of their more economically well-off counterparts.

K–12 Academic Standards and the College Disjuncture

In recent years, a movement to increase academic standards has swept across the United States. Forty-nine states have created K–12 academic content standards in most academic subjects, and all but Iowa have statewide K–12 student achievement tests. These efforts have two interrelated goals: clarifying what students must know and be able to do in the K–12 grades and aligning standards, assessments, textbook selection, and accountability measures across those grades. The reforms, however, have ignored the lack of coherence in content and assessment standards between K–12 and higher education. Only Oregon considered postsecondary education systems in designing their K–12 standards (Kirst and Venezia 2004). Until educators address this issue, secondary schools and their students will have no clear sense of what knowledge and skills constitute an adequate preparation for higher education. The current K–16 scene is a Babel of standards rather than a coherent strategy.

Colleges and universities rely on the SAT and ACT to provide some national assessment uniformity, but neither of these tests is aligned with the recent reforms in K–12 standards. The relationship between K–12 standards and college placement tests is even more chaotic. In 1992, for example, universities in the southeastern United States devised 125 combinations of 75 different placement tests, with scant regard to secondary school standards (Abraham 1992).

Tests at each level—K–12 achievement tests, standardized college entrance exams, and college placement assessments—use different formats, emphasize different content, and are given under different conditions. For example, high school assessments in Illinois and Florida rely heavily on written work, but ACT and some Florida college placement exams use multiple-choice tests to assess students' writing skills. Massachusetts's K–12 assessment also contains performance items that are dissimilar to the closed-end multiple-choice format of the SAT and ACT. California's newly augmented STAR test includes math that is considerably more advanced and difficult than the SAT and ACT, even as Alabama's high school assessment includes less algebra and geometry than the SAT. Some state K–12 assessments permit students to use calculators, but the college placement exams do not. Texas has a statewide postsecondary placement test (TASP), but many Texas universities also use their own placement exams. High school students in Texas are either confused by or ignorant of college placement standards (Venezia 2000).

In addition, many secondary school state assessments do not go beyond tenth grade and stress minimal high school graduation standards. Such scores cannot be used for college admissions or placement. By contrast, Illinois and Colorado designed a new state test given in eleventh grade that combines a state standards-based assessment with all of the ACT.

Universities provide some good arguments to explain why they pay little attention to K–12 standards or assessments. First, the universities emphasize that they are not involved in creating or refining the K–12 standards. Second, the universities observe that both politics and technical problems effect frequent changes in state K–12 standards. Third, they note that the K–12 assessments have not been evaluated to see how well they predict freshman grades, though such evaluations are not difficult to conduct (Kirst and Venezia 2004). Before discussing improved policies, it is important to examine how deeply rooted the disconnects are.

Historical Evolution of the Disjuncture

The origin of the disjuncture between lower and higher education in the United States stems, in part, from the laudable way the nation created mass education systems for both K–12 and higher education. The American comprehensive high school was designed for many purposes, not primarily college preparation. It includes vocational education, the worthy use of leisure (for example, jewelry making), home economics, driver education, and many elective courses. The American high school has conflicting principles within it—democratic, practical, and meritocratic. College preparation can be relegated to a minority of students that are in a track of challenging courses (Ravitch 2000). In Europe, by contrast, the higher grades of secondary education were designed for an elite group who would be going on to universities. European universities still play a major role in determining the content of the secondary school curriculum and both the content and format of secondary school examinations. Professors at British universities such as Cambridge and Durham, for example, grade the A levels taken by students during their last year of secondary education, and these essay exams figure critically in a student's chances for university admission.

Over time, the chasm between lower and high education in the United States has grown greater than that in many other industrialized nations (Clark 1985), but at one time U.S. colleges and universities did play an important role in the high schools. In 1900, for example, the College Board set uniform standards for each academic subject and issued a syllabus to help students prepare for college entrance subject-matter examinations. Before that, each college had had its own entrance requirements and examinations. Soon after, the University of California began to accredit high schools to ensure that their curriculums were adequate for university preparation.

In the postwar years, however, the notion of K–16 academic standards vanished. Aptitude tests like the SAT replaced subject-matter standards for college admission, and secondary schools added elective courses in nonacademic areas, including vocational education and life skills. Today, K–12 faculty and college faculty may belong to the same discipline-based professional organizations, but they rarely meet with one another. K–12 policy makers and higher education policy makers cross paths even less often. It was not until 1982 that the Carnegie Foundation organized the first national meeting between K–12 state school superintendents and college presidents (Stocking 1985, 258). The only nationally aligned K–16 standards effort is the advanced placement program—a stalactite that extends from universities, which dictate the course syllabus and exam.

With that exception, there are no major efforts to provide curricular coherence and sequencing between upper secondary grades and postsecondary education. The role of the last two years of high school as a basis for post-secondary general education preparation is rarely discussed. Nor is there any consensus on a conception of college liberal education that relates the academic content of the secondary schools to the first two years of college. Instead, many students in broad access postsecondary education face an "eclectic academic muddle in Grades 10–14" (Orrill 2000) until they select a college major. In Ernest Boyer's metaphor, postsecondary general education is usually the spare room of the university, "the domain of no one in particular" whose many functions make it useless for any one purpose (Boyer and Levine 1981). The more functional rooms are the departmental majors (Clark 1993).

In sum, the high school curriculum is not tied to the freshman and sophomore college curriculum or to any continuous vision of liberal education. In California, the focus of high school English course work for college preparation is literature. But the initial community college courses focus on grammar and writing, and the University of California stresses rhetoric. Policy makers for the secondary and postsecondary schools work in separate orbits that rarely interact, and the policy focus for K–16 has been more concerned with access to postsecondary education than with the academic preparation needed to complete a postsecondary degree or certificate. Access, rather than preparation, is also the theme of many of the professionals who mediate between the high schools and the colleges: high school counselors, college recruiters, college admissions personnel, and financial aid officers. The modal high school student does little home-work and has an outside job. Most students know they can attend post-secondary education with minimal preparation.

The number and influence of mediating groups such as the College Board, Education Testing Service, and ACT is for Stocking an indicator of the "amount of disorder and confusion that has grown through the years in the relationship between the school and the university in America" (1985, 263). In addition to the mediating professionals employed by the high schools and the colleges, "a major role is assumed by the major private testing organizations, whose tests have become powerful tools for allocating students to different types of universities and colleges. And increasingly prominent is the mediating influence of federal government as it has attempted to increase equity in American education and now . . . seeks to emphasize excellence" (263). She concludes that secondary and higher education systems diverge, and are pulled apart by different agendas.

In the United States, the relationship between the secondary school and the university is complex and ambiguous. The educational system is both decentralized and very large. The connections between these two levels of education vary from the public to the private sector, from one state to another, within states from one school district to another, and nationally from one type of college to another. It becomes a major enterprise to describe the variety in student selection, training, certification, and ideology, the mechanisms through which the school is considered to shape the university.

Some of the fastest-growing courses are college courses in high school (for example, advanced placement) and remedial education in postsecondary education. This trend demonstrates that the better high school students are becoming more closely aligned with higher education, but the weaker students are more disconnected. Most broad-access postsecondary students regress academically during their senior year (Conley 2005). They rarely take a math course oriented to college and study very little.

The customary fragmented manner in which policy is made on issues that span the K–16 continuum—such as finance, curricula, assessments, accountability, teacher education, data collection, and data usage—suggests a need for a better understanding of the state governance structures that will permit improved planning and connections across the education sectors. In addition, the very structure and organization of legislative committees traditionally serves to reinforce the divide between K–12 and postsecondary education. Georgia and New York have separate K–12 and higher education committees in both houses. Oregon and Florida have committees that oversee both, in both houses. Florida has K–20 committees, and it will be important to learn from their work over time. Having separate bodies makes policy making and appropriating funds across sectors very difficult. Appropriations committees are critical and usually have different lower and higher education subcommittees, making it virtually impossible to change the status quo.

Higher education governance structures, in general, can be a major impediment to K–16 reform. They are a reason why there is no one-size-fits-all model for reform. The variation in state higher education governance is significant. Some states, such as California, have three tiers, whereas Georgia has a single board of regents governing community colleges through research universities. In addition, almost every state has a coordinating board of higher education, and a separate K–12 state board of education.

Community Colleges

Community colleges are the point of entry into higher education for many students across the United States. More than 45 percent of undergraduates attend a community college, an increase of 10 percent in the last decade (Marcus 2005). This number has been increasing because of the heavy use of community colleges in fast growing states like California, Texas, and Florida. California, for example, enrolls two-thirds of its college freshmen into the community college system (Hayward et al. 2004).

Many of the students who enter community colleges fit the characteristics of those who are less likely to have access to college information and preparation. Community colleges serve a large proportion of low-income, ethnic minority, and first-generation college students (Tinto 1993). Despite low transfer and completion rates, community colleges continue to be an attractive option because of their proximity to students' residence, low enrollment fees, and open door policy that admits students with few entrance standards. Unfortunately, students often mistake the open door policy to mean that the college has few achievement standards. Students often believe that they are free to enter any courses, including college-level courses, they choose (Rosenbaum 2001).

High school counseling for prospective community college students is particularly weak and students receive vague signals about the college's academic demands. According to James Rosenbaum (2001), the level of high school achievement needed to succeed in the community college is not communicated to high school students. Students are told what it takes to enroll into a community college, but not what it takes to complete it. Because their performance in high school does not affect their enrolling in a community college, students are led to believe that what they do or do not achieve in high school does not matter. They are not told that it will affect how long it will take them to finish transfer requirements, thus decreasing their chances of ever completing college.

It is very difficult to make generalizations about the community college's structure and operations. There is no typical community college, but after 1960 it nonetheless became the primary institution for increasing college opportunity. Originally, community colleges were funded like public schools with mostly local support, state supplements, and no tuition. In California, community colleges originated as part of the local K–12 system and considered thirteenth and fourteenth grades. But four-year systems dictated much of their curricula to facilitate transfer (Callan 1997). Not until 1950 did community colleges across the nation begin to have their own governing boards and to be termed junior colleges.

Between 1950 and 1970, the number of community colleges more than doubled and enrollment increased from 217,000 to 1,630,000. Between 1969 and 1974, enrollment increased by 174 percent, versus the 47 percent for four-year institutions (Callan 1997). Growth was accompanied by a much expanded mission and a loss of interaction with and focus on secondary education. Colleges expanded their mission to vocational education and community service. New and neglected populations were added, including displaced housewives, immigrants, older adults, and laid-off industrial workers. The comprehensive community college became detached from secondary education and sent fewer and less clear signals to high school students about necessary academic preparation and skills needed to obtain vocational certificates.

Of all the English and math courses offered at the community college, 29 percent and 32 percent, respectively, are remedial (Cohen and Brawer

2003). The majority of the students enrolled in these remedial courses (60 percent) are traditional college age and enter the college directly after high school. This implies that the high level of remediation is not simply a result of having to refresh the skills of individuals who have been out of school for a while, but also of having to teach skills that were not received in high school (see chapter 4).

Increasingly, four-year institutions transfer their remediation of first-time students to community colleges. Ten states currently discourage four-year universities from offering remedial education by not providing state funding (Jenkins and Boswell 2002). Two states that have gotten much attention for shifting the responsibility of remedial education over to the community colleges are New York and Illinois. Both the City University of New York (CUNY) and Illinois universities began phasing out remedial education during the 1990s. Students who would have taken remedial courses in these systems are now being sent to the community colleges (Jenkins and Boswell 2002).

Incentives to Improve Disjunctures

One of the most important, and difficult, issues that states must tackle is creating the motivation and pay-off for systems, institutions, and people to overcome the disjunctures between the systems as a result of this historical evolution. Incentives must be developed for both systems, and in ways that tie them together. Haycock outlined two basic ways to create incentives:

> The first, and probably the most popular, is to put dollars on the table for joint K–16 work. Those dollars can be made conditional on the creation of a K–16 governance structure and/or on the willingness to undertake particular actions . . . This approach has the advantage of getting lots of activity underway quickly. But it has several disadvantages as well, not the least of which is that these activities tend to remain at the fringes of institutional life and institutional priorities. And when the dollars dry up . . . the activity goes away. The alternative is to approach this issue through the lens of accountability. The core idea is simple. Policy makers should design their accountability systems for both K–12 and higher education to include outcomes that each system cannot possibly deliver alone. K–12, for example, might be held accountable not only for improving student achievement and closing gaps between groups, but also for assuring that all of its secondary teachers have deep and substantial knowledge in the subject areas they are teaching. Similarly, higher education can be held accountable for decreasing the number of minority freshmen requiring remediation. (2002, 16)

Although money helps motivate, the key to success is avoid programmatic allocations that keep K–16 reform on the edges of institutions and systems. There is little incentive, for example, for an institution to work with K–12 to reduce the number of students who require remediation because those students bring with them valuable funds. One strategy is to "use the 'push' of a reconstructed accountability system together with the 'pull' of recaptured funding for institutional or departmental priorities" (Haycock 2002, 18).

Peter Ewell (2004) wrote that current incentives are not, from a K–16 accountability perspective, effective. One reasonable objective of a K–16 system would be to ensure that a greater percentage of traditionally underrepresented students persist throughout the education systems and complete some form of postsecondary education. For postsecondary institutions, however, two ways to improve completion rates are to be highly selective and diminish access, or to reduce both standards and the worth of a credential. But some broad access postsecondary institutions use a "student churn business model" to survive. These institutions contend that it costs less to let students drop out than to provide the intensive student services to help unprepared students stay enrolled. As long as the number of incoming students equals or exceeds those dropping out, the broad access institution is financially viable. A good K–16 accountability system might counteract these student churn financial policies. Ewell notes three typical state policy mechanisms regarding accountability: direct regulation, performance reporting, and performance funding but none of them have had much impact on the K–16 disjuncture (2004).

In many states, the elite selective institutions are in a separate postsecondary policy orbit, such as the University of California and the University of Michigan, that is not closely connected to most broad access institutions. The California community colleges are locally governed and see their mission as quite different from the University of California. The former normal and teaching training institutions that have become state universities see their role as more expansive than the flagship selective state university. Consequently, leadership and leverage that trickles down from elite postsecondary to broad access postsecondary is likely to be very limited.

Improving Secondary School Transition

Four policy levers are available for states, K–12 schools and districts, postsecondary institutions and systems, and the federal government to use to improve the transition from high school to college for students in broad-access postsecondary education.

The first is alignment of coursework and assessments. States need to align the content of their courses and assessments from the early grades through grade fourteen or later. A second lever is state finance. Statewide goals for grades K–16 should be integrated into state education finance systems. A third is data systems. States must create high-quality data systems than span the K–16 continuum. Last is accountability. States need to connect their accountability systems for K–12 and postsecondary education.

Improving State Alignment Policies

The first of the three steps involved in realignment is examining the relationship between the content of postsecondary education placement exams and K–12 exit-level standards and assessments to determine if more compatibility is necessary and possible. K–12 standards and assessments that are aligned with postsecondary education standards and assessments can provide clear signals and incentives, if they are high enough quality.

The second step is allowing students to take placement exams in high school so that they can prepare, academically, for college and understand college-level expectations. These assessments should be diagnostic so that secondary school students, their parents, and teachers know how to improve students' preparation for college.

The third involves using the senior year of high school to make up college readiness deficiencies, and sequencing undergraduate general education requirements so that appropriate senior-year courses are linked to postsecondary general education courses.

State Finance

Most state systems perpetuate the divide between K–12 and higher education by creating separate, aggregated, streams of financial support for each sector. State budgets lack incentives to promote college-readiness reforms. For example, states could offer financial incentives to both systems to offer dual enrollment or to reduce remediation. No state has fully established an integrated K–16 finance model, but Oregon may be moving in that direction. The Oregon Business Council analyzed state expenditures in 2002 and 2003 for both schools and colleges as though they came from one budget, and found that the per student level of investment varied by grade and degree—with community colleges receiving the least state aid and K–12 special education receiving the most. It recommended to the governor that Oregon reform its system so that, among other things, budgets would explicitly decide the level of support per student for different services and the measurable outcomes anticipated. The governor and a joint board that includes members from both the state board of education and the board of higher education have called for the establishment of a unified education system with curriculum alignment and a budget that connects all sectors. More states should follow a similar path.

State financial aid, a traditional means for broadening access to college, can also be used to leverage college-readiness reforms. Indiana's Twenty-first Century Scholars Program is an excellent model for how a state can both broaden access to college and improve college readiness. It promises the future payment of college tuition for middle school students who qualify for the federal free and reduced lunch program. It targets low-income students in the eighth grade and requires each participating student to complete a pledge to finish high school, maintain at least a C average, remain drug- and alcohol-free, apply for college and financial aid, and enroll in an Indiana postsecondary institution within two years of completing high school. In return, Indiana encourages the scholars to pursue a college preparatory curriculum, provides support services for them and for those who fulfill the pledge, and pays their tuition and fees (after other financial aid awards) at a public institution in Indiana or contributes a similar portion for tuition at an independent college. The program pays for 80 percent of the approved tuition and fees for students completing a regular high school diploma, for 90 percent of tuition and fees for students completing a more rigorous high school diploma (called a Core 40), and 100 percent of tuition and fees for students completing the most rigorous diploma (called Academic Honors). Through these incentives, the program sends clear signals to students regarding academic preparation for college. The results are encouraging. In 1992, Indiana was thirty-fourth in the nation in terms of the percent of high school graduates who enrolled in college immediately after graduation. In 2002, it was tenth. It is hoped that improvements in postsecondary completion will follow. An important next step would be to align high school graduation and college entrance and placement standards.

Better State Data Systems

Currently most states are unable to determine if their efforts to improve student readiness for college are having any impact. Many are working to improve their ability to gather information—Florida, for example, already has a model system up and running that links K–12 and postsecondary education, along with other public data. Few, if any, however, currently link information from schools and colleges. Some do not even collect data on the course-taking patterns of their high school students.

Consequently, in those states, it is impossible to determine the relationships between the courses that high school students take and students' persistence and success in college. Likewise, it is impossible to identify and analyze success rates for students who enter college from the workforce, students who attend part time, or students who attend multiple institutions. In short, the lack of reliable facts and figures that connect different levels of education makes it difficult to assess needs accurately, identify the worst problems, work toward finding solutions, and evaluate reforms.

States should be able to use their data systems to answer a variety of questions:

- How do students who take college-preparatory courses in high school perform in postsecondary education?
- Of those students who require remediation in college, what percentage took a college-preparatory curriculum in high school?

- How do students who earn a proficient score on a state's K–12 assessment perform in college?

- What pedagogical approaches are common among high school teachers who consistently send well-prepared students to college?

- Given their students' performance in college, how can high schools change their curricula and instruction to improve student readiness for college?

To be effective in improving college readiness, states should establish student-achievement objectives that require the education systems to collaborate on reaching them. Determining how to use the information to improve teaching and learning is an ideal area in which high schools and colleges should collaborate. For example, high schools should use data about their graduates' performance in college to improve their curricula, instruction, and grading practices.

Requiring educational institutions to report data to state departments of education, however, will not make the systems more accountable for student achievement. States need to work with educational leaders to develop clear student achievement targets that will require K–12 and postsecondary systems to achieve them jointly. Ultimately, primary outcomes for state accountability systems should include the percentage of the young population completing high school prepared for college (college readiness), the percentage enrolling in college (participation and access), the percentage staying in college (persistence), and the percentage graduating (completion). In addition, key indicators at various stages can include, for example, high school graduation and transfers from community colleges to four-year institutions.

The Role of Governance

To carry out the reforms we have recommended, states need to provide incentives to integrate governance structures across the education sectors. They should establish and support cross-sector commissions, charge them with specific responsibilities, provide the requisite resources, give them enough influence and authority to make real change, and hold them accountable for their performance. The agencies and groups involved with education within each state must also collaborate. Finally, strong leadership from both governors and legislative leaders, depending on the state, is needed to frame the college readiness issue to build public support.

The Federal Role

The federal government should also play an enhanced role in high school to college transition. One such function would be to expand the focus of federal programs to include not just access to college but access to success in college—access to the resources and information students need to prepare well for college. A second would be to expand the twelfth grade National Assessment of Educational Progress to include state-level data and link its standards to college readiness standards. A third would be to explore the possibility of using Indiana's Twenty-first Century Scholars Program as a model for a federal financial aid program that combines need and incentives for rigorous course-taking. A fourth would be to create incentives for states to collect and connect K–12 and postsecondary data, establish voluntary data collection standards, and provide technical assistance to help states develop high-quality data systems.

Overcoming Resistance

Any of the changes recommended in this chapter, however, confront the public's high approval rating for the current performance of postsecondary education, and satisfaction with the higher education status quo. Colleges and universities earned a respectable B in a 2001 nationwide random sample, but secondary schools were a full grade or more lower (Immerwahr 1999). The public's collective advice is that colleges and universities continue to focus on what they do best. According to public opinion, college students themselves, as adults, bear a considerable share of responsibility for succeeding in higher education. The public feels generally assured about the performance and academic quality of higher education. Only 12 percent of the public would raise entrance standards to postsecondary education.

The public believes that college students are less prepared than a decade ago, but only 11 percent hold postsecondary institutions responsible for students' failure to persist. Half of a national sample thinks that students are to blame. Another 40 percent think that it is a failure of high schools that causes students to drop out of colleges. Very few respondents think the presence or absence of K–16 services such as better counseling or higher education working with public schools is a primary cause of student success or failure. Moreover, most of the public think that minority students have about the same opportunities as their counterparts. This public opinion poll concluded, "there is no mandate for change—or even a suggestion of what kind of [higher education] change would prove necessary." The public message seems to be "stay the course" (Immerwahr 1999, 10). A major public information campaign is needed to highlight the lack of persistence and completion in broad access postsecondary education.

Research is needed on the critical levers and policies to overcome K–16 disjunctures. The basic issue is how to get K–12 and postsecondary education to work together (Venezia et al. 2005). Neither level working alone can do very much to improve signals that students and parents receive. We know very little about the incentives that will overcome the deeply rooted historical chasm. What mix of economics, social, and moral incentives will be effective? The two levels of education have so little social contact among faculty, administrators, and policy makers that there is unlikely to be much pressure from educators to change the current condition.

In many ways, the United States produces the college outcomes its systems of education were designed to produce. Its K–12 system was developed to provide education to everyone; its college and university systems were developed when only a few were expected to attend and complete college. This historical separation of missions needs to be overcome.

Endnotes

1. Calculations were based on data from Carnegie Foundation for the Advancement of Teaching. 2001. *The Carnegie Classification of Institutions of Higher Education,* Menlo Park, California. Researchers checked the Carnegie classifications with College Board data concerning the percentage of applicants accepted by postsecondary institutions and with data compiled by Thomas Mortenson (1998).
2. Data provided by National Center for Higher Education and Public Policy, San Jose, California, and the Southern Education Foundation.

References

Abell Foundation. 2002. *Baltimore City Community College at the Crossroads.* Baltimore, Md.: Abell Foundation.

Abraham, A. A., Jr. 1992. *College Remedial Studies: Institutional Practices in the SREB States.* Atlanta, Ga.: Southern Regional Education Board.

ACT Policy Report. 2005. *Courses Count: Preparing Students for Postsecondary Success.* Iowa City: ACT, Inc.

Adelman, Clifford. 1999. *Answers in the Toolbox: Academic Intensity, Attendance Patterns, and Bachelor's Degree Attainment.* Washington: U.S. Department of Education.

———. 2001. "Putting on the Glitz: How Tales From a Few Elite Institutions Form America's Impressions About Higher Education." *Connection: New England Journal of Higher Education* 15(3): 24–30.

———. 2005. *Academic Momentum from High School Through College.* Washington: U.S. Department of Education, Office of Vocational and Adult Education.

American Council on Education. 2002. *Access and Persistence.* Washington, D.C.: ACT, Inc.

———. 2003. "American College Testing (ACT)." Report. Iowa City, Iowa : ACT, Inc. Available at: http://www.act.org/news/releases/2003/pdf/english.pdf.

Bensimon, Estela. 2003. *Measuring the State of Equity in Public Higher Education.* Paper presented at Harvard Civil Rights Conference. Sacramento, Calif. (2003).

Bishop, John. 2003. "Nerds and Freaks: A Theory of Student Culture Norms." In *Brookings Papers in Education Policy,* edited by Diane Ravitch. Washington, D.C.: Brookings Institution.

Bowen, William G., Martin A. Kurzweil, and Eugene M. Tobin. 2005. *Equity and Excellence in American Higher Education.* Charlottesville: University of Virginia.

Boyer, Ernest, and Arthur Levine. 1981. *A Quest for Common Learning*. Princeton, N.J.: The Carnegie Foundation for the Advancement of Teaching.

Callan, Patrick M. 1997. "Stewards of Opportunity: America's Public Community Colleges." *Daedalus* 126(4): 95–112.

Carroll, Stephen, Cathy Krop, Jeremy Arkes, Peter A. Morrison, and Ann Flanagan. 2005. *California's K–12 Public Schools: How Are They Doing?* Santa Monica, Calif.: Rand.

Clark, Burton R. 1985. *The School and the University*. Berkeley: University of California Press.

———. 1993. *The Problem of Complexity in Higher Education*. Cambridge: Cambridge University Press.

Cohen, Arthur M., and Florence Brawer. 2003. *The American Community College*. San Francisco: Jossey-Bass.

Committee for Economic Development (CED). 2005. *Cracks in the Education Pipeline*. Washington, D.C.: The Committee for Economic Development.

Conley, David. 1996. "Where's Waldo: The Conspicuous Absence of Higher Education from School Reform and One State's Response." *Phi Delta Kappan* 78(4): 309–15.

———. 2005. *College Knowledge*. San Francisco, Calif.: Jossey-Bass.

Ewell, Peter. 2004. "An Accountability System for 'Doubling the Numbers.' " In *Double the Numbers: Increasing Postsecondary Credentials for Underrepresented Youth*, edited by Richard Kazis, Joel Fargas, and Nancy Hoffman. Cambridge, Mass.: Harvard Education Press.

Greenwald, Rob, Larry V. Hedges, and Richard Laine. 1996. "Interpreting Research on School Resources and Student Achievement: A Rejoinder to Hanushek." *Review of Educational Research* 66(3): 411–16.

Hanushek, E. A. 1997. "Assessing the Effects of School Resources on Student Performance: An Update." *Educational Evaluation and Policy Analysis* 19(2): 141–64.

Haycock, Kati. 2002. "Why Is K–16 Collaboration Essential to Educational Equity?" In *Gathering Momentum: Building the Learning Connection Between Schools and Colleges*. Washington, D.C.: The National Center for Public Policy and Higher Education, and The Institute for Educational Leadership.

Hayward, Gerald C., Dennis P. Jones, Aimes C. McGuinness, and Allene Timar. 2004. *Ensuring Access with Quality to California's Community Colleges*. San Jose, Calif.: The National Center for Public Policy and Higher Education.

Henry, Gary T., and Ross Rubenstein. 2002. "Paying for Grades: Impact of Merit-Based Financial Aid on Education Quality." *Journal of Policy Analysis and Management* 21(1): 93–109.

Immerwahr, John. 1999. *Doing Comparatively Well*. San Jose, Calif.: National Center for Higher Education and Public Policy.

Jenkins, Davis, and Katherine Boswell. 2002. *State Policies on Community College Remedial Education: Findings from a National Survey*. Education Commission of the States. Denver, Colo.: Center for Community College Policy.

Kahlenberg, Richard D. 2004. *America's Untapped Resource: Low Income Students in Higher Education*. New York: Twentieth Century Fund.

Kirst, Michael W. 2001. *Overcoming the High School Senior Slump: New Education Policies*. San Jose, Calif.: The National Center for Public Policy and Higher Education.

Kirst, Michael W., and Andrea Venezia. 2004. *From High School to College*. San Francisco, Calif.: Jossey-Bass.

Koski, William. 2004. "What Educational Standards Do Students Need to Meet California Education Standards?" *Teacher College Record* 106(10): 1907–35.

Marcus, Jon. 2005. "CUNY Sheds Reputation as Tutor U." *CrossTalk* 13(2)(Spring). http://www.highereducation.org/crosstalk/ct0205/news0205-cuny.shtml

Mortenson, Thomas G. 1998. "Freshman-to-Sophomore Selectivity and Degree Level, 1983 to 1998." *Postsecondary Education OPPORTUNITY*74(August).

Oakes, Jeanie. 1985. *Keeping Track*. New Haven, Conn.: Yale University Press.

Orrill, Robert. 2000. *Grades 11-14: The Heartland or Wasteland of American Education*. Princeton, N.J.: Woodrow Wilson National Fellowship Foundation.

Porter, Andrew. 1995. "The Uses and Misuses of Opportunity-to-Learn Standards. Research News and Comment." *Educational Researcher* 31(7): 3–14.

Ravitch, Diane, ed. 2000. *Brookings Papers in Education Policy*. Washington, D.C.: Brookings Institution Press.

Rosenbaum, James. 2001. *Beyond College for All*. New York: Russell Sage Foundation.

Roza, Marguerite. 2005. *District Fiscal Practices and Their Effects on School Spending*. Seattle: University of Washington, Center for Reinventing Public Education.

Schmidt, William H. 2002. "Too Little, Too Late: American High Schools in an International Context." In *Education Policy*, edited by Diane Ravitch. Washington, D.C.: Brookings Institution Press.

Schneider, Barbara. 2003. "Strategies for Success: High School and Beyond." In *Education Policy*, edited by Diane Ravitch. Washington, D.C.: Brookings Institution Press.

Stocking, Carol. 1985. "The United States." In *The School and the University*, edited by Burton Clark. Berkeley: University of California Press.

Tierney, William. 2004. *Nine Propositions Relating to the Effectiveness of College Preparation Programs*. New York: SUNY Press.

Tinto, Vincent. 1993. *Leaving College*. Chicago: University of Chicago.

U.S. Code. 1994. *Goals 2000: Educate America Act*. Public Law No. 103–227, *U.S. Statutes at Large* 108 (1994): 125.

U.S. Department of Education. 2001. *The Condition of Education*. Washington: Government Printing Office.

Venezia, Andrea. 2000. "Connecting California's K–12 and Higher Education Systems: Challenges and Opportunities." In *Crucial Issues in California Education 2000: Are the Reform Pieces Fitting Together?* Berkeley: Policy Analysis for California Education.

———. 2007. *Uneven Opportunity to Learn in California Schools*. Berkeley: Policy Analysis for California Education.

Venezia, Andrea, Michael Kirst, and Anthony Antonio. 2003. *Betraying the College Dream: How Disconnected K–12 and Postsecondary Education Systems Undermine Student Aspirations*. Stanford, Calif.: The Stanford Institute for Higher Education Research.

Venezia, Andrea, Michael Kirst, Patrick Callan, and Michael Vadan. 2005. *The Governance Divide*. San Francisco: National Center for Education and Public Policy.

Young, Jeffrey R. 2004. "Students' Political Interest Hits Highest Level in Decade." *Chronicle of Higher Education* 50(21)(January): 30–32.

Part II

The Role of Institutions

Chapter 4

Remedial and Developmental Courses

ERIC P. BETTINGER AND
BRIDGET TERRY LONG

A CADEMIC PREPARATION is an important predictor of success in college. Numerous studies link the types of courses students take in high school to their performance in higher education. Clifford Adelman (1999), for example, provides a detailed study of college access and degree completion among a cohort of students who were in the tenth grade in 1980. He finds that a student's academic background, defined by measures of academic content and performance in secondary school (such as high school curriculum intensity, class rank, and GPA), is the most critical factor in determining college enrollment and success. However, the preparation students have when entering college often is below what is required and varies greatly by background. Adelman finds that students differ significantly in the types of courses they take and how well they perform by background. In a recent update (2006), he finds curriculum to be even more compelling in terms of its role in degree completion. In another study, Jay Greene and Greg Foster (2003) found that only 32 percent of students leave high school at least minimally prepared for college. The proportion is much smaller for black and Hispanic students—20 and 16 percent, respectively.[1] Gaps in test scores by race and income are also significant (Jencks and Phillips 1998). Therefore, though academic preparation is a problem for many students entering college, it is a problem that affects low-income and minority students in particular.

One solution has been to place students in remedial courses. Also called developmental or basic skills courses, these classes are designed to address the deficiencies and prepare student for subsequent college success.[2] This practice has been around as early as the seventeenth century, when Harvard College assigned tutors to underprepared students studying

Latin (Phipps 1998). However, during the twentieth century, the increased demand for higher education by students from all backgrounds accelerated the need for remediation in higher education. Moreover, given the correlation between income and educational inequality and the need for remediation, remediation has become a popular policy tool aiming to reduce inequalities. By 1995, 81 percent of public four-year colleges and 100 percent of two-year colleges offered remediation (NCES 1996).

In 2001, colleges required nearly one in three first-year students to take remedial courses in reading, writing, or mathematics (NCES 2003). Moreover, there is some evidence that the proportion of students in need of college remediation has been growing. According to the NCES (1996), 39 percent of colleges surveyed reported that remedial enrollments had increased during the last five years. In Ohio, though only 17.8 percent of recent high school graduates enrolled in math remediation in 1988, the proportion had risen to 30 percent by 2004 (Ohio Board of Regents 2005). This growth has been principally located at community and technical colleges (Secondary and Higher Education Remediation Advisory Commission 1997).

Although the use of remedial courses by postsecondary institutions is widespread, little is known about the effectiveness of such interventions. It appears that states and colleges know little about whether their remediation programs are successful along any dimension. According to the Southern Regional Education Board, few states have exit standards for remedial courses (Crowe 1998). Moreover, a study of 116 two-year and four-year colleges found only a small percentage performed any systematic evaluation of their programs (Weissman, Rulakowski, and Jumisko 1997). On one hand, the courses may help underprepared students gain the skills necessary to excel in college. On the other hand, by increasing the number of requirements, extending the time to degree, and effectively restricting the majors available to students (due to the inability to enroll in advanced coursework until remedial courses are completed) remediation may negatively impact college outcomes such as persistence and long-term labor market returns. Moreover, it is not obvious what level of proficiency is required for college success and how this differs by subject area. According to Ronald Phipps (1998, 2), "conjecture and criticism has filled the void created by the lack of basic information."

At an estimated annual cost in the billions (Breneman and Haarlow 1998), the debate about the merits of investing in remediation has intensified in recent years. There are many questions about whether remediation is worthwhile. Do the courses help students succeed in college? What is the best way to perform remediation? Could the courses be offered in more limited, less expensive ways? States are currently confronting these questions by considering ways to limit remediation, shift its location, or pass on the costs of the courses to students or high school districts. However, they do so with little information on the students who need remediation and the effects of the courses on their outcomes. We attempt to address this hole in the literature by examining the role of remediation in higher education.

Context of the Study

This chapter reviews information on remediation nationwide, but the empirical analysis focuses on students attending public colleges and universities in Ohio. Using a unique database of college students maintained by the Ohio Board of Regents (OBR), we provide a detailed picture of remediation in the fifth largest public higher education system in the country. With longitudinal information from college transcripts, applications, and standardized tests, the analysis tracks Ohio students who began at a public college in fall 1998 over the course of six years.[3] Despite the focus on remediation in Ohio, the results are important and should also have external validity. Ohio's college enrollment and remediation rates are similar to national patterns. The percentages of Ohio public school students who graduate from high school and enter college the following fall are near the national averages (Mortenson 2002). Similarly, 27 percent of first-time freshmen enrolled in remedial math nationally in 1995 (NCES 1996), and 29 percent did so in Ohio.

Ohio is an exemplary case for studying remediation because the state is confronting many of the questions and concerns surrounding the debate on remediation. The magnitude of the number of students involved and the costs of remediation have parents, students, and policy makers in Ohio concerned about the value of the programs (Ruth Sternberg and Alice Thomas, "Ohio's Remedial College Courses costs Millions." *The Columbus Dispatch,* August 12, 2002, pg. 01A.). Another compelling reason to study Ohio is that it plays a prominent role in higher education. The only states with greater numbers of students in public colleges are California, Texas, New York, and Illinois (NCES 2000). Moreover, Ohio reflects the complete spectrum of communities, labor markets, and higher education options that exist across the nation. Ohio has a mixture of selective and nonselective four-year institutions as well as two-year community and technical colleges spread geographically across the state.

Table 4.1 provides summary statistics of the sample of Ohio students. As is typical in higher education, the sample is slightly more female (53.5 percent), and the percentage of the sample that is African American is similar to national college proportions (Hispanic and Asian students are underrepresented). A little over half of the first-time students for the fall 1998 term are full time and a quarter take fewer than six credits. The columns display mean statistics for the different types of institutions within the state. As expected, students at the selective four-year universities had a higher mean ACT score than those at other schools.[4] Students at the

Table 4.1 Public Higher Education in Ohio, First-Time Undergraduates

	All Schools	Four-Year Universities			Two-Year Colleges	
		Selective	Nonselective	Branch	Community	Technical
Age in 1998	21.78	18.55	21.20	21.76	24.23	26.34
	(7.88)	(1.94)	(6.88)	(8.19)	(9.57)	(11.25)
Female	53.51	55.20	53.75	55.46	50.66	58.14
White	80.52	85.53	71.01	82.82	78.66	92.04
Black	10.33	6.06	16.43	2.53	13.86	4.88
Hispanic	1.89	1.88	1.79	0.59	2.49	0.63
Asian	1.57	2.57	1.55	0.49	1.18	0.47
Race unknown	4.29	2.67	7.93	13.06	1.91	1.43
Ohio resident	91.92	85.03	93.59	94.09	95.61	97.85
Full-time fall 1998	54.73	82.38	56.46	53.17	30.75	25.55
Part-time fall 1998	20.19	11.88	21.56	20.54	26.00	31.38
Less than part-time	25.08	5.75	21.99	26.29	43.24	43.07
Four-year degree intent	—	—	—	—	35.24	10.22
Two-year degree intent	—	—	—	—	28.48	50.40
ACT composite score	21.37	23.31	20.73	19.77	19.25	18.61
(maximum 36)	(4.36)	(3.99)	(4.31)	(3.68)	(3.79)	(3.56)
	[37,227]	[16,103]	[8,041]	[4,204]	[7,816]	[1,063]
Observations	65,977	20,538	12,145	6,280	23,385	3,629

Source: Authors' computations using data from the Ohio Board of Regents.

Note: Four Ohio colleges without clear records on which courses were considered remedial during the 1998–99 school year are excluded (Kent State University, University of Cincinnati, Hocking Technical College, and Lima Technical College).
Standard deviations are shown in the parentheses. The complete sample is not used in calculating the means for full/part/less than part-time due to missing information for approximately seven percent of the sample.
The number of observations used to calculate the mean ACT score (the number who took the exam) is shown in brackets. The selective universities are defined as "competitive" institutions by Barron's Educational Guides (1997). Full-time is defined as taking twelve or more credit hours during the first term (Fall 1998); part-time constitutes taking six to eleven credits, and less than part-time means students took less than six credits during the first term. Four-year degree intent means the student noted wanting to get a bachelor's degree or transfer to a four-year college.

selective institutions also tend to be younger, white, and full time. The two-year colleges instead serve older students, students of color, and part-time students. Students at the state and local community colleges as well as the technical colleges report their educational intent. Approximately 64 and 61 percent report wanting to advance to receive either an associate's or bachelor's degree, respectively. However, only 10 percent of students at the technical colleges report intent to go onto a four-year degree, whereas 35 percent of students at a state or local community college plan to continue for a bachelor's degree.

One limitation of the data is that it does not include students who attended private colleges. However, public colleges educate a much larger share of students than the private sector and are the places where the role of remediation is most significant. According to the NCES (2003), only 12 percent of students take remedial courses at private, four-year colleges. Excluding these schools therefore does not present a serious impediment in assessing the effects of remediation. Unfortunately, because we are unable to track students who transfer to private institutions or schools outside of Ohio, these students are indistinguishable in the data from students who drop out of college completely. However, this potential measurement error is likely to be very small because the percentage of students thought to transfer to such schools is a small fraction of the total number of observed dropouts.[5]

The Institutional Side of Remediation

States and university systems often set the policies that govern where, how, and who pays for remediation at public institutions within their borders. In 1995, state policies or laws governed remedial offerings at one in three institutions nationwide (NCES 1996). In recent years, states have become even more involved. Some, such as Connecticut and Arizona, do not allow remedial education at public institutions (Breneman and Haarlow 1998). Other state systems have chosen to expel students with severe academic deficiencies. During the fall of 2001, for example, the California State University system "kicked out more than 2,200 students—nearly 7 percent of the freshman class—for failing to master basic English and math skills" (Rebecca Trounson, "Cal State Ouster Rate Rises Slightly," *The Los Angeles Times*, January 31, 2002, pg. B1). Among the 22 percent of colleges that do not offer remediation, approximately 27 percent note having an institutional policy that prohibited the offering of remedial courses (NCES 1996). Supporters of such measures suggest that remedial courses remove the incentive to adequately prepare for college while in high school. Additionally, they question the appropriateness of work below college level at a postsecondary institution. Among the institutions not offering remedial courses, nearly one in four reported fielding the courses out to other institutions (NCES 1996).

Although most two-year public colleges were required to offer courses, 15 percent of public four-year institutions in 1995 were discouraged from offering the courses or restricted in some way from doing so (NCES 1996). At least eight states, including Florida and Illinois, restrict remediation to two-year institutions. Several other states have recently considered such policies along with state college systems. With 70 percent of entering freshmen failing at least one of the three placement tests and nearly 20 percent of all students taking remedial basic-skills courses, the CUNY system joined this group during the late 1990s. After much debate and revision to the original proposal, the final decision was made in November 1999 to phase out most remedial education at the system's four-year colleges beginning in 2000 (Hebel 1999).

Focusing on the finances behind remediation, states such as Texas, Tennessee, and Utah have imposed or are considering limits on the government funding of remedial coursework (Education Commission of the States, 2003). Time limits were imposed on remediation at about one in four institutions across the country (NCES 1996). For example, the California State University system imposes a one-year limit on remedial work. Finally, several initiatives seek to pass on the costs of remediation to students. In Florida, for example, the legislature elected to require college students to pay the full cost of their remedial course work, an expense estimated to be four times greater than the regular tuition rate (Ignash 1997).

Many blame the increasing role of college remediation on the K–12 system. During the CUNY controversy, Rudolph Giuliani voiced the sentiment of numerous government officials when he said that the "university system currently devotes far too much money and effort to teaching skills that students should have learned in high school" (Schmidt 1998, A33). Some officials have therefore targeted the secondary school system for funding the courses. For a short time, Minnesota allowed colleges to bill secondary schools for the cost of their graduates' remedial classes, and several secondary school districts in Virginia guarantee their diplomas by paying the remedial expenses of their former students (Wheat 1998). However, this type of action would not fully address the problem of remediation as only 64 percent of students earn a standard high school diploma, and many argue that high school graduation standards do not coincide with the competencies needed in college (McCabe 2001).

Organization and Delivery

The purpose of remedial education in most college systems is to provide underprepared students the skills necessary to complete and succeed in college. In addition, remediation may serve several institutional needs. First, it allows colleges to offer access to growing numbers of students. It also provides individual departments the ability to generate enrollment, particularly in English and math departments. Moreover, by separating weaker students into remedial courses, remediation allows colleges to protect institutional selectivity, regulate entry to upper level courses, and maintain the research functions of the college. Finally, remediation may serve as a tool to integrate students into the school population (Soliday 2002). The bulk of remediation is provided by nonselective public institutions, the point of entry for 80 percent of four-year students and virtually all two-year students.

Within the state of Ohio, public colleges and universities are independent and autonomous. Therefore, as shown by a 1995 study by the Ohio Legislative Office of Education Oversight (LOEO), each is free to set their admissions, placement, and remediation policies.[6] With the exception of two campuses, Miami University and Central State University, all public colleges in Ohio offer remedial courses to entering freshmen.[7] However, most remedial students take their courses at the community colleges. For example, about 55 percent of traditional-age, first-time freshmen at community colleges enroll in remedial courses (Ohio Board of Regents 2001). Half of two-year colleges provide remedial or developmental courses to local business and industry as well as to their traditional students (NCES 1996). As noted, the practice of focusing remediation at the community colleges is similar to the experience in other states, and recent developments suggest more systems are moving more toward this model. Even though four-year colleges in Ohio offer remediation, some require students to take remedial courses at their satellite campuses.

Nationally, institutional policy on remedial courses varies. About 10 percent of higher education institutions offer no academic credit for remedial courses. All public colleges in Ohio offer credit for remedial courses, though at most schools it does not count toward degree completion and simply becomes a part of the student's record (LOEO 1995). Campuses also vary in the extent to which they require versus suggest that underprepared students enroll in remedial or developmental work (Ohio Board of Regents, 2002).

Remedial courses are often the gateway for students to enroll in upper level courses. About two-thirds of campuses nationally restrict enrollment in some classes until remediation is complete (NCES 1996). This is also the case in Ohio where, similar to national trends, most schools prohibit students from taking college-level courses in the same subject area until remediation is complete. Some go even further by barring students from taking any college-level work while enrolled in remediation (LOEO 1995).[8] This requirement may restrict students' class schedules and, to the extent that remediation affects the classes that students can take, it may also discourage students from focusing on certain majors. For example, some majors are extremely demanding in terms of required credit hours and have little leeway for students to enroll in non-required classes. Students in remediation may have to take a semester's worth of preparatory classes before they start the major; however, given course scheduling, the student may fall a year behind. On the one hand, this rigidity may just increase the time to graduation; however, it also discourages certain majors. One college administrator, for instance, claimed that students needing remediation in their first year often "have no possibility of completing an engineering degree and must choose other majors" (Dodd 2002).

At some colleges, remedial courses are offered institution-wide whereas at others the courses are housed in individual departments. Another option for institutions and states is to outsource the remediation. Kaplan Educational Centers and Sylvan Learning Systems are major providers of remediation (Phipps 1998). An evaluation of the relative effectiveness of Sylvan in serving students of Howard Community College found results at least as equal to the rates of success for those enrolled in a traditional course (Copenhaver, Irvin, and Novak 1996). In our review, we focus on identifying whether remedial policies affect students' educational outcomes. There may be other benefits in terms of earnings and career. All measurable benefits, however, should be contrasted with the cost of remedial programs. Although we review what is known about the costs of remediation, the primary data used in our analysis unfortunately do not include cost information nor data on students' work outcomes. We leave it for future analyses to determine whether the remediation programs are cost-effective.

The Remedial Placement Process

Because the average college student attends a nonselective institution to which he or she is almost assured admission, the remediation placement exam taken when first arriving on campus has become the key academic gate-keeper to postsecondary study. As Michael Kirst notes in chapter 3, because admission is virtually certain, students' first hurdle is their placement test. Nationally, the most widely used placement exams are the Computerized Adaptive Placement Assessment and Support Systems (COMPASS) and the Assessment of Skills for Successful Entry and Transfer (ASSET), each published by the ACT. The tests consist of a variety of tests to measure students' skill level. For example, the asset exam is a written exam with as many as twelve subsections, including in depth assessment of students' writing, numerical, and reading skills.[9] Most students are identified using placement exams in reading, writing, and mathematics, but some schools also use standardized test scores and high school transcripts to make assignments. After students have taken the placement exam, colleges assign them to a specific math course, oftentimes a remedial course, based on their scores. Typically, administrators make these designations based on cutoffs: students scoring below a given threshold are assigned to a remedial course.

In Ohio, all colleges require entering freshman to take placement exams, but due to the autonomous nature of each institution, the instruments vary by institutions. Colleges use different combinations of ACT and SAT scores, sections of the ASSET test, and institutionally developed subject-area tests to determine remedial placement. Although there are statewide standards in Ohio to distinguish between remedial and college-level work, institutions differ in how they interpret the standards at the campus level. For example, the cut-off scores used to determine placement differ among institutions, reflecting the varying interpretations of what comprises college-level coursework (LOEO 1995). A survey performed by Raymond Walters Colleges on placement mechanisms found significant differences in the level of performance required to qualify for college-level writing courses at colleges around Ohio. The cut-off scores for placement into writing remediation varied from 17 to 20 for the ACT, from 410 to 580 for the SAT, and from 26 to 44 for the ASSET test (Secondary and Higher Education Remediation Advisory Commission 1997). A student who might be placed into college-level courses at some Ohio colleges would therefore be put in remediation at others.

Institutional rules on placement into remediation might differ for a number of reasons. First, placement policies and rates vary due to differences in schools' student bodies. For example, Ohio State University (OSU) is one of the most selective schools in the state and its remediation program differs from that of Cuyahoga Community College (CYCC), the largest community college in the state. Students at OSU typically have higher test scores and more college preparation than students at CYCC, and the demands of the curriculum at OSU are higher. However, even schools with similar student bodies vary in their remediation policies. This may be partly due to differences in the preferences of the administration likely to influence the role of remediation at a school. For example, the University of Toledo recently decided not to offer remediation courses due a change in the college leadership. Students requiring remediation are now referred to Owens Community College (Robert Sheehan, personal communication, September 18, 2002). The preferences of the departments responsible for remediation courses are also likely to be important in determining an institution's view of remediation. Some colleges in Ohio, the University of Toledo and Case Western Reserve University are good examples, use different placement exams or give different weight to high school background and preparation. The measurement error in the tests and the difference in weighting creates variation across similar students at different universities.

Another reason remediation may differ across colleges is costs. If the price attached to remediation differs across schools, then colleges will vary in their placement policies. Particularly over time, as college budgets become more or less stringent, institutions may be more or less willing to spend money on remediation. Finally, the political economy of the surrounding area could explain differences in remediation. Local colleges and universities repeatedly report the percentage of students requiring remediation. Because students living nearby are more likely to attend a given college, the college by necessity must develop a relationship with nearby secondary schools. A more expansive remediation policy might be an indictment of the quality of local education and political pressure may indicate or require less formal remediation. The political economy and secondary schools of the surrounding area might also be important in determining the role of remediation at a college, but it is worth noting that Bettinger and Long (2005) found that the characteristics of the local high schools and community were not related to the cutoffs for placement into remediation.

The Cost of Remediation

David Breneman and William Haarlow (1998) estimate that remediation costs $1 billion a year, but this figure does not include private or proprietary colleges and most states surveyed had little data from which to give accurate assessments. When considering the costs, it is important to distinguish between recent high school graduates and nontraditional college students, including adult learners and immigrants. Although critics blame the K–12 system for the remediation of its recent graduates and suggest that high schools should contribute to the costs associated with these students, most treat older students returning to higher education to upgrade their skills as a separate category.

In 2000, Ohio public colleges spent approximately $15 million teaching 260,000 credit hours of high school–level courses to freshmen; another $8.4 million was spent on older students (Ohio Board of Regents 2001). These figures take into account only state subsidies because the state of Ohio offers instructional subsidies for courses granting academic credit. However, additional costs associated with items such as tuition expenditures, financial aid resources, and lost wages are not included in this estimate. The cost of remediation for the 20,000 freshmen in the state amounted to an additional $15 million in tuition.

According to the Arkansas Department of Higher Education (1998), remedial education is less costly than or approximately the same as core academic programs. An analysis of expenditure data in the 1996–1997 school year found that the direct and indirect costs per FTE were $7,381 for remediation at four-year colleges and $6,709 at two-year colleges.[10] In comparison, the cost of core programs ranged from $7,919 to $12,369 at the four-year colleges and $6,163 to $8,235 at the two-year colleges. The two primary reasons for the cost differences are class size and faculty compensation. For example, large courses taught by adjuncts are far less expensive than small seminars taught by full professors. Furthermore, the use of equipment and technology can affect the cost of providing a course (Phipps 1998).

In the CUNY system during the 1996–1997 school year, a Price Water-house study found that colleges spent $124 million on remediation. This constituted 23 percent and 5 percent of expenditures at two-year and four-year colleges, respectively. Further analysis suggests that the cost of remediation courses was approximately one-third less than the cost of other academic courses. At community colleges, schools spent $4,660 per full-time equivalent (FTE) student for remediation courses and $7,079 per FTE for all other academic programs. The courses were more expensive at four-year institutions: $6,350 per FTE on remediation versus $9,754 overall. Two-thirds of the costs for remediation were covered by tuition and student aid with city and state funding providing for the rest (City University of New York, 1999).

The social costs of not offering remediation, however, are likely to be much higher than the institutional costs of the programs. Whereas long-term solutions may rely on changes in K–12 and reforms that better link high school and college, several present and short-term concerns must be considered. Unskilled individuals have expenses associated with them, such as unemployment costs, government dependency, crime, and incarceration. Moreover, the increasing demands of the economy in terms of skill encourage the nation to find an effective way to train its workers. As noted in a *Time* magazine article, eliminating remediation in higher education could "effectively end the American experiment with mass postsecondary education" (Cloud 2002).

The Student Side of Remediation

We now address what is known about the students placed into remediation, reviewing the research literature and examining data from the public higher education system in Ohio. The results highlight how the backgrounds and level of academic preparation differ for students who participate in the courses versus those who avoid remediation.

Participation in Remedial Education

The first major group of students in remedial education is underprepared recent high school graduates, many of whom leave secondary school without grade-level competency or the proper preparation for college-level material. In Ohio, 37 percent of first-year students under the age of nineteen fit into this category, having graduated from high school without a college-prep curriculum (Ohio Board of Regents 2002). In addition, a substantial number of adult students enroll in developmental courses.

Table 4.2   Remediation in Ohio Public Higher Education

	All Schools	Four-Year Universities	
		Selective	Nonselective
In Math or English			
Remediation	36.18%	14.25%	34.65%
In Remedial Math	29.70%	11.07%	25.29%
In Remedial English	20.08%	5.72%	21.27%
Observations	65,977	20,538	12,145

	All Schools	Two-Year Colleges		
		Branch	Community	Technical
In Math or English				
Remediation	36.18%	43.90%	52.20%	48.83%
In Remedial Math	29.70%	36.89%	45.64%	34.75%
In Remedial English	20.08%	19.17%	29.69%	36.98%
Observations	65,977	6,280	23,385	3,629

Source: Authors' computations using data from the Ohio Board of Regents.
Notes: The credits completed are totals up to the spring 2002 term (four years). Credits earned at colleges with the quarter system have been converted to semester hours. The selective universities are defined as competitive institutions by Barron's Educational Guides (1997) and include Bowling Green State University, Miami University, Ohio State University, Ohio University, and Youngstown State University.

Many of these were displaced by structural shifts in the labor market and seek developmental courses to acquire the skills necessary for re-employment. Others are often recent immigrants or welfare recipients. Nationally, about 27 percent of remedial students were over the age of thirty (IHEP 1998).

In Ohio during the fall of 1998, approximately 36 percent of first-time freshman were placed in remediation. As shown in table 4.2, nearly 30 percent were placed in remedial math and 20 percent in remedial English. Although the numbers in math remediation were greater, participation in English remediation may be more serious as some evidence suggests that the seriousness of academic deficiencies differs by subject. Robert McCabe (2000) asserts that reading remediation puts students at a greater disadvantage than math remediation.

The proportion in remediation differs considerably by type of institution. Remediation rates are highest at the two-year colleges. More than half of first-time freshmen took at least one remedial course during the fall 1998 term at the state and local community colleges. In contrast, only 14 percent of students at selective colleges took remedial math or English. This variation is at least partly explained by differences in the student bodies of the schools.

The Backgrounds of Remedial Students

A detailed picture of the students in remediation by background is presented in table 4.3, which itemizes the mean characteristics of students in and out of different types of remediation. At the four-year colleges, female students are overrepresented in math remediation and underrepresented in English remediation. Additionally, black and Hispanic students are more likely to be found in remediation, particularly in both courses. Similar trends are also found at the two-year colleges. Full-time students and those seeking a four-year degree are also less likely to be in remediation than part-time or less than part-time students or those seeking a two-year degree.

Table 4.4 provides another perspective on which types of students end up in remediation. For each group as defined in the first column, the percentages denote the proportion of that group that was placed in math or English remediation. For example, 37 percent of students aged eighteen to twenty and 46 percent of those aged twenty-one to twenty-three were in remediation. At most of the institutions, except at the university branch campuses and selective four-year universities, remediation is concentrated among younger students. It is also more likely among female than male students at the community and technical colleges. In terms of race, remedial placement is more likely for black and Hispanic students, though one-third of white and one-quarter of Asian students are also in the courses. Part-time students are the most likely to be in remediation.

Table 4.5 examines the relationship between family income and being placed in college remediation. Information on family income is derived from a survey of a large subset of Ohio students. One must be cautious in interpreting the results because children often do not know their parents' income. However, students were given a choice of various income ranges and asked to choose the appropriate category, which likely reduces inaccurate responses as students are probably not off the correct answer by more than one category. The higher categories represent higher incomes. The percentages shown in table 4.5 also denote the proportion of each group that was placed in or out of remedial courses. As expected, placement into remediation declines as family income increases. This is likely related to differences in high school quality by income.

Academic Preparation and the Need for Remediation

Research has established that the need for remediation in college is closely tied to the high school course of study of a student. A 2002 study by the Ohio Board of Regents found that students who had completed an academic core curriculum in high school were half as likely to need remediation in college when compared to students without this core. Jeff Hoyt

Table 4.3 Placement In and Out of Remediation by Background (Means)

	Four-Year Colleges				Two-Year Colleges			
	None	Math	English	Math and English	None	Math	English	Math and English
Age in 1998	19.47	19.71	19.41	20.15	26.39	21.82	21.72	21.43
	(4.70)	(4.49)	(4.10)	(4.63)	(11.44)	(6.89)	(6.93)	(6.11)
Female	54.41	62.87	44.74	52.87	48.52	59.34	48.87	55.55
White	83.52	75.60	68.90	54.19	83.21	86.03	80.43	70.30
Black	6.43	16.05	20.25	35.09	6.60	7.81	12.40	22.97
Hispanic	1.73	2.52	1.29	2.79	1.34	2.04	2.46	3.03
Asian	2.42	0.98	2.52	0.96	0.95	0.98	1.17	0.96
Ohio Resident	86.74	92.95	92.90	94.92	93.25	97.65	97.79	98.09
Full-time fall 1998	79.34	55.00	58.80	36.11	31.49	42.40	38.02	34.35
Part-time fall 1998	11.82	28.57	22.84	31.89	19.37	30.37	27.60	33.90
Less than part-time	8.84	16.43	18.36	32.00	49.14	27.23	34.37	31.76
Four-year degree intent	—	—	—	—	40.11	55.20	43.32	45.32
Two-year degree intent	—	—	—	—	18.74	28.90	36.76	33.94
Observations	25,549	3,377	1,788	1,969	16,559	7,245	2,484	7,006

Source: Authors' computations using data from the Ohio Board of Regents.
Notes: Standard deviations are shown in the parentheses. The complete sample is not used in calculating the means for full/part/less than part-time due to missing information for approximately seven percent of the sample. Full-time is defined as taking twelve or more credit hours during the first term (Fall 1998); part-time constitutes taking six to eleven credits, and less than part-time means students took less than six credits during the first term. Four-year degree intent means the student noted wanting to get a bachelor's degree or transfer to a four-year college. Students at university branch campuses (two-year institutions) are assumed as having four-year degree intent.

Table 4.4   Percentage of Group Placed in Remediation

	All Schools	Four-Year Universities		Branch	Two-Year Colleges	
		Selective	Nonselective		Community	Technical
Age 18 to 20	37.12	13.78	37.31	48.20	66.36	60.78
Age 21 to 23	45.70	35.08	28.21	55.66	51.39	55.30
Age 24+	31.69	40.53	26.19	27.61	32.29	37.54
Male	34.23	14.23	33.13	43.01	46.92	46.94
Female	37.87	14.26	35.95	44.62	57.34	50.19
White	33.90	12.91	29.96	47.97	49.29	47.75
Black	59.84	35.37	57.89	65.41	69.78	66.67
Hispanic	46.79	18.60	41.74	72.97	65.35	56.52
Asian	25.41	6.45	33.51	29.03	52.17	82.35
Full-time fall 1998	27.30	10.41	26.77	42.98	62.16	52.29
Part-time fall 1998	53.15	29.90	48.66	64.50	60.39	67.75
Less than part-time	38.55	33.70	42.14	29.68	40.56	34.31
Four-year degree intent	—	—	—	—	64.20	54.72
Two-year degree intent	—	—	—	—	64.38	60.03

Source: Authors' computations using data from the Ohio Board of Regents.
Notes: The figures reflect the percentage of that group that was placed in remediation at that type of institution. The selective universities are defined as competitive institutions by Barron's Educational Guides (1997) and include Bowling Green State University, Miami University, Ohio State University, Ohio University, and Youngstown State University. Full-time is defined as taking twelve or more credit hours during the first term (Fall 1998); part-time constitutes taking six to eleven credits, and less than part-time means students took less than six credits during the first term. Four-year degree intent means the student noted wanting to get a bachelor's degree or transfer to a four-year college.

Table 4.5   Percentage of the Income Group Placed in Remediation

Financial Background	No Remediation	Remediation	Observations
Less than $18,000	50.23	49.77	2,196
$18,000 to $24,000	55.58	44.42	2,008
$24,000 to $30,000	62.24	37.76	2,227
$30,000 to $36,000	64.19	35.81	2,642
$36,000 to $42,000	65.24	34.76	3,245
$42,000 to $50,000	67.05	32.95	4,136
$50,000 to $60,000	69.68	30.32	4,697
$60,000 to $80,000	72.31	27.69	5,597
$80,000 to $100,000	78.90	21.10	2,957
More than $100,000	82.06	17.94	2,743
Total Sample	68.09	31.91	32,448

Source: Authors' computations using data from the Ohio Board of Regents.

and Colleen Sorensen (1999) found a similar pattern when examining the need for remediation at Utah Valley State College. Interestingly, the Ohio Board of Regents records that 36 percent of first-year students aged nineteen or younger attending any public Ohio campus graduated from high school without a college prep curriculum. This is exactly the same proportion of students who enrolled in at least one remedial course in their first year of college (Ohio Board of Regents 2001). As Michael Kirst notes in chapter 3, graduation from high school does not ensure that a student has completed a curriculum adequate for easy entry into college.

Table 4.6 examines how the level of high school preparation and achievement differs by remedial placement. Most students in Ohio take the ACT exam and the proportion is highest at the four-year colleges. Our data include the highest score received by the student and his or her most recent responses to the ACT survey, which includes self-reported information on high school preparation and performance. As expected, the mean ACT scores of students are higher among those not placed into remediation. For instance, at selective four-year universities, students not in remediation had an average score of 24 and those in the courses an average score of 19.

In terms of math remediation, we find that students not in remediation had higher grades in high school math and took more semesters of the subject. This is similar to the results found by both the Ohio Board of Regents and Hoyt and Sorensen. Likewise, the mean math ACT scores are also higher for nonremediated students. Similar patterns can be found for those students in English remediation. Indeed, academic preparation seems to play an important role in the need for remediation.

However, many students who had successfully completed upper-level math courses still required remedial math or needed to repeat subjects in

Table 4.6   Remedial Placement Compared to Academic Preparation and Achievement

	Selective Four-Year Colleges		Nonselective Four-Year Colleges		Two-Year University Branches		Community Colleges	
	None	Remed.	None	Remed.	None	Remed.	None	Remed.
Took ACT	78.20	79.67	67.10	64.52	65.29	69.06	29.13	37.35
ACT overall score (36 max)	24.03	19.03	22.29	17.69	21.22	18.02	21.17	17.88
	(3.67)	(3.01)	(4.08)	(2.90)	(3.63)	(2.90)	(3.89)	(3.06)
Placement into Math Remediation								
Average HS math GPA	3.35	2.65	3.10	2.48	3.03	2.51	2.92	2.46
	(0.61)	(0.70)	(0.75)	(0.78)	(0.75)	(0.79)	(0.76)	(0.78)
# Semesters of math in HS	7.70	7.04	7.48	6.95	7.31	6.89	7.20	6.84
	(0.80)	(1.24)	(1.04)	(1.37)	(1.15)	(1.42)	(1.22)	(1.39)
ACT math score (36 max)	24.03	18.27	22.09	17.39	21.04	17.46	20.77	17.51
	(4.28)	(2.92)	(4.66)	(3.00)	(4.02)	(2.81)	(4.16)	(2.90)
Placement into English Remediation								
Average HS English GPA	34.61	29.68	32.15	27.74	31.80	28.32	30.51	27.39
	(5.23)	(6.30)	(6.51)	(6.35)	(6.30)	(6.57)	(6.88)	(6.65)
# Semesters of English in HS	7.91	7.82	7.87	7.74	7.82	7.72	7.81	7.70
	(0.53)	(0.73)	(0.64)	(0.92)	(0.70)	(0.90)	(0.74)	(0.92)
ACT English Score (36 max)	23.51	18.42	21.55	16.73	20.47	17.09	20.35	16.90
	(4.22)	(3.97)	(4.61)	(3.78)	(4.46)	(3.87)	(4.63)	(4.01)
ACT reading Score (36 max)	24.47	19.41	22.68	17.80	21.51	18.36	21.63	18.09
	(5.12)	(4.74)	(5.36)	(4.46)	(5.17)	(4.62)	(5.39)	(4.68)
Observations	13,773	2,331	5,326	2,715	2,300	1,904	3,256	4,559

Source: Authors' computations using data from the Ohio Board of Regents.
Notes: Standard deviations are shown in the parentheses. The number of observations is the number who took the ACT at that institution (not the full sample number). The selective universities are defined as "competitive" institutions by Barron's Educational Guides (1997) and include Bowling Green State University, Miami University, Ohio State University, Ohio University, and Youngstown State University.

college. In Ohio, 25 percent of those with a known core high school curriculum still required remediation in either math or English (Ohio Board
of Regents 2002). Therefore, though course selection problems in high
school contribute to the need for remediation, requiring college preparation
classes may not fully eliminate the need for remediation. Some suggest
high school courses are not rigorous enough. Additionally, high school
courses often do not teach the competencies necessary in college. Andrea
Venezia, Michael Kirst, and Anthony Antonio (2003) detail how differences
between what high schools expect and what colleges demand undermine
student access and success in postsecondary institutions. This research
suggests that straightforward high school preparation is not sufficient
to curb the need for remediation.

As illustrated here, then, substantial numbers of college students participate in remediation. They often have less academic preparation than
their counterparts, but other differences in background, enrollment intensity, and institutional choice also distinguish students in remediation. We
now discuss whether remediation helps these students to be successful in
college in terms of subsequent course performance and degree completion, and why determining the causal effects of remediation is difficult
and one possible empirical strategy to deal with the inherent biases surrounding this issue.

The Effects of Remediation on Student Outcomes

Despite the growing debate on remediation and the thousands of underprepared students who enter the nation's higher education institutions
each year, little sound research exists on the causal effects of remediation
on student outcomes.

Why Is It Difficult to Identify the Effects of Remediation?

One major problem is a lack of good data. Most states and colleges do
not have exit standards for remedial courses and therefore do not collect
performance information on their students. A 1991 internal report by the
Ohio Board of Regents found that "very few institutions conduct consistent
follow-up studies of students completing developmental programs or track
the students to completion of their educational goals" (Legislative Office
of Education Oversight 1995, 7). Other studies also document the lack of
systematic evaluations of remedial programs (Crowe 1998; Weissman,
Bulakowski, and Jumisko 1997). There are also no current benchmarks
by which to judge the success of higher education's remediation efforts
(Ohio Board of Regents 2001).

Studies that have been able to overcome the information barrier often focus on a particular institution. Researchers have simply compared students in remediation with those not in the courses. Because the data used are often proprietary, the results are often not published or easy to obtain. One exception is a large-scale study released by NCES in 1996, which suggests that freshmen enrolled in remedial classes are less likely to persist into their second year of college. However, given the differences in preparation outlined, this finding is not surprising, nor are those of similar studies that fail to control for characteristics related to ability. Students with less ability and preparation are more likely to be placed in remediation. Even without remediation, they are less likely to complete a degree. One must therefore develop a way to separate the effects of lower preparation and ability from the effects of a remedial course.

Issues of selection, or the fact that students who are placed in remedial courses differ from those who are not, are major concerns when examining the effects of remediation. These differences, such as gaps in student preparation, make direct comparisons between students in and out of remediation inaccurate. The first major concern is ability bias and differences in achievement by placement status. Most studies, such as the NCES report, fail to account for student ability in models that examine the effects of remediation, such as whether students in remedial courses are less likely to graduate. However, controlling for ability by using conventional measures—such as test scores, GPAs, or the years a student has taken certain subjects—is probably not enough given the difficulty of measuring true ability or preparation. A second concern is college choice. Enrollment in a particular college may be an outcome reflecting both student ability and preferences about remediation. For example, a student wishing to avoid remediation might choose a college with a very low placement cutoff. As a result, to establish the causal effects of remediation, one must develop strategies to overcome such biases.

Thus far, few have developed satisfactory methodologies to do so. Two reviews of the literature on remedial and developmental education found the bulk of studies to be "methodologically weak" with almost two-thirds reflecting "serious methodological flaws" (O'Hear and MacDonald 1995; Boylan and Saxon 1999). Although little is known about the causal impact of remediation, the literature highlights factors that might matter in the success of a remediation program. These factors include clearly specified goals and objects, a high degree of structure, the provision of counseling and tutoring components, and the use of a variety of approaches and methods in instruction (O'Hear and MacDonald 1995). However, far more work is needed to compare the relative effectiveness of different models of delivery.

Another concern is that most studies often do not track students for long and so do not have information on outcomes such as degree completion.

Those datasets that have longer term data do not allow researchers to account for the possible movement of students across colleges. Therefore, researchers may be incorrectly labeling transfer students as dropouts.

Is Remediation Likely to Be Helpful or Harmful?

Before reviewing evidence on the effects of remediation, we first consider what theory predicts about the effects of remediation. Remedial classes are designed to address academic deficiencies and prepare students for subsequent college success. By teaching students the material they have not yet mastered, the courses may help underprepared students gain skills necessary to excel in college. In comparison, students with similar concerns who are not in remediation may never develop an adequate academic foundation. Without the structure and diagnostic elements of a remediation program, underprepared students may struggle to have their needs addressed or to face their academic problems directly. Remedial courses may also provide a safe environment in which students receive other kinds of support as they make the transition from high school to college. These additional benefits of remediation may include instructors especially attentive to developmental needs, tutoring services, and support from peers in similar situations.

However, remedial courses may in fact have the opposite effect for several reasons. For instance, by increasing the number of requirements and extending the time to degree, remediation may lower the likelihood that a student earns a degree. The literature also suggests that the stigma associated with remediation may also negatively affect students. Research suggests that stigmas attached to underprepared students is real and can be harmful to students (Basic Skills Agency 1997; MacDonald 1987). Remediation, as perceived by other students and faculty, may equate to a Scarlet Letter effect—that is, could amount to a psychological burden that has a negative effect on outcomes. In sum, if remedial students feel that their colleges are singling them out as poor performers, they may be discouraged from making any additional effort.

Remedial courses may also be filled with negative peer effects. Recent work in economics suggests that students who interact with higher-achieving peers tend to improve (see Sacerdote 2000; Zimmerman 2003; Hoxby 2000). For example, Bruce Sacerdote (2000) found that having a roommate with higher standardized test scores appears to have a positive effect on a student's college achievement. Remediation, much like dorm room assignments, will group certain types of students. In doing so, colleges may be fostering negative peer effects amongst students with lower abilities. In contrast, students with fewer abilities not placed in remediation might benefit from positive peer effects by interacting with students with more ability in standard classes.

A Simple Comparison

Table 4.7 displays the course-taking patterns of students in and out of remediation who began in Ohio public colleges and universities from the fall of 1998 until the spring of 2004 (six years). Some of the credits earned may be from campuses other than the campus a student first attended. First, students not placed in remediation completed more credit hours than students in the remedial courses. Nearly 50 percent of the credits these students took were in courses that lead to a baccalaureate degree. Another 42 percent were in general courses that could lead to a certificate but did not fulfill requirements for a four-year degree. At the two-year colleges, most of the courses qualified for general or technical course credit. In contrast, students in remediation took up to one-third of their courses in remedial subjects. The highest percentage was for students at two-year colleges who placed in math and English remediation. Meanwhile, students at four-year colleges might take only one course in remedial math.

Table 4.8 displays the outcomes of students after four and six years. The simple comparison of the outcomes of students placed in remediation and those not placed suggests that remedial students fared less well. Within four years, 61 percent of students at four-year colleges earned a bachelor's degree but only 13 percent of those in math and English remediation did so. The difference is not as great when looking at degree completion over six years. This is likely due to the fact that remediation lengthens the time to degree so that four years is no longer realistic. Similar patterns can be found among two-year college students with two-year or four-year degree intent. Interestingly, slightly more remediated students completed a college certificate than their counterparts, but this is most like due to differences in the types of students that completed certificates rather than degrees.

Students who needed remediation were more likely to stop out of college before completing their studies. Given the system-wide nature of the data, students who transfer to other Ohio public colleges are not counted as stop outs. At the four-year colleges, differences in the likelihood of stopping out arise during the second term, meaning that students in remediation are less likely to return to college their sophomore year. At the two-year colleges, the pattern appears almost immediately, during the first term. Overall, there is a huge difference in the likelihood of stopping out by remedial status, though the differences are not as great at the two-year colleges. These tables, as we have noted, do not demonstrate evidence of the causal effects of remediation, given the significant differences in the underlying samples. We now turn briefly to attempts to address this issue of bias.

Table 4.7 College Course-Taking Behavior over Six Years

	Four-Year Universities				Two-Year Colleges			
	None	Math Remed.	English Remed.	Math and English	None	Math Remed.	English Remed.	Math and English
Total credit hours	104.80	78.90	72.09	57.15	37.74	51.39	41.14	38.72
	(50.71)	(52.41)	(54.35)	(48.63)	(46.6)	(46.18)	(42.49)	(39.05)
Remedial courses:								
Total credit hours	—	2.75	3.32	6.15	—	3.14	3.03	7.09
		(2.76)	(2.83)	(5.13)		(3.22)	(3.35)	(6.18)
Proportion of credits in remedial courses	—	0.06	0.10	0.21	—	0.13	0.16	0.33
Baccalaureate courses:	57.43	35.24	32.48	20.60	9.46	10.97	6.50	4.44
Total credit hours	(37.12)	(35.60)	(35.92)	(29.53)	(22.84)	(22.15)	(17.94)	(13.43)
Proportion of credits in baccalaureate courses	0.49	0.33	0.33	0.23	0.13	0.12	0.08	0.06
General courses:	38.84	35.52	31.15	25.58	16.80	27.05	18.66	17.79
Total credit hours	(19.33)	(21.03)	(21.98)	(20.85)	(22.05)	(23.49)	(20.26)	(20.09)
Proportion of credits in general courses	0.42	0.53	0.49	0.48	0.41	0.56	0.46	0.42
Technical courses:	1.94	3.75	4.02	4.35	10.29	9.40	12.62	9.19
Total credit hours	(7.36)	(9.90)	(9.71)	(10.33)	(16.04)	(15.65)	(18.33)	(15.78)
Proportion of credits in technical courses	0.03	0.06	0.07	0.08	0.44	0.19	0.30	0.20
Observations	25,419	3,373	1,788	1,967	16,559	7,245	2,484	7,006

Source: Authors' computations using data from the Ohio Board of Regents.
Notes: Standard deviations are shown in the parentheses. The number of observations is the number who took the ACT at that institution (not the full sample number). The selective universities are defined as competitive institutions by Barron's Educational Guides (1997) and include Bowling Green State University, Miami University, Ohio State University, Ohio University, and Youngstown State University.

Table 4.8   Remedial Placement and College Educational Outcomes

	Four-Year Colleges				Two-Year Colleges (with degree intent)			
	None	Math Remed.	English Remed.	Math and English	None	Math Remed.	English Remed.	Math and English
After four years (up to spring 2002)								
Bachelor's degree	60.55	31.57	27.40	12.75	13.16	9.37	5.93	2.97
Associate's degree	3.89	4.62	4.98	4.47	21.61	18.28	19.91	12.59
Certificate	0.97	0.68	0.50	0.25	1.77	1.51	2.26	1.89
After six years (up to spring 2004)								
Bachelor's degree	64.73	36.27	33.05	18.99	16.08	12.56	7.64	4.47
Associate's degree	4.25	5.36	5.87	5.18	22.62	19.84	20.86	14.21
Certificate	1.02	0.77	0.50	0.36	1.84	1.61	2.36	2.11
Transferred up during period	2.01	2.70	3.02	2.54	22.41	19.86	15.18	10.75
Stopped out, no return	26.18	45.95	49.89	60.65	58.10	60.61	65.16	70.97
Stopped out term 1	4.47	4.42	5.98	5.29	19.76	9.67	16.24	11.04
Stopped out term 2	4.99	8.18	11.19	11.08	11.20	12.10	15.43	16.37
Stopped out year 2	5.00	8.75	10.01	13.47	9.03	13.05	11.41	14.96
Stopped out year 3	3.55	7.14	7.27	9.71	6.00	8.37	7.59	10.48
Stopped out year 4	3.39	7.59	5.87	8.29	4.94	7.01	6.33	7.26
Transferred down	13.82	24.58	20.08	27.05	4.25	4.96	4.07	3.35
Observations	25,444	3,373	1,788	1,967	9,744	6,093	1,989	5,553

Source: Authors' computations using data from the Ohio Board of Regents.
Notes: The sample of students at two-year colleges had degree intent (associate's or bachelor's degree). Stopping out means the student did not return to *any* institution within the Ohio public higher education system during the entire period. Transferring up is defined for nonselective, four-year colleges as a transfer to a selective university, for university branches as a transfer to a selective or nonselective four-year college, and for community colleges as a transfer to any four-year institution. Transferring down is the opposite motion in the hierarchy of institutions.

Estimates of the Causal Effects of Remediation

Little analysis has been undertaken on the causal impact of remedial courses on students. Leona Aiken and her colleagues, however, do provide a rare example in their 1998 study evaluating the impact of a one-semester remedial English course at a large university. Because their main intent is to compare different kinds of research designs, they estimate the results using a randomized experiment, nonequivalent control group design, and regression discontinuity. The results using each method are similar, and suggest that the remedial writing courses did not improve students' skills beyond those of the standard freshman composition course. However, this study exemplifies the limitations of most of the research on remediation. It is based on one institution and has a very small sample (375 students). Whether the results are representative for larger groups of students or institutions is therefore unclear. Additionally, the Aiken et al. analysis compares only students in remediation to those taking college-level courses in the same subject. It does not comment on situations in which students could be taking courses in other subjects—that is, their intended major—and avoiding remediation. A third limitation is that students are followed for one year only. To truly understand the impact of remediation, longer term outcomes are needed. However, even if Aiken and her colleagues could follow the students additional years, they would probably not be able to distinguish between those who drop out of college completely and those who transfer to another school, which failure would lead to measurement error in the outcomes.

In other work using data from the Ohio Board of Regents, we provide much more information on the causal impact of remedial courses (Bettinger and Long 2005). The analysis is likely to be much more representative of remediation in general because it includes forty-five colleges and thousands of students and tracks students over six years throughout the entire Ohio public higher education system. The results thus give a sense of the longer term outcomes related to remediation without as much concern about incorrectly categorizing transfer students as dropouts.

In our 2005 study, we focus on only a subset of the sample of Ohio public college students who entered during the fall 1998 term: traditional-age college undergraduates who attended full time, took the ACT, and signified the intent to complete a degree on their college application.[11] The demographics and outcomes of this selected group are shown in table 4.9. Nearly the entire group is from Ohio and relatively few are black, Hispanic, or Asian; more than half are female. This group has higher mean ACT scores, but significant numbers still need remediation. There are also gaps in degree completion by experience with remediation. A simple comparison of the outcomes among this sample of students by remedial

Table 4.9   Students with Degree Intent

| | Four-Year Universities | | Two-Year Colleges | |
	Selective	Non-selective	University Branch	Community
Demographic characteristics and achievement				
Age in 1998	18.35	18.44	18.42	18.47
	(0.49)	(0.56)	(0.54)	(0.58)
Female	57.98	55.07	57.13	57.68
Black	4.28	9.61	1.29	5.86
Hispanic	1.53	1.26	0.48	1.56
Asian	2.51	1.63	0.55	1.24
Ohio resident	99.86	99.96	99.96	100.00
ACT composite score	23.66	21.65	20.23	19.53
(maximum 36)	(3.86)	(4.28)	(3.60)	(3.62)
Educational outcomes after four years				
In Remedial Math	8.31	17.15	33.16	54.69
In Remedial English	4.28	15.47	16.51	29.35
Experience with remediation				
Completed No remediation	77.78	57.12	43.28	16.45
bachelor's In remediation	54.75	32.27	27.63	10.87
degree				
Completed No remediation	2.01	5.86	32.51	47.58
associate's In remediation	3.96	5.82	20.68	31.65
degree				
Stopped out No remediation	10.35	20.68	25.45	33.74
In remediation	21.53	33.31	36.23	44.88
Observations	13,326	4,841	2,708	2,814

Source: Authors' computations using data from the Ohio Board of Regents.
Notes: The sample is restricted to full-time students aged eighteen to twenty with degree intent who were first-time freshmen in fall 1998. Additionally, to be included in the sample, students must have taken the ACT and had valid zip code information.
Standard deviations are shown in the parentheses. Stopping out means the student did not return to *any* institution within the Ohio public higher education system during the entire period. Technical colleges are excluded.

status suggests, not unlike the patterns shown in table 4.8, remediation has a negative effect.

As noted earlier, each institution in Ohio is permitted to set its own remedial placement policies, and two similar students who attend different colleges may therefore have different experiences with remediation. Which college a student attends is largely dictated by proximity (most students in Ohio attend a college within thirty miles of their home), meaning that the likelihood of being placed in remediation is influenced by the distance of the student's home to colleges with stringent rather than lax remediation policies. We document this pattern in our 2005 study and compare similar students who placed in or out of remediation due to this institutional variation. Because that research focuses on students for whom the probability of remediation differs according to the college they attend, the results do not reflect the impact of remediation on students with severe academic deficiencies.

The 2005 study estimates paint a sharply different picture of the impact of remedial courses. Once using a more relevant control group by comparing similar students who are placed in and out of remediation because of the institutional policies of their colleges, remediation appears to decrease the likelihood of stopping out of college. The estimates suggest that students in math or English remediation are nearly 10 percent less likely to stop out over six years. This is in comparison to similar students in terms of background, preparation, and performance who did not take remedial courses. Remediated students are also more likely to complete a bachelor's degree. For example, students in math remediation are nearly 10 percent more likely than similar students to complete a college degree in four years. English remediation is estimated to have an even larger effect because students were found to be 17 percent more likely to graduate by spring 2002 than their counterparts.

It is important to note, however, that many students do not complete their remediation. In the Ohio data, 64 and 69 percent of students completed all of the math and English remediation courses, respectively, in which they enroll. Table 4.10 displays how the likelihood of completing remediation differs according to the amount of remediation attempted. The bottom cells in each column highlight the percentage of students who complete 100 percent of the remedial courses they attempt. In general, the percentage who complete all of the courses falls as the number of credits increase. Less than a quarter of students who are required to take approximately three courses (nine credits) complete their remediation.

Students who do not complete their courses do not necessarily receive the full "treatment" of remediation. The results described therefore concern the intention to treat students with remediation. Little is known about the treatment on the treated impact of remediation. Because completion of the remedial courses is not likely to be random, estimating the treatment on the treated has additional selection issues that must be addressed before causal results can be estimated.

Conclusion

In summary, remediation is widespread and an important part of American higher education. Postsecondary institutions invest significant resources in the courses to address the academic deficiencies of entering students.

Table 4.10   Remedial Credits Attempted and Completed

Credits Completed	Credits Attempted								
	1	2	3	4	5	6	7	8	9
Math remediation									
0	100.0	28.16	34.57	38.34	18.66	22.84	21.99	16.2	19.5
1	0.0	0	0	0	0	0	0	0	0
2		71.84	0	1.84	23.33	2.5	2.63	7.85	5.35
3			65.43	0	0.52	28.85	26.5	1.96	18.24
4				59.83	0	0.44	15.6	17.79	2.83
5					57.49	0	3.01	7.8	0.94
6						45.37	0	2.83	29.25
7							30.26	0	0
8								45.57	0
9									23.9
English remediation									
0	37.78	22.3	24.32	30.63	25.39	26.31	13.79	17.86	18.25
1	62.22	0	0.11	0.73	0	0	1.72	0.08	0
2		77.7	0.11	3.14	11.29	0.64	13.79	5.74	1.59
3			75.45	0.58	0.52	8.56	24.14	0.56	22.22
4				64.92	0	0.54	13.79	11.88	5.56
5					62.81	0	8.62	11.24	0
6						63.95	0	0.56	25.4
7							24.14	0	1.59
8								52.07	0.79
9									24.6

Source: Authors' computations using data from the Ohio Board of Regents.

Although little research has been undertaken to establish the causal impact of remedial programs, our own research suggests that institutions can play a significant positive role in addressing inequities in preparation. However, further research is needed to more fully understand the effects of remediation, especially for students who are extremely underprepared for college-level work. It may also be the case that certain types of instruction and supports are more beneficial than others. Research is needed to identify which programs and practices are the most effective.

Additional research on how to maximize the benefits of remediation is imperative as the cost of not offering the courses appears to be expensive. Individuals with less education are more burdensome on the economy in terms of higher probabilities of unemployment, welfare dependency, and incarceration. Moreover, the increasing demands of the economy in terms of skill encourage the country to find an effective way to train its workers.

Given persistent concerns about the abilities of high school graduates, higher education must find ways to address the needs of underprepared students.

Implications for Policy

States are currently considering a number of policies related to remediation. Some policy makers have argued, for example, that community colleges should be the principal provider of remedial courses, and thus are either reducing remediation at four-year universities or limiting the number of courses students can take at these institutions. Given the dearth of information available on the effects of remediation and the lack of a set of best practices on how to deliver remediation, these reforms should be approached with caution. Our 2005 research certainly suggests that remediation improves student outcomes. Additionally, given the large numbers of students who need remediation, exclusionary admissions policies are likely to have widespread effects on many parts of higher education and long-term labor market quality. Community colleges are also often strapped for funding and may not have the resources to provide effective remedial programs.

It is also important to note that the need for remediation is rooted in the K–12 system, and that reform efforts may therefore be better served by focusing on this level of education. As noted, students often do not take the appropriate courses. Investments in guidance counseling could have profound effects. In urban school districts, because counselors are sometimes responsible for more than 700 students, students may not be adequately served. However, even students who take an academic core in high school sometimes still need remediation. As Venezia, Kirst, and Antonio (2003) suggest, high schools need to find out more about the expectations of colleges.

One promising policy that combines efforts to improve student advising while conveying the expectations of higher education is early placement testing. Several states—Ohio, Kentucky, Oklahoma, and North Carolina among them—have begun to use the remediation placement exam ordinarily given to college freshmen on students who are still in tenth or eleventh grade. The results of the test are then shared with the students and their parents as a way to inform all parties of the competencies that still need to be mastered. With their teachers and counselors, students can then determine what courses they need to take while still in high school to avoid college remediation. As long as students graduate from high school underprepared, remediation will continue to be pervasive. Efforts should therefore focus on policies that could lower the need for remediation but still help those no longer in high school to gain the skills that can help them succeed in higher education.

Endnotes

1. Jay Greene and Greg Foster (2003) define being minimally "college ready" as: graduating from high school, having taken four years of English, three years of math, and two years of science, social science, and foreign language, and demonstrating basic literacy skills by scoring at least 265 on the reading NAEP.
2. We refer to all types of courses below the college level as remedial. This includes basic skills training and nontraditional coursework, which are other names for developmental courses. We acknowledge that different areas of the country and stakeholders may prefer other terminology.
3. Four Ohio colleges without clear records on which courses were considered remedial during the 1998–1999 school year are excluded—Kent State University, University of Cincinnati, Hocking Technical College, and Lima Technical College.
4. The selective universities are defined as competitive institutions by Barron's Educational Guides (1997) and include Bowling Green State University, Miami University, Ohio State University, Ohio University, and Youngstown State University.
5. According to information from the Integrated Postsecondary Education Data System (IPEDS), approximately 700 Ohio students transfer to the non-Ohio schools each year. This assumes that transfer students are geographically representative of the incoming freshman classes of these schools. If we assume that all these transfer students had just finished their first year of college, then only 5 percent of observed dropouts are mislabeled.
6. Seven Ohio public institutions—University of Akron, Cleveland State University, Central State University, Shawnee State University, University of Toledo, Wright State University, and Youngstown State University—are subject to the state's open admissions law that requires high school graduates to be admitted to the public school of their choice with certain exceptions. Students who have completed a college prep curriculum are generally accepted unconditionally. The other public four-year colleges—Bowling Green State University, University of Cincinnati, Kent State University, Miami University, Ohio State University, and Ohio University—have selective admissions based on academic background (Ohio Board of Regents 2001).
7. Miami University also sends students to satellite campuses for remediation.
8. More than four in five campuses nationally restrict enrollment in some college-level classes until remediation is complete, and most require those in need of remediation to participate in the courses (NCES 2003).
9. Complete information on both the asset and compass exams is available at http://www.act.org.
10. Because these figures include indirect costs such as libraries, registration, and plant maintenance, they should not be used to determine the savings associated with eliminating remediation.
11. These restrictions are necessary because the methodology of Eric Bettinger and Bridget Long (2005) requires preparation and achievement information from the ACT survey. Furthermore, so that degree completion is a relevant indicator of success, students needed to signify in some way wanting to get a degree and being able to complete it in reasonable time (beginning college full-time).

References

Adelman, Clifford 1999. *Answers in the Toolbox: Academic Intensity, Attendance Patterns, and Bachelor's Degree Attainment.* U.S. Department of Education. Washington: U.S. Department of Education.
———. 2006. *The Toolbox Revisited: Paths to Degree Completion From High School Through College.* Washington: U.S. Department of Education.
Aiken, Leona S., Stephen G. West, David E. Schwalm, James L. Carroll, and Shenghwa Hsiung. 1998. "Comparison of a Randomized and Two Quasi-Experiments in a Single Outcome Evaluation: Efficacy of a University-Level Remedial Writing Program." *Evaluation Review* 22(2): 207–44.
Arkansas Department of Higher Education. 1998. *Arkansas Academic Cost Accounting.* Little Rock: Arkansas Department of Higher Education.
Barron's Educational Guides. 1997. *Barron's Profiles of American Colleges, 21st Edition.* Hauppauge, N.Y.: Barron's Educational Series.
Basic Skills Agency. 1997. *Staying the Course: The Relationship between Basic Skills Support, Dropout, Retention and Achievement in Further Education Colleges.* London: Basic Skills Agency.
Bettinger, Eric, and Bridget T. Long. 2005. "Addressing the Needs of Under-Prepared College Students: Does College Remediation Work?" *NBER* Working Paper 11325. Cambridge, Mass.: National Bureau of Economic Research.
Boylan, Hunter, and D. Patrick Saxon. 1999. "What Works in Remediation: Lessons from 30 Years of Research." Prepared for The League for Innovation in the Community College. Boone, N.C.: National Center for Developmental Education. http://www.ncde.appstate.edu/reserve_reading/what_works.htm.
Breneman, David W., and William N. Haarlow. 1998. *Remedial Education: Costs and Consequences.* Washington, D.C.: Thomas B. Fordham Foundation.
City University of New York. 1999. *Report I: Financial Analysis of Remedial Education at the City University of New York.* New York: Mayor's Advisory Task Force on the City University of New York.
Cloud, John. 2002. "Who's Ready for College." *Time* 160(16, October 14): 44.
Copenhaver, Carol, Zoe Irvin, and Ginny Novak. 1996. *Howard Community College: Developmental Math Study.* Columbia, Md.: Howard Community College.
Crowe, Edward. 1998. *Statewide Remedial Education Policies—State Strategies that Support Successful Student Transitions from Secondary to Postsecondary Education.* Denver, Colo.: State Higher Education Executive Officers and ACT, Inc.
Dodd, Timothy. 2002. Personal communication, March 2002.
Education Commission of the States. 2003. *State Files.* Denver, Colo.: The Center for Community College Policy. http://www.communitycollegepolicy.org/html/top.asp?page=/html/state_files_main.asp.
Greene, Jay, and Greg Foster. 2003. "Public High School Graduation and College Readiness Rates in the United States." Education Working Paper No. 3, September. New York: Manhattan Institute, Center for Civic Information.
Hebel, Sara. 1999. "N.Y. Board of Regents Approves CUNY Plan to Limit Remedial Education." *The Chronicle of Higher Education* 46(15)(December 3): A33.
Hoxby, Caroline. 2000. "Peer Effects in the Classroom: Learning from Gender and Race Variation." *NBER* Working Paper 7867. Cambridge, Mass.: National Bureau of Economic Research.

Hoyt, Jeff E. 1999. "Remedial Education and Student Attrition." *Community College Review* 27(2): 51–72.

Hoyt, Jeff E., and Colleen T. Sorensen. 1999. *Promoting Academic Standards?: The Link between Remedial Education in College and Student Preparation in High School.* Department of Institutional Research & Management Studies. Orem, Utah: Utah Valley State College.

Ignash, Jay. 1997. "Who Should Provide Postsecondary Remedial/Developmental Education?" In *Implementing Effective Policies for Remedial and Developmental Education,* edited by Jay Ignash. New Directions for Community Colleges No. 100. San Francisco: Jossey-Bass.

Jencks, Christopher, and Meredith Phillips. 1998. *The Black-White Test Score Gap.* Washington, D.C.: The Brookings Institution.

Legislative Office of Education Oversight (LOEO). 1995. *Remedial and Developmental Programs in Ohio's Public Colleges and Universities.* Columbus: Ohio General Assembly.

MacDonald, Ross B. 1987. "Evaluation of an Alternative Solution for the Assessment and Retention of High-Risk College Students." Presentation at the American Educational Research Association. Washington, D.C. (1987).

McCabe, Robert H. 2000. *No One to Waste: A Report to Public Decision-Makers and Community College Leaders.* Washington, D.C.: Community College Press.

———. 2001. "Developmental Education: A Policy Primer." *League for Innovation in the Community College* 14(1) (February). Downloaded November 4, 2002. Available at: http://www.league.org/publication/abstracts/leadership/labs0201.htm.

Mortenson, Thomas G. 2002. "Chance for College by Age 19 by State in 2000." *Postsecondary Education OPPORTUNITY* 123(September): 1.

National Center for Education Statistics. 1996. *Remedial Education at Higher Education Institutions in Fall 1995.* Washington: Office of Educational Research and Improvement.

———. 2000. *Digest of Education Statistics.* Washington: U.S. Department of Education.

———. 2003. *Remedial Education at Degree-Granting Postsecondary Institutions in Fall 2000.* Washington: Department of Education.

O'Hear, M., and R. MacDonald. 1995. "A Critical Review of Research in Developmental Education, Part I." *Journal of Developmental Education* 19(1): 2–6.

Ohio Board of Regents. 2001. *Ohio Colleges and Universities 2001: Profile of Student Outcomes, Experiences and Campus Measures.* Columbus, Ohio: Ohio Board of Regents.

———. 2002. *Making the Transition from High School to College in Ohio 2002.* Columbus, Ohio: Ohio Board of Regents.

———. 2005. *Ohio's College and Universities: Profile of Student Outcomes, Experiences, and Campus Measures 2005.* Columbus, Ohio: Ohio Board of Regents.

Phipps, Ronald. 1998. *College Remediation—What it is, What it Costs, What's at Stake.* Washington, D.C.: Institute for Higher Education Policy.

Sacerdote, Bruce. 2000. "Peer Effects with Random Assignment: Results for Dartmouth Roommates." *NBER* Working Paper No. 7469. Cambridge, Mass.: National Bureau of Economic Research.

Schmidt, Peter. 1998. "A Clash of Values at CUNY over Remedial Education." *The Chronicle of Higher Education* 44(28)(March 20): A33–A34.

Secondary and Higher Education Remediation Advisory Commission. 1997. *A Total Approach: Improving College Preparation in Ohio.* Columbus: Ohio Board of Regents.

Soliday, Mary. 2002. *The Politics of Remediation.* Pittsburgh: The University of Pittsburgh Press.

Venezia, Andrea, Michael Kirst, and Anthony Antonio. 2003. *Betraying the College Dream: How Disconnected K–12 and Postsecondary Education Systems Undermine Student Aspirations.* Stanford, Calif.: The Stanford Institute for Higher Education Research. Available at: www.stanford.edu/group/bridgeproject/betrayingthecollegedream.pdf.

Weissman, Julie, Carol Bulakowski, and Marci Jumisko. 1997. "Using Research to Evaluate Developmental Education Programs and Policies." In *Implementing Effective Policies for Remedial and Developmental Education,* edited by Juan M. Ignash. New Directions for Community Colleges No. 100. San Francisco: Jossey-Bass.

Wheat, I. David. 1998. "Deficient Diplomas: Is It Time for a Graduate Warranty Program?" *Thomas Jefferson Institute for Public Policy* Working Paper. Springfield, Va.: Thomas Jefferson Institute for Public Policy.

Zimmerman, David. 2003. "Peer Effects in Academic Outcomes: Evidence from a Natural Experiment." *Review of Economics & Statistics* 85(1): 9–23.

═ Chapter 5 ═

Community Colleges

DAN GOLDHABER AND GRETCHEN K. PERI

THE EVIDENCE that higher education is a key to economic advancement is uncontested. Relative to those who fail to attain a college diploma, graduates of four-year colleges[1] tend to be significantly more successful in the labor market. In 2004, for instance, the annual average unemployment rate for persons with a bachelor's degree or higher was 2.7 percent as compared to 3.7 percent for those with an associate's degree, 4.5 percent for those with some college but no degree, and 5.0 percent for high school graduates without any college attendance (U.S. Bureau of Labor Statistics 2005).[2] In 2003, college graduates with a bachelor's degree had a median income $14,200 higher than nongraduates (see figure 5.1) (The College Board 2004a).[3] There is also evidence that college graduates tend to live healthier, happier lives (Michael 1972; Kenkel 1991; Grossman 1975, 1982; Berger and Leigh 1989; Behrman and Wolfe 1989; The College Board 2004a).[4]

There is some question as to whether the benefits of college attendance accrue primarily as a consequence of human capital accumulation resulting from college training or from the screening role that colleges play in identifying individuals who are productive (Spence 1973; Dale and Krueger 2002; Becker 1964; Groot and Oosterbeek 1994; Layard and Psacharopoulos 1974). The answer to this question is important in determining the societal benefits associated with college attendance but, regardless of the reasons for the benefits, it is clear that college completion is one of the best ways to ensure economic success.

Far less is known about an increasingly important part of the postsecondary schooling world: community colleges. The number of undergraduate students attending any type of college has grown considerably over the last thirty years, but this growth has occurred disproportionately in the community college sector. In 1970, the share of postsecondary undergraduate students enrolled in community colleges was just over 30 percent. In 2003, it had risen to about 45 percent.[5] Furthermore, community colleges appear to be particularly important for lower-income and minority

Figure 5.1   Median Earnings by Education, 2003

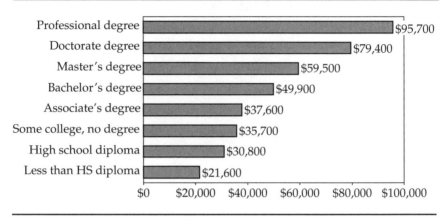

Source: The College Board (2004a, figure 1).
Note: Includes full-time year-round workers aged twenty-five and older.

students. In 2002, for example, 43 percent of African American and 58 percent of Hispanic postsecondary students were attending two-year colleges. In the same year, minority students constituted 36 percent of total enrollment at two-year institutions versus about 25 percent at four-year colleges (NCES 2005a). In 2000, low-income students were almost twice as likely as high-income students to spend their first year of undergraduate study at a community college (The College Board 2004a).

Does the existence of community colleges lead to reductions in educational inequality that in turn translates into a reduction in society's economic inequalities? The answer is complicated. It depends both on whether community colleges encourage greater educational attendance and how well community college students fare in the labor market compared with those who graduate from traditional four-year institutions. A fair amount of research covers how community college students compare to four-year college students, but far less on how the existence of community colleges affects the choices of prospective postsecondary students.

Here we explore the role of community colleges in postsecondary schooling as it relates to alleviating or exasperating access, persistence and success in higher education, and what this in turn portends for their influence on economic inequalities in society.

Trends in (Community) College Attendance

Postsecondary college attendance increased significantly after World War II. In the last three decades alone, the percentage of high school graduates attending at least some college has grown from 51 to 64 percent (NCES

Figure 5.2   Undergraduate Enrollment in Two-Year Colleges as a Percentage of Total Undergraduate Enrollment in Degree-Granting Two- and Four-Year Postsecondary Institutions: Fall 1970 to 2003

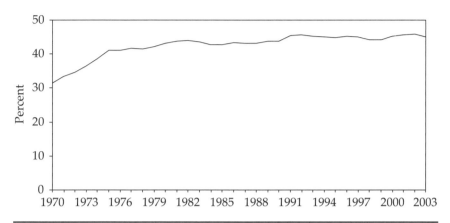

Source: National Center for Education Statistics (2005a, table 7-1).
Note: Includes both full-time and part-time undergraduates. Enrollment in 2003 is projected based on data through 2000 and alternative assumptions (see NCES 2005-065 for more detail).

2005b).[6] Enrollment is projected to continue this upward trend through at least 2014. This growth, however, has occurred disproportionately among community colleges (see figure 5.2).[7]

Much of this increase in attendance has been among low-income students, and it appears that a shift is occurring in the distribution of students across different types of institutions. In both 1990 and 2000, for instance, about 50 percent of full-time undergraduates in the lowest quarter of family income attended public four-year institutions. However, the percentage of the lowest-income students attending private four-year colleges decreased from 31 to 24 percent but increased from 18 to 26 percent at public two-year institutions over the same period (see figure 5.3). It is safe to assume that at least part of this shift in the distribution of attendance is in response to tuition increases, since studies show that low-income students are highly sensitive to tuition (as well as financial aid) levels when making the decision to attend college (Heller 1997; Hossler, Hu, and Schmit 1998; St. John 1994). Research also shows that when the cost of attendance increases, low-income students tend to enroll in less expensive institutions (McPherson and Schapiro 1998; St. John 1994).

Community colleges also appear to be particularly important for minority students. In 2002, the percentage of white students receiving some type of postsecondary training who were enrolled in a two-year college was about 37 percent. By contrast, the percentage of minority

Figure 5.3   Distribution of Full-Time, Full-Year Dependent Undergraduates by Type of Institution, by Family Income

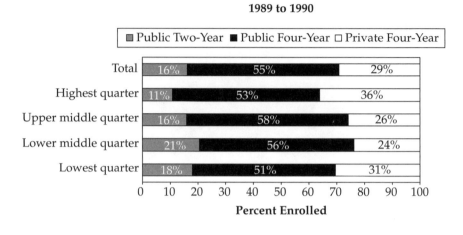

1989 to 1990

□ Public Two-Year ■ Public Four-Year □ Private Four-Year

	Public Two-Year	Public Four-Year	Private Four-Year
Total	16%	55%	29%
Highest quarter	11%	53%	36%
Upper middle quarter	16%	58%	26%
Lower middle quarter	21%	56%	24%
Lowest quarter	18%	51%	31%

Percent Enrolled

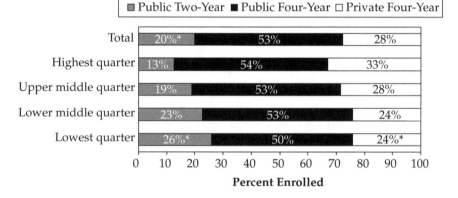

1999 to 2000

■ Public Two-Year ■ Public Four-Year □ Private Four-Year

	Public Two-Year	Public Four-Year	Private Four-Year
Total	20%*	53%	28%
Highest quarter	13%	54%	33%
Upper middle quarter	19%	53%	28%
Lower middle quarter	23%	53%	24%
Lowest quarter	26%*	50%	24%*

Percent Enrolled

Source: National Center for Education Statistics (2004, table 1); Authors' calculations.
* Indicates a statistically significant change from the 1989–1990 school year.
Notes: Values may not sum to 100 percent due to rounding. These figures include only full-time, full-year dependent undergraduates and therefore differ from figure 5.2. However, almost 50 percent of all students are financially independent and these students are both more likely to be from lower-income families and are largely concentrated in community colleges. Table 5.1 includes private for-profit less-than-four-year institutions, which have been omitted here and the resulting percentages were recalculated.

students—including American Indian, Asian–Pacific Islander, African American, and Hispanic—was 48 percent. In the case of Hispanics, nearly 60 percent of those attending postsecondary schooling were enrolled in two-year colleges (NCES 2005a). It is perhaps not surprising that community colleges are particularly important for minority students, given that they tend to be more economically disadvantaged than their white counterparts (Alon 2001).

The growing importance of community colleges in serving the needs of low-income and minority students means that the impacts of community colleges as a postsecondary educational option have a potentially profound effect on the distribution of income in society by students' socioeconomic background, race, and ethnicity. The actual picture is of course more nuanced, but, in short, if the existence of this option tends to be a net positive for those who attend, then community colleges serve to decrease economic stratification, and the converse is also true. The research we review later provides a starting point in determining the policy impacts of community colleges, but first we look briefly at the reasons students attend two-year colleges.

Why Do Students Choose Community Colleges?

Although community colleges are generally thought of as providing a bridge to four-year colleges or as a means to complete a vocational or technical degree, in actuality they serve a variety of functions. Much of the retraining of displaced workers, for instance, occurs in community college courses (Jacobson, LaLonde, and Sullivan 2004). A large number of students with bachelor's degrees also attend two-year colleges for additional training or technical skills, especially in information technology (Lerman, Riegg, and Salzman 2000).

Traditional students (that is, those who enroll in postsecondary institutions immediately after high school) attend community colleges as well, for a number of reasons. Some benefit from remedial help provided at a community college prior to enrolling in a four-year institution, or they may be required to attend remedial classes. Many public universities have reduced their remedial class offerings in recent years (Kane and Rouse 1999) and, as chapter 4 discusses further, several states have reassigned all remedial courses to their community colleges. Other students may attend a community college to demonstrate that they can handle college-level work.[8]

For traditional students given the choice between a public university and a community college, several factors weigh in on their decision. Student ability, perceived institutional attributes (campus life, quality, and the like), proximity, price of attendance, educational and occupational aspirations, socioeconomic status, and parental encouragement are some of the common aspects involved in student attendance decisions. Research shows, for instance, that parental encouragement affects a student's decision of whether to go to college after high school and has some bearing on what type of institution a student attends. A study by Mary Conklin and Ann Dailey (1981) finds that students who enrolled in four-year colleges were more likely to report receiving consistent parental encouragement during ninth through twelfth grades, whereas students attending two-year institutions were more likely to report receiving mixed parental support.

Not surprisingly, a significant body of research (Behrman et al. 1992; Ganderton 1992; Hilmer 1998) confirms that academic performance, measured by student performance on standardized tests, is a good predictor of postsecondary attendance. It also appears to play an important role in the type of institution chosen. Michael Hilmer (1998), for instance, provides evidence that the probability of college attendance—at either a university or a community college—is strongly related to academic performance: as test scores increase, the probability of attending increases and the probability of not attending decreases, which is not a surprising finding. However, he also found that the probability of attending community college appears to have a nonlinear relationship with test performance. The likelihood increases with test scores up to a point (roughly the sample average test score), and then decreases as test scores increase further. This pattern makes sense given that the lowest performers are unlikely to complete any postsecondary schooling, and at the higher end of the test distribution students are more likely to be making a choice between two- and four-year schools.

Among the various factors that contribute to a student's decision to attend a community college over a four-year university, however, cost is paramount. Recent articles in popular press with headlines such as "Tuition Shock," "State's Poor being Priced out of College," "Tuition to Soar for State Undergraduate Students," and "How Much More can Tuition-Payers Afford?" have raised concerns over the increasing cost of four-year college attendance. Although these stories may exaggerate the degree to which students are really being priced out of college, postsecondary education has without question grown more expensive.

After relative stability throughout the 1970s, average undergraduate tuition and fee charges began to climb in the 1980s. Figure 5.4 shows the increase in the price of college tuition and fees at all types of institutions. Since 1977, average full-time undergraduate tuition and fees (in current dollars) have increased more than 600 percent at all types of institutions (see chapter 7 for an in-depth examination of college prices). Although the real inflation-adjusted figures are substantially more modest, the point is still clear: the cost of attending college has increased.

The increase in college tuition and other necessary expenses does not directly equate to a matching increase in the out-of-pocket costs of college

Figure 5.4   Average Published Tuition and Fee Charges

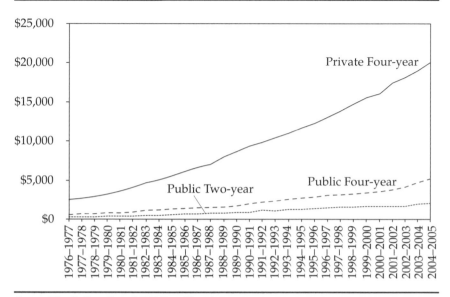

Source: The College Board (2004b, table 4a).
Note: Enrollment weighted. Current dollars.

attendance. In fact, as Amy Schwartz explains in chapter 7, increases in financial aid have compensated for much of the increase in the price of postsecondary education. Since 1990, the percentage of students from all income groups and at all types of institutions receiving financial aid has increased, as has the average amount they receive (NCES 2004). Today, the great majority of students receive some form of financial assistance for their postsecondary education.[9]

The composition of financial aid, however, has changed. Although both loans and grants increased in real terms between 1990 and 2000, average loan amounts increased more quickly than grants. This is an important consideration, as some evidence suggests that students from various socioeconomic backgrounds respond differently to various types of financial aid in their decision to attend college (Manski and Wise 1983; Berkner and Chavez 1997; Jackson 1978). A study by Edward St. John (1990), for instance, finds that low-income students in general are highly responsive to financial aid in the form of grants but largely unresponsive to loans in their decision, whereas low-middle and middle income students are responsive to both. Therefore, to get an accurate picture of how the cost of college affects attendance decisions, it is necessary to take the differential effects of financial aid into account.

In the last decade, borrowing has become an increasingly popular way to finance educational expenses, and average borrowing levels have increased for students at all income levels and types of institutions.[10] Loans reduce the current expense of education costs and therefore postpone the burden of paying for college, but do not directly reduce the cost of attendance as grants do. Between 1990 and 2000, increases in financial aid compensated for much of the increased costs of attendance, except at community colleges, when both grants and loans are considered (NCES 2004). However, if grants alone are taken into account, over the same decade the average net price of attendance—including tuition, fees, books, and living expenses—for full-time dependent undergraduates generally increased after adjusting for inflation at all types of institutions (NCES 2004, table 5).[11] Loans have filled much of the remaining gap in the amount students are able to pay and the required cost of attendance. In general, due to increases in tuition and the greater role of loans in financing higher education, it can be argued that the burden of paying for postsecondary education has increased over the last decade.[12]

Although the absolute cost of college is an important consideration in students' decisions, so is the relative cost among types of institutions. In 1980, average tuition and fees at two-year institutions were almost 50 percent of those charged at public four-year universities. In 2005, they were only 40 percent (The College Board 2004b). There was also a small reduction in the relative cost between two-year colleges and private four-year universities over the same period. In 1980, tuition and fees at community colleges were, on average, 11 percent of average private university charges, twenty-five years later they were 10 percent. As the result of both their absolute and relative cost advantage over other four-year institutions, community colleges are a financially attractive postsecondary option for many students.

Several studies also suggest that the cost advantage provided by community colleges is a primary reason students pursue this type of postsecondary education (Hilmer 1998; Surette 2001; Kane and Rouse 1999). Hilmer found that students were less likely to attend a community college and more likely to attend a four-year college when community college tuition became more expensive. In the opposite case, an increase in university tuition significantly decreased the probability of university attendance and had, in general, almost no impact on the likelihood of attending a community college.[13] However, the measured response to tuition increases was more pronounced for low-income students, for whom an increase in university tuition led to a small decrease in community college attendance (Hilmer 1998). This is consistent with the notion that community colleges and four-year universities are what economists would refer to as complementary goods—those that tend to be purchased in conjunction with one another such that an increase in price

for one causes the demand for it to fall and the demand for the complementary good to also fall, or when the price falls for one causing the demand
for it to rise, the demand for the complementary good also rises. Thus,
community colleges and four-year universities appear to be complements
for many students. Increases in university tuition lead to only a small
increase in community college attendance because many students who opt
to attend a community college eventually plan to transfer to four-year
institutions, which are now more costly to attend. Were community colleges and four-year institutions pure substitutes for one another such that
an increase in university tuition caused students to attend community colleges instead, we would expect four-year college tuition hikes to cause a
large increase in community college attendance.

This finding confirms what has been generally acknowledged. For many
students, community colleges serve as a bridge to eventual enrollment in a
four-year institution. Empirical evidence indicates that community colleges
are increasingly important in serving this purpose. For example, a sample
of students from the mid-1970s showed that about 9 percent of university
graduates had started at a community college (Tinto 1987). A more recent
survey showed that this proportion had increased to roughly 20 percent for
a sample of 1999 and 2000 college graduates (NCES 2003a). This is not ter-
ribly surprising given that community college systems have grown considerably in many states since the 1970s (NCES 2003b).[14] Because more
students are choosing community colleges for their postsecondary education, it is important that we know how the existence of this option affects
overall education levels and economic inequality.

Research on the Impacts of
Community Colleges

There is little doubt that students are better off in the labor market with
a degree from a community college rather than simply a high school
diploma. On average, those with a community college degree have lower
unemployment rates, 3.2 percent versus 4.5 percent, and higher salaries,
$37,600 versus $30,800 (see figure 5.1), than those with only a high school
degree. Thus, for those students who otherwise would not have received
a college education, the existence of a community college sector appears
to be quite beneficial.

Despite the potential benefits of community colleges, there is some
question as to their net effects. In the counterfactual situation, where community colleges were not an option, some of the individuals who attend
community colleges would have received a four-year college degree. The
economic returns to having a bachelor's diploma far exceed those of a
community college degree, so those individuals who are diverted from
four-year institutions are likely to be worse off over the course of their

lifetime. On the other hand, those who receive postsecondary schooling because of the availability of community colleges are likely to be better off financially. Thomas Kane and Cecilia Rouse (1999) estimated the private return to a year of community college and found that forgone earnings and tuition costs of one year of community college attendance is roughly similar to the present value of the lifetime future earnings differential associated with that year of college completion. They also found that completing an associate's degree appears to be associated with a larger increase in annual earnings than two years of community college attendance, implying that future lifetime earnings are likely to more than cover both the direct and indirect costs of community college attendance.

As this discussion implies, the total community college impact ultimately depends on how the existence of a community college sector affects three groups: those who attend community colleges and without them would not receive any college training, those who attend community colleges and transfer and graduate from a four-year college, and those who are diverted from attending and graduating from a four-year college because of community colleges.[15] The idea that community colleges increase years of schooling by enhancing access to postsecondary education is commonly referred to as their democratization effect, and the notion that the existence of community colleges diverts students away from four-year colleges is called their diversion effect.

From a research perspective the difficulty in analyzing the effects of community colleges is significant. No good counterfactual would allow an assessment of what students would do in the absence of community colleges: they might not go to college at all or alternatively might enroll directly in a four-year institution. Much of the research we discuss estimates the effects of community colleges by comparing the behavior of students in the face of cross-sectional variation in college availability or costs, as well as the outcomes of students who attend community colleges to those who attend four-year colleges. The potential problem with focusing on students who opt for one or another type of institution is that students who attend one may be fundamentally different from those who attend another in ways not readily apparent from available data. This raises the concern over attributing individual unobserved differences that may tend to exist between the individuals attending different postsecondary institutions to the availability of those institutions. For example, if we observed that community college students were less likely to complete their degree, that is, finish two years of postsecondary schooling, than four-year college students were likely to complete two years of college, we would not necessarily want to conclude that community colleges have a diversionary impact.[16] Unobserved differences might in fact reflect personal characteristics of community college attendees, such as lower parental support or desire to complete a four-year degree.

Given that a perfect counterfactual does not exist for studying community colleges, a key concern is that researchers appropriately account for the various factors that influence schooling decisions in their models. Most of the research we describe tries to accomplish this by including controls for the demographic and family background characteristics of students, for example, race-ethnicity, socioeconomic status, and so on. Other researchers go a step further to try to account for self-selection of students into schools by including variables designed to capture the educational environment in prospective students' homes. Finally, at least one attempts to deal explicitly with the potential problem of selection through her statistical modeling technique (Rouse 1995). She estimates a two-stage model: the first stage estimates the probability of attending either a community or four-year college, and the second stage estimates the effect of attending each type of institution on years of educational attainment.[17] Although we cannot say definitively which of these studies adequately account for the differences between individuals, in general those that explicitly attempt to account for selection or include variables attempting to factor in the home environment are somewhat more convincing.

It is important to note that research on one aspect of the democratization effect is relatively scarce. Does the existence of community colleges increase the amount of postsecondary education among those individuals who never end up at a four-year college—that is, do they increase the proportion of high school graduates who receive at least some college? A Kane and Rouse review (1999) suggests that although some community college students go on to obtain a degree at a four-year college, more than half are non-traditional, such as displaced workers who are retraining or students who have already earned a bachelor's degree, and therefore unlikely to subsequently attend four-year colleges (Rouse 1995, 1998). In this case, community colleges do in fact increase aggregate educational attainment.

Attendance at a community college appears to increase wages even if students do not finish their degrees, suggesting that community colleges are contributing to human capital accumulation (Jacobson, LaLonde, and Sullivan 2004; Kane and Rouse 1995). Louis Jacobson and his colleagues, who focus on workers who attended community colleges after being displaced from their jobs, estimate that completion of an academic year at a community college increases earnings by 10 to 15 percent (2004). However, these average effects mask considerable variation contingent on the type of courses completed. Technically oriented courses, for example, have a much larger positive effect on earnings than nontechnical courses, which have little or no positive effect.

Far more research exists on whether community colleges increase or decrease the likelihood that students earn a bachelor's degree. Much of the early work in this area was completed by Rouse (1995) and Kane and

Rouse (1999). Using High School and Beyond data for the class of 1982, Kane and Rouse (1999) find that within ten years of completing high school more than 50 percent of all the students who attended community college did not complete any type of degree, 16 percent completed an associate's degree, another 16 percent went on to finish a bachelor's degree or higher, and roughly 15 percent received a certificate.

Rouse's earlier research (1995) finds that starting at a two-year college did not affect the likelihood of completing a bachelor's degree because those students starting at a community college would have been unlikely to complete a bachelor's degree even if they had begun their postsecondary education at a four-year institution. She also finds that the democratization effect of community colleges is stronger than the diversion effect and therefore the presence of two-year colleges increases aggregate educational attainment. Specifically, her research findings suggest that students who began at a two-year college, and who otherwise would have attended a four-year institution, complete at the most one year less of schooling than those who begin at a four-year college—this is the diversion effect. However, because her estimate of the democratization effect (one to one and a half years) is larger than the diversion effect, with roughly the same number of students falling into each group, Rouse concludes that the increase in college attendance attributable to the existence of community colleges slightly outweighs the decrease in schooling that results from diversion.

Others' studies have also tried to estimate the democratization and diversion effects of community colleges. Duane Leigh and Andrew Gill (2003), for example, find that on net community colleges slightly increase schooling by between 0.1 and 0.3 year. When the authors control for students' desired education level, they find that community colleges decrease schooling by about 1.04 years as a consequence of the diversion effect, but increase it by 1.15 years because of the democratization effect. The primary difference between the Leigh and Gill findings and those of Rouse is that Rouse's estimates of the effect of community colleges do not consider levels of desired education, and the two studies measure accessibility differently.[18]

Recall that it is difficult to accurately account for the causal impacts of community colleges because the students who attend each type of college may differ in ways that are unobservable to the researcher. For example, educational aspirations are likely to affect a student's schooling perseverance and thus educational attainment. Research by Leigh and Gill (2004) focuses on this issue using data from the *National Longitudinal Survey of Youth* (NLSY) to investigate whether Kane and Rouse overstate the diversion effect of community college. Leigh and Gill note that students who enroll initially in community colleges tend to have a lower graduation rate than students who enroll directly in four-year institutions, and are careful to try to take this into account in estimating the effects of community colleges. Specifically, they control for students' educational aspirations early and late in their high school years in models estimating graduation likelihood.[19] Evidence from this study suggests that there are important differences in educational aspirations and that accounting for these differences influences estimates of the diversion effect. In fact, Leigh and Gill estimate the community college "differential aspirations effect"[20] to be in the range of −0.43 to −0.68 of a year, which is less than half that of previous effect estimates from Kane and Rouse (1999), Rouse (1995), and Leigh and Gill's earlier research (2003). This difference is attributed to the fact that Leigh and Gill's 2004 study includes changes in educational aspirations during the first two critical years of college. Their study also finds evidence of a strong democratization effect, which they estimate at 1.81 years of school completed. They attribute this positive impact, in part, to an increase in the educational aspirations of students who attend community colleges.

Leigh and Gill's 2004 research also looks at how different categories of students are affected by the democratization and diversion effects. The authors find that the effect of community colleges on increasing the educational aspirations of disadvantaged students (that is, Hispanics, African Americans, low-income, and students with neither parent having attended college) is higher than the comparison group (white students with at least one parent having attended college). In terms of diverting students from additional years of schooling, Leigh and Gill also find that none of the disadvantaged groups are diverted more than the comparison group and, in fact, Hispanic students are diverted less. Their research suggests that community colleges have a larger positive effect on years of desired education for disadvantaged students than for their white counterparts.

It is evident that a big part of the democratization effect of community colleges is the role they play as a stepping-stone for students who will eventually enroll in four-year institutions. A 2001 report by the National Center for Education Statistics (NCES) found that an overwhelming 71 percent of the 1989–1990 school year beginning community college cohort expected to complete a bachelor's degree or higher. Using the NCES 1990 *Beginning Postsecondary Students Longitudinal Study* (BPS: 1990/1994), the authors found that, of students enrolled in a community college in the 1989–1990 school year, 25 percent had transferred to a four-year institution by the spring of 1994. The transfer rate was higher than 50 percent for students beginning at a two-year college who were pursuing a specific major and taking courses that would apply to a bachelor's degree. Furthermore, as figure 5.5 illustrates, transfer rates appeared to be strongly related to students' socioeconomic status (SES), with those with the highest SES being far more likely to transfer.

A central issue in determining the net impact of community colleges is assessing the educational outcomes of transfer students. Research by Ronald Ehrenberg and Christopher Smith (2004) investigates how attendance at a community college affects the likelihood of ultimate graduation

Figure 5.5   Transfer Behavior of Students Enrolled in Public Two-Year Institutions, by Socioeconomic Status

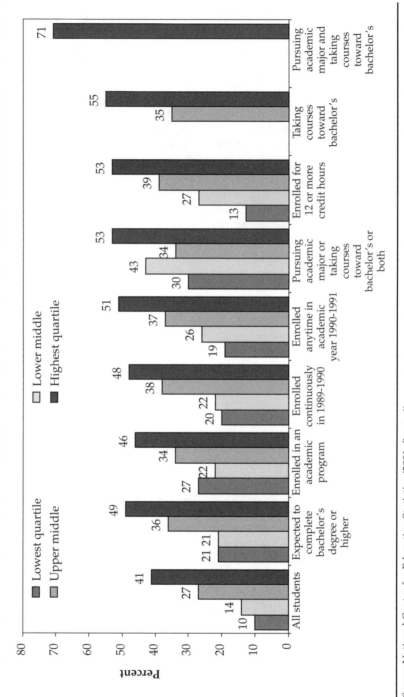

Source: National Center for Education Statistics (2001, figure 6).
Notes: Among 1989 to 1990 beginning postsecondary students. Variables are as of the 1989–1990 school year unless explicitly specified otherwise.
Categories not shown are due to small sample sizes.

from a four-year college. They find that students who transfer after earning an associate degree are more likely to graduate from a four-year university than those who transfer without completing a degree. Others argue that community colleges actually impede the educational attainment of students interested in completing a bachelor's degree, because the cost of transferring can be burdensome and because four-year institutions can better help students to stay focused on completing the bachelor's degree (Brint and Karabel 1989; Clark 1960; Pincus 1980). Philip Ganderton and Richard Santos (1995) find evidence that enrolling in a community college and subsequently transferring to a four-year university versus enrolling directly at a four-year college decreases the probability of completing a bachelor's degree by 10 percent for Hispanics, 13 percent for African Americans, and 22 percent for whites.

An important related question is whether attendance at a community college might influence the quality of four-year institution that students choose to attend. On the one hand, one might hypothesize that students who attend a community college would be better academically prepared, and would therefore opt to attend a more selective four-year college than they would have directly out of high school. On the other hand, having possibly forgone acceptance at a university straight out of high school, community college attendees may end up transferring to less rigorous four-year institutions (Hilmer 1997).

This is an important area of study, given that college selectivity has been shown to influence lifetime earnings. Dominic Brewer, Eric Eide, and Ronald Ehrenberg (1999), for instance, find that graduating from the most selective colleges and universities, based on the *Barron's Profiles of American Colleges* rankings, can increase earnings by nearly 40 percent over graduating from the least selective schools, and that the premium associated with graduating from more selective schools has been increasing over time. Michael Hilmer (1997) focuses on this issue and finds that, on average, students who first attend community colleges choose higher-quality universities than those who enroll in four-year institutions directly out of high school.[21]

Interestingly, Hilmer's study suggests that the impact of first attending a community college on the quality of the university subsequently attended differs for various types of students. Attendance at a community college has the largest impacts on students who perform poorly in high school, come from a poor family, or are of low ability.[22] Hilmer estimates that low-ability students who attend a community college first, transfer to universities whose mean SAT scores for incoming freshman are, on average, 75 points higher than those at the universities attended by comparable low-ability students who choose to enroll directly at four-year institutions. For those with low grades, the differential is about sixty SAT points, and for those from the lowest income group the differential is nearly fifty points. These results

Figure 5.6   Highest Education Level by Race-Ethnicity, 2002

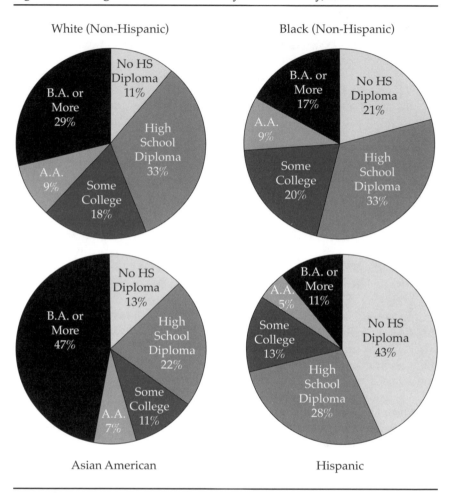

Source: The College Board (2004a, figure 25).
Notes: Includes persons twenty-five and older. Values may not sum to 100 percent because of rounding.

imply that there may be important distributional consequences of community colleges, a point we discuss further in the next section.

Conclusions

It is not surprising that the racial, ethnic, and socioeconomic backgrounds of students in higher education institutions attract considerable attention. The disparities in educational attainment between individuals of different backgrounds are striking (see figures 5.6 and 5.7). For instance, only 16 per-

Figure 5.7   Education Level in 2000 by Socioeconomic Status:
1992 High School Graduates

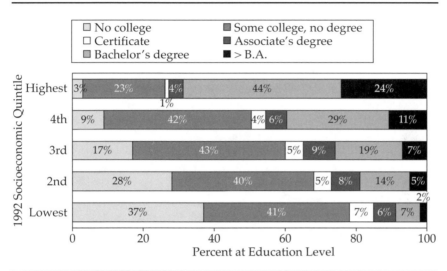

Source: The College Board (2004a, figure 27).
Notes: Values may not sum to 100 percent due to rounding. Socioeconomic status is determined by family income, parent occupation, and the highest level of education attained by parents. Highest level of education completed by December 2000 and includes class of 1992 students who had received a high school diploma by July 1993.

cent of Hispanics and 26 percent of African Americans have received a postsecondary degree, versus 38 percent of whites and 54 percent of Asians.[23] Similar disparities exist for students from different socioeconomic backgrounds. High-income students are six times more likely to complete a bachelor's degree than low-income students, and twelve times less likely to have never attended college after graduating from high school.[24]

Differences in the types of institutions attended among students of various backgrounds are considerable as well (see figure 5.3), a point also made clear in chapter 5, which focuses on programs aimed at increasing opportunities for low-income students to attend selective colleges.[25] Although the percentage of full-time dependent undergraduates within each income bracket who choose public four-year institutions was roughly similar in 2000, differences in attendance at public two-year and private four-year colleges is substantial. Of full-time dependent undergraduates, low-income students are twice as likely as high-income students to be enrolled in a community college and nearly 10 percentage points less likely to attend a private four-year university.[26]

It is well established that attending a two- or four-year college has significant economic value for individuals and that those who do not attend college will, on average, have significantly less upward economic mobility. Clearly, access to educational opportunities beyond high school plays an important role in determining the magnitude of economic inequality in society. Therefore, the composition of groups attending higher education is important for a society concerned about economic inequality that is strongly correlated with immutable background characteristics (race, for example). Community colleges appear to be particularly important institutions for students from disadvantaged backgrounds and minorities. On the whole, we believe that the relatively sparse body of available empirical evidence implies that their existence serves to reduce economic inequality among these groups by increasing educational attainment for society's disadvantaged populations.[27]

Interestingly, an area of study that has failed to receive any empirical attention is how specific state policies might influence education attainment rates. Almost all states have some transfer and articulation policies in place, but variation across states is significant. As of 2000, forty had cooperative agreements between institutions, thirty-three had procedures for reporting transfer data, thirty had legislation on transfer policies, twenty-six had a statewide articulation guide, twenty-three had a common core curriculum, eighteen provided incentives or rewards for transfer students, and eight even had common course numbering (NCES 2005a). However, it is interesting to note that not one state had all of these policies in place.

State policies that define the relationships between community colleges and four-year institutions are likely to influence the extent to which community colleges have democratization or diversion effects. It is therefore essential that empirical research on community colleges take the variation in state policies into account. In fact, the variation in previous findings on these two effects discussed in the previous section may be partly attributable to the weight (the influence of the observations from each state) of the study sample from states with different transfer and articulation policies.

Although data collection procedures for transfer students have improved considerably in recent years, little is known about how state transfer policies affect college attendance decisions and the performance of transfer students. Research by Jane Wellman (2002) analyzes state transfer policies for six states. Florida, New York, and North Carolina were given high grades for student retention and degree completion by the National Center for Public Policy and Higher Education report *Measuring Up* (2000), and Arkansas, New Mexico, and Texas were assigned low grades.[28] Wellman finds that all six are similar in their general approaches to transfer policies, for example, cooperative agreements, transfer incentives, and a common course system. What distinguishes the high-performing from the low-performing states, however, is the structure of governance. States receiving high grades had stronger statewide structures of higher education governance, whereas those with low grades had separate institutional

Table 5.1   Selected State Undergraduate Enrollment as Percentage of
             National, 2004

	All Postsecondary Undergraduate Enrollment	Public Four-Year University Undergraduate Enrollment	Community College Undergraduate Enrollment
California	15.7%	9.2%	24.4%
Texas	7.0%	7.1%	8.1%
New York	6.1%	5.5%	4.0%
Florida	4.9%	4.0%	5.7%
Illinois	4.6%	2.9%	5.7%
All other states (total)	61.7%	71.2%	52.2%

Source: National Center for Public Policy and Higher Education (2004); authors' calculations.
Note: Enrollment includes all full- and part-time undergraduate students at public two-year and public and private four-year institutions. Totals may not sum to 100 due to rounding.

governing structures. In New York, for instance, community colleges and public four-year institutions report to the same governing board. A state-centered approach to transfer and articulation policies facilitates stronger transfer performance between community colleges and public as well as private four-year universities (Wellman 2002).

The community college systems of some states are clearly more developed than others, and it is striking that in 2004, nearly half of all community college enrollments were in five states: California, Florida, Illinois, New York, and Texas. As table 5.1 shows, community college enrollment (as a percentage of total two-year enrollment) in all but one of these, New York, far exceeds the state's percentage of total postsecondary and public four-year institution enrollment. This is interesting because it portends a mismatch between enrollments in two- and four-year institutions that could conflict with the notion that community colleges serve as a stepping-stone to public four-year universities for their students.[29] The little available empirical evidence on the interaction between public higher education institutions suggests that states choose to develop and invest in either a community college system or a public university system (Rouse 1998).[30]

There has been some experimentation with actual partnerships, as opposed to just articulation agreements, between universities and community colleges. In Oregon, for example, Portland State University (PSU) recently signed a memorandum of understanding with four community colleges to integrate student admissions, enrollment, academic planning, and support services. PSU began creating co-admission agreements with community colleges in 1997 when it entered into a partnership with Clackamas Community College. The co-admission agreements, subsequently formed with three additional community colleges, admits students to both institutions. Students can thus take courses at either institution to satisfy their individual educational goals. The program also provides students with collaborative advising, coordinated financial aid and scholarships, aligned curriculum, and library and computer lab access at both campuses. The memorandum signed between all five institutions in March 2006 will further integrate admissions, registration, and financial aid among the consortium of participating institutions.

Well-designed partnerships between two-year colleges and four-year universities are thought to provide advantages for both types of institutions. Community colleges benefit from the ability to better align their course instruction with the curriculum expectations of the partner university, and four-year universities save considerable amounts of financial aid by having students spend their first two years at community colleges. These partnerships may assist with retention and degree completion as students starting at a community college are immediately affiliated with the university and may remain more focused on the baccalaureate degree. They also help to ensure that students who intend to eventually transfer to four-year universities are adequately prepared.

An issue related to the two-year versus four-year transfer debate is how well high schools prepare their students for college-level work. Inadequate readiness for university study is an important reason that many students attend community colleges. Michael Kirst describes in chapter 3 the disconnect that can occur between K–12 and higher education in the United States. Secondary schools and their students have little (or inaccurate) information regarding the academic standards that colleges and universities expect from incoming students. The result is that high schools are failing to equip their students with the competencies needed to perform in college. Bettinger and Long also discuss this point in chapter 4 and describe how some state officials and administrators, blaming the secondary school system for the poor preparation of many of their students, have proposed that high schools should bear the financial responsibility for the remedial courses their students must take.

Another area ripe for investigation is the relationship between community colleges and local labor markets. Given their relatively smaller size, two-year institutions are likely to be more flexible than public universities in adapting programs to meet local labor market needs. Although community colleges have always played an important role in workforce development, there has been a proliferation of contract training engagements and partnerships between local employers and community colleges over the last few decades. In some cases, the role of community colleges in filling labor market niches is itself subject to state policies. The teacher labor market is a classic example of this. For example, North Carolina recently passed a law that allows community colleges to play a central role in the preparation of the state's teachers. Formerly the courses that enable noneducation college graduates to become licensed teachers were reserved for four-year institutions, but now they are being offered at community colleges (Silberman and Simmons, "2-Year Colleges to Help Teachers," *Raleigh News & Observer,* July 20, 2005).

Research on the role that community colleges play in reducing or exacerbating economic inequality is complex given their interactions with K–12 schooling, public universities, and the labor market. This research is not in its infancy, as the literature in the previous section shows, but it clearly has not reached its teenage years either. On the whole, the literature presented here appears to suggest that the existence of community colleges provides postsecondary schooling opportunities that ultimately serve to democratize higher education. But the question of what community colleges do in general is in some ways not the relevant question for policy makers. Instead, we would urge researchers to move beyond a focus on community colleges writ large and toward a focus on the effects of higher education policy. As we described, state policies that delineate the linkages between two- and four-year colleges are quite likely determining the extent to which they are substitutes or complements for one another and how they affect access, persistence, and success in higher education.

It is certainly not novel for researchers to call for more research on a topic, but we believe this chapter makes a strong case that several lines of research on community colleges would greatly enhance our ability to make astute higher education policy decisions. For instance, far more work is necessary to learn how to craft coherent transfer and articulation policies, and thoughtful community college policy making is particularly important, given the increasingly prominent role that community colleges play as an initial access point to higher education for minorities and students from disadvantaged backgrounds.

Endnotes

1. The terms university, four-year institution, and four-year college, are used interchangeably throughout this chapter, as are community college, two-year institution, and two-year college. The text is explicit when referring to either public or private universities and, though there are private two-year colleges, the authors generally refer to publicly funded institutions when discussing two-year colleges.
2. For the civilian noninstitutional population twenty-five years old and over. The unemployment rate for high school dropouts was 8.5 percent.
3. University graduates earned about $12,000 more than those with an associate degree only.
4. It is important to consider that these differences may not be attributable to the level of education attained. The amount of education people complete is typically correlated with a variety of other factors that may or may not be responsible for part of the differences in economic and social livelihood.

5. From 1973 to 2003, overall postsecondary undergraduate enrollment rose from 8.3 million to 14.5 million—an increase of approximately 75 percent. However, much of that growth occurred in community colleges, where enrollment grew from 3.0 million to 6.5 million during that same time period—an increase of about 117 percent (NCES 2005a).

6. These numbers are likely to be underestimates because they are based on the percent of total high school completers who are enrolled in college in the year of completion for 1975 and 2003, and therefore do not include students who return to school after some time off.

7. Figure 5.2 includes both full-time and part-time undergraduates. Part-time students are especially important for two-year institutions; 65 percent of students attending community colleges are enrolled part-time versus around 28 percent at both public and private four-year universities (The College Board 2005).

8. As with four-year universities, whether community colleges serve to increase students' knowledge base (that is, human capital) or to play a role in screening out motivated individuals for prospective employers is open to debate. Although researchers attempt to control for characteristics associated with educational attainment and achievement (for example, socioeconomic status, family stability, and the like), research on community college attendees and transfer students is complicated by the possibility that these students may be different from direct university attendees in unobservable ways.

9. In the 1999–2000 school year, the percentage of full-time undergraduate students receiving financial aid was 50.6 percent for public two-year institutions; 70.8 percent for public four-year institutions; and 84.8 percent for private four-year institutions (NCES 2004).

10. The 1992 Reauthorization of the Higher Education Act made changes to the Stafford loan program that impacted both the percentage of students who borrowed and the average loan amount. New unsubsidized Stafford loans for students regardless of financial need, higher loan limits for the subsidized loan program participants, and changes in need analysis that lowered the average expected family contribution (thereby increasing the number of eligible students) all served to increase the percentage of students borrowing and the average amount borrowed (NCES 2004).

11. The increase is not statistically significant for community college students in the lowest income quarter.

12. It is important to remember that this discussion considers average aid amounts for students who actually enrolled in college. It thus excludes those for whom the cost of college precluded their attendance.

13. The relationship between tuition increases and attendance probability is not the same for both types of institutions: a tuition increase at a university reduces the likelihood that a student will attend a university four times more than a tuition increase at a community college.

14. The number of public two-year institutions has grown from 654 in 1970 to 1,101 in 2002.

15. The effect is actually slightly more complicated because the three groups are not mutually exclusive. Some students who would not have enrolled in college were it not for community colleges end up transferring to four-year colleges because of their community college experience.

16. Similarly, students are confronted with different options in terms of college geographic accessibility and cost. We would not want to inappropriately mis-attribute the impact of cost or availability to the effect of attending a particular type of institution, unless we viewed these as part of the effect of the institution. For example, one might consider "relatively low cost" as part of the community college treatment and it would therefore be appropriate to compare the completion rates at low-cost community colleges to educational attainment at higher-cost four-year institutions.

17. The instruments—variables that are thought to influence the first stage probability of college attendance models but not the second stage years of educational attainment models—she uses for identification of the effect of institution type are distance to the closest two- and four-year schools and two- and four-year college tuition.

18. Duane Leigh and Andrew Gill (2003) include general and financial constraints whereas Cecilia Rouse (1995) uses proximity from high school to nearest two-year or four-year college and average state tuition to measure college access.

19. To account for educational aspirations, they use two questions from the NLSY: "What is the highest grade or year of regular school, that is, elementary school, high school, college, or graduate school that you would like to complete?" and "As things now stand, what is the highest grade or year you think you will actually complete?"

20. Leigh and Gill (2004) use the term "differential aspirations effect" to refer to the two-year–four-year college difference in educational aspirations in order to reserve the term diversion for differences in educational attainment.

21. One might imagine that students who graduate from a four-year institution after transferring from a community college would have different labor market outcomes than those who matriculate directly into a four-year college, because students would accumulate different amounts of human capital in the first few years of college. This does not appear to be so, at least in the case of earnings. Michael Hilmer (2002) finds no statistically significant difference between the earnings of those who transferred from a community college and subsequently graduated from a four-year institution and those who graduated from a four-year university after matriculating directly from high school.

22. Students characterized as low-ability had math and reading test scores lower than one standard deviation below the mean on the High School and Beyond survey, and students considered to have performed poorly in high school are those with grades lower than one standard deviation below the mean.

23. An astounding 70 percent of Hispanics receive no postsecondary education.

24. It is important to note that figure 5.7 shows the attendance decisions of students who received a high school diploma. The disparity is even more pronounced when one also considers high school graduation rates by SES.

25. Interestingly, there are considerable differences in postsecondary attendance among children from the same level of socioeconomic status. Kim Lloyd, Martha Tienda, and Anna Zajacova (2001) found that in 1994 40 percent of Hispanic and African American youth from low SES families attended postsecondary institutions versus 30 percent of white youth and 77 percent of Asian youth.

26. Figure 5.3 understates the point that students from lower SES backgrounds are more likely to enroll in community colleges than those from middle- and higher-income families, because it omits students who are financially independent of their parents. Independent students are disproportionately from low-income families, more heavily concentrated in community colleges, and make up almost half of all postsecondary students (The College Board 2004a).
27. It is worth stressing that this conclusion is based on a relatively thin body of evidence and is far from universally held (see, for example, Alon 2001).
28. Wellman chose these states because their community college sector is an important starting point for many low-income students who eventually complete a bachelor's degree. She did not choose California, the state with the largest number of community college students, because it received midrange scores in the report.
29. It is in fact an oft-stated function of community colleges to prepare students for their transfer to four-year institutions (Brawer and Cohen 1987; Brint and Karabel 1989).
30. Of course, this is a complex issue because the cost of educating a college student is likely to depend on each student's educational focus and year in school. Furthermore, state funding formulas will influence the extent to which relying on transfers is financially beneficial to public four-year colleges.

References

Alon, Sigal. 2001. "Racial, Ethnic and Socioeconomic Disparities in College Destinations, 1982 and 1992." Princeton, N.J.: Princeton University, Office of Population Research. http://www.opr.princeton.edu/papers/opr0102.pdf.

Becker, Gary S. 1964. *Human Capital.* New York: National Bureau of Economic Research.

Behrman, Jere R., and Barbara L. Wolfe. 1989. "Does More Schooling Make Women Better Nourished and Healthier—Adult Sibling Random and Fixed Effects Estimates for Nicaragua." *Journal of Human Resources* 24(4): 644–63.

Behrman, J. R., L. G. Kletzer, M. S. McPherson, and M. O. Schapiro. 1992. *The College Investment Decision: Direct and Indirect Effects of Family Background on Choice of Post-secondary Enrollment and Quantity.* Arthur Anderson Working Paper Series 9201. Los Angeles: University of Southern California Department of Economics.

Berger, Mark C., and J. Paul Leigh. 1989. "Schooling, Self-Selection, and Health." *Journal of Human Resources* 24(3): 433–55.

Berkner, Lutz, and Lisa Chavez. 1997. *Access to Postsecondary Education for the 1992 High School Graduates.* Washington, D.C.: National Center for Education Statistics.

Brawer, Florence B., and Cohen, Arthur M. 1987. *The Collegiate Function of Community Colleges.* San Francisco, Calif.: Jossey-Bass Inc.

Brewer, Dominic J., Eric R. Eide, and Ronald G. Ehrenberg. 1999. "Does it Pay to Attend an Elite Private College? Cross-Cohort Evidence on the Effects of College Type on Earnings." *Journal of Human Resources* 34(1): 104–23.

Brint, Steven, and Jerome Karabel. 1989. *The Diverted Dream: Community Colleges and the Promise of Educational Opportunity in America, 1900–1985.* New York: Oxford University Press.

Clark, Burton R. 1960. "The 'Cooling-Out' Function in Higher Education." *The American Journal of Sociology* 65: 569–76.

Conklin, Mary E., and Ann R. Dailey. 1981. "Does Consistency of Parental Educational Encouragement Matter for Secondary Students?" *Sociology of Education* 54(4): 254–62.

Dale, Stacey B., and Alan B. Krueger. 2002. "Estimating the Payoff to Attending a More Selective College: An Application of Selection on Observables and Unobservables." *Quarterly Journal of Economics* 117(4): 1491–1527.

Ehrenberg, Ronald G., and Christopher L. Smith. 2004. "Analyzing the Success of Student Transitions from 2- to 4-Year Institutions within a State." *Economics of Education Review* 23(1): 11–28.

Ganderton, Philip T. 1992. "The Effect of Subsidies in Kind on the Choice of College." *Journal of Public Economics* 48: 269–91.

Ganderton, Philip T., and Richard Santos. 1995. "Hispanic College Attendance and Completion: Evidence from the High School and Beyond Surveys." *Economics of Education Review* 14: 35–46.

Groot, Wim, and Hessel Oosterbeek. 1994. "Earnings Effects of Different Components of Schooling: Human Capital versus Screening." *The Review of Economics and Statistics* 76(2): 317–21.

Grossman, Michael. 1975. "The Correlation between Health and Schooling." In *Household Production and Consumption*, edited by N. E. Terleckyj. New York: National Bureau of Economic Research.

———. 1982. *Determinants of Children's Health.* Report PHS 81–3309 and NTIS P380–1636603. Bethesda, Md.: National Center for Health Services Research.

Heller, D. E. 1997. "Student Price Response in Higher Education: An Update to Leslie and Brinkman." *Journal of Higher Education* 68(6): 624–59.

Hilmer, Michael J. 1997. "Does Community College Attendance Provide a Strategic Path to Quality Education?" *Economics of Education Review* 16(1): 59–68.

———. 1998. "Post-Secondary Fees and the Decision To Attend a University or a Community College." *Journal of Public Economics* 67: 329–48.

———. 2002. "Student Migration and Institution Control as Screening Devices." *Economics Letters* 76: 19–25.

Hossler, Don, Shouping Hu, and Jack Schmit. 1998. "Predicting Student Sensitivity to Tuition and Financial Aid." Paper presented at the annual meeting of the American Educational Research Association, San Diego, Calif. (April 1998).

Jackson, Gregory A. 1978. "Financial Aid and Student Enrollment." *Journal of Higher Education* 49(6):548–74.

Jacobson, Louis, Rover LaLonde, and Daniel G. Sullivan. 2004. "Estimating the Returns to Community College Schooling for Displaced Workers." *Institute for the Study of Labor* Discussion Paper 1017. Chicago: Federal Reserve Bank.

Kane, Thomas J., and Cecilia Rouse. 1995. "Labor Market Returns to Two- and Four-Year Colleges." *American Economic Review* 85(3): 600–14.

———. 1999. "The Community College: Educating Students at the Margin between College and Work." *The Journal of Economic Perspectives* 13(1):63–84.

Kenkel, Donald S. 1991. "Health Behavior, Health Knowledge, and Schooling." *Journal of Political Economy* 99(2):287–305.

Layard, Richard, and George Psacharopoulos. 1974. "The Screening Hypothesis and the Returns to Education." *Journal of Political Economy* 82: 985–98.

Leigh, Duane E., and Andrew M. Gill. 2003. "Do Community Colleges Really Divert Students from Earning Bachelor's Degrees?" *Economics of Education Review* 22(1): 23–30.

———. 2004. "The Effect of Community Colleges on Changing Students' Educational Aspirations." *Economics of Education Review* 23: 95–102.

Lerman, R. I., S. K. Riegg, and H. Salzman. 2000. *The Role of Community Colleges in Expanding the Supply of Information Technology Workers.* Washington, D.C.: The Urban Institute. http://www.urban.org/pdfs/comm_colleges.pdf

Lloyd, Kim, Martha Tienda, and Anna Zajacova. 2001. "Educational Achievement Trends of Minority Students since Brown v. Board of Education." Presented at the Millennium Conference: Achieving High Educational Standards for All. National Academy of Sciences, Washington, D.C. (September 21–22, 2001).

Manski, Charles F., and David A. Wise. 1983. *College Choice in America.* Cambridge, Mass.: Harvard University Press.

McPherson, Michael S., and Morton O. Schapiro. 1998. *The Student Aid Game: Meeting Need and Rewarding Talent in American Higher Education.* Princeton, N.J.: Princeton University Press.

Michael, Robert T. 1972. *The Effect of Education on Efficiency in Consumption.* New York: Columbia University Press.

National Center for Education Statistics (NCES). 2001. *Community College Transfer Rates to 4-year Institutions Using Alternative Definitions of Transfer.* Washington: Government Printing Office.

———. 2003a. *A Descriptive Summary of 1999–2000 Bachelor's Degree Recipients 1 Year Later.* Washington: Government Printing Office.

———. 2003b. *Digest of Education Statistics.* Washington: Government Printing Office.

———. 2004. *Paying for College: Changes between 1990 and 2000 for Full-Time Dependent Undergraduates.* Washington: Government Printing Office.

———. 2005a. *The Condition of Education 2005.* Washington: Government Printing Office.

———. 2005b. *Youth Indicators 2005: Trends in the Well-Being of American Youth.* Washington: Government Printing Office.

National Center for Public Policy and Higher Education. 2000. *Measuring Up 2000: The State-by-State Report Card for Higher Education.* San Jose, Calif.: National Center for Public Policy and Higher Education.

———. 2004. *Measuring Up: The National Report Card on Higher Education.* San Jose, Calif.: National Center for Public Policy and Higher Education. Available at : http://measuringup.highereducation.org.

Pincus, F. L. 1980. "The False Promises of Community Colleges: Class Conflict and Vocational Education." *Harvard Educational Review* 50: 332–61.

Rouse, Cecilia E. 1995. "Democratization or Diversion? The Effect of Community Colleges on Educational Attainment." *Journal of Business & Economic Statistics* 13(2): 217–24.

———. 1998. "Do Two-Year Colleges Increase Overall Educational Attainment? Evidence from the States." *Journal of Policy Analysis and Management* 17(4): 595–620.

Spence, Michael. 1973. "Job Market Signaling." *Quarterly Journal of Economics* 87(3): 355–74.

St. John, Edward P. 1990. "Price Response in Enrollment Decisions: An Analysis of the High School and Beyond Sophomore Cohort." *Research in Higher Education* 31(2): 161–76.

———. 1994. *Prices, Productivity, and Investment: Assessing Financial Strategies in Higher Education.* ASHE-ERIC Higher Education Reports no. 3. Washington, D.C.: George Washington University Press.

Surette, B. J. 2001. "Transfer from Two-Year to Four-Year College: An Analysis of Gender Differences." *Economics of Education Review* 20: 151–63.

The College Board. 2004a. *Education Pays 2004.* Washington, D.C.: The College Entrance Examination Board. http://www.collegeboard.com/prod_downloads/press/cost04/EducationPays2004.pdf

———. 2004b. *Trends in College Pricing 2004.* Washington, D.C.: The College Entrance Examination Board. http://www.collegeboard.com/prod_downloads/press/cost04/041264TrendsPricing2004_FINAL.pdf

———. 2005. *Trends in College Pricing 2005.* Washington, D.C.: The College Entrance Examination Board. http://www.collegeboard.com/prod_downloads/press/cost05/trends_college_pricing_05.pdf

Tinto, Vincent. 1987. *Leaving College: Rethinking the Causes and Cures of Student Attrition.* Chicago: University of Chicago.

U.S. Bureau of Labor Statistics. 2005. *Current Population Survey.* Washington: Government Printing Office. http://www.bls.gov/cps/cpsaat7.pdf.

U.S. Census Bureau. 2003. *Educational Attainment in the United States: March 2002.* Washington: Government Printing Office. http://www.census.gov/population/www/socdemo/education/ppl-169.html

———. 2004. *Annual Social and Economic Supplement. Current Population Reports.* Washington: Government Printing Office. http://ferret.bls.census.gov/macro/032004/perinc/new03_010.htm

Wellman, Jane V. 2002. *State Policy and Community College-Baccalaureate Transfer.* National Center Report #02-6. Washington: The National Center for Public Policy and Higher Education and the Institute for Higher Education Policy.

═ Chapter 6 ═

Access to Elites

Amanda Pallais and Sarah E. Turner

S TUDENTS FROM relatively low-income families are persistently under-represented in the most selective institutions of higher education (see, for example, Bowen, Kurzweil, and Tobin 2005). This is true among the most expensive private colleges and universities as well as many selective public universities with more modest tuition charges. Because selective colleges and universities are perceived to be important stepping-stones to professional and leadership positions, the representation of students from a broad range of socioeconomic backgrounds at these institutions is a significant demonstration of commitment to opportunity and intergenerational mobility.[1] With increased public attention to the underrepresentation of low-income students at selective colleges and universities, a number of leading universities have responded with aggressive initiatives intended to increase opportunities for low-income students.

The direct costs of college have risen substantially over the past decade, particularly at selective colleges and universities, and there is little indication that this trend will abate. This reality has increased the degree of concern about the capacity of elite colleges and universities to provide opportunities for students from low- and moderate-income families. Although the direct charges at selective public universities remain well below those at private universities, the combination of decreased state support, rising costs, and the need to raise tuition prices to maintain the quality of program offerings contributes to a sense that costs may exacerbate the difficulty in enrolling low-income students at state flagship universities (see Schwartz, in chapter 7, for more on college costs). At issue is whether aggressive recruiting and generous financial aid can counteract the effects of high tuition at selective universities to increase the representation of students from the most economically disadvantaged families.

128

Researchers and the press have shone a brighter spotlight on the under-representation of low-income students at the most selective institutions. One indication of the prominence of the issue is that the most recent *U.S. News and World Report* college rankings includes a section highlighting the colleges with a particularly high representation of low-income students. Colleges and universities have responded proactively, with the most selective at the forefront of initiatives to increase the enrollment of low-income students.

A number of colleges and universities are making aggressive and visible efforts to increase the availability of need-based financial aid to increase the representation of low-income students in their entering classes. In the fall of 2005, we identified ten such efforts, many with catchy titles such as AccessUVa, Illinois Promise, and Carolina Covenant. In the course of a year, a significant number of universities announced new programs and others announced expanded offerings. Among the private universities, Harvard, Yale, Brown, and—more recently—MIT have each announced programs. There is a common theme among these efforts. In all cases, the universities are making a direct and public case that a college education is affordable to low- and moderate-income students.[2] Because these programs are so new, however, it is far too early to evaluate their effects on outcomes such as college completion.

Stating the Problem

Overall, there is clear evidence that low-income students are under-represented in the post-secondary pipeline. Table 6.1 shows the college enrollment rates of dependent students between age eighteen and twenty-four from national data in 2003. Although the overall difference between the enrollment rate of the top two income groups (69 to 71 percent) and the bottom two (37 to 44 percent) is significant, the large difference between students from different economic circumstances in enrollment at four-year institutions is even more striking. Among college students, those in the higher income groups are appreciably more likely to enroll in four-year colleges and universities, which often provide the most direct path to gaining a degree. Overall, the gap in college enrollment between students in the highest and the bottom income quartiles narrows to about 15 percentage points when high school achievement is taken into consideration (Ellwood and Kane 2000).

Beyond aggregate gaps in college enrollment rates, students from low-income families are particularly underrepresented in the most selective colleges and universities, both private and public. Table 6.2 shows data on applications, admission, and matriculation in relation to economic circumstances of those entering college in 1995 for the nineteen selective colleges and universities in the Expanded College & Beyond database

Table 6.1   College Enrollment Rates for Dependent Individuals
Ages Eighteen to Twenty-four, 2003

| | Two-Year | | Four-Year | | Total |
| | Full-Time | Part-Time | Full-Time | Part-Time | Post-secondary |
Family Income					
Total	0.10	0.03	0.31	0.03	0.55
Less than $10,000	0.04	0.02	0.14	0.01	0.37
$10,000 to $14,999	0.06	0.03	0.20	0.03	0.44
$15,000 to $19,999	0.09	0.05	0.18	0.01	0.44
$20,000 to $29,999	0.09	0.03	0.20	0.02	0.45
$30,000 to $39,999	0.11	0.02	0.24	0.04	0.50
$40,000 to $49,999	0.10	0.07	0.23	0.03	0.50
$50,000 to $74,999	0.11	0.03	0.32	0.03	0.56
$75,000 to $99,999	0.11	0.05	0.38	0.03	0.64
$100,000 to $149,999	0.13	0.03	0.44	0.05	0.71
$150,000 and over	0.10	0.02	0.47	0.03	0.69
Not reported	0.07	0.03	0.31	0.02	0.53

Source: U.S. Census Bureau (2003, table 14).
http://www.census.gov/population/socdemo/school/cps2003/tab14_06.xls.

Table 6.2   Low-Income Students at Selective Colleges and Universities,
1995 Entering Cohort

| | Share Bottom Income Quartile | | | |
	Apply	Admit	Enroll	Graduate
All expanded college and beyond	12%	9%	11%	11%
Ivy League universities	12%	8%	9%	8.2%
Public universities	12%	11%	12%	10.5%
Liberal arts colleges	11%	8%	10%	9.9%
Women's colleges	17%	13%	16%	15.5%

Source: Bowen, Kurzweil, and Tobin (2005, figure 5.1). Reprinted with permission.

collected by the Andrew W. Mellon Foundation. Overall, fewer than 11 percent of first-year students matriculating at these institutions were from the bottom income quartile. Such results are echoed in Catherine Hill's and Gordon Winston's (2005) examination of selective private institutions, twenty-three schools among the membership of the Consortium on Financing Higher Education (COFHE). About 10 percent of matriculating students were from families with incomes less than $41,000. About 70 percent were from families with incomes exceeding $91,000. Still, within the group of selective schools, heterogeneity in the representation of low-income students is considerable. It is unambiguously the case that low-income students are much better represented at some universities than

Figure 6.1   **Poverty and Enrollment at the University of Virginia by District**

Panel A. Percent of Children Living Below the Poverty Line

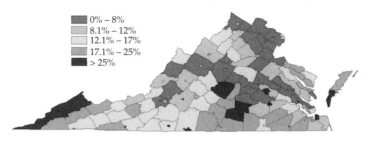

	0% – 8%
	8.1% – 12%
	12.1% – 17%
	17.1% – 25%
	> 25%

Panel B. Percentage of Students Graduating from Public High Schools Attending the University of Virginia

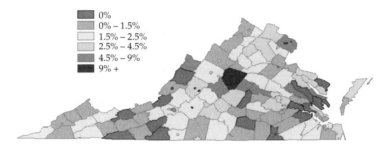

	0%
	0% – 1.5%
	1.5% – 2.5%
	2.5% – 4.5%
	4.5% – 9%
	9% +

Source Panel A: Census 2000 Summary File 3 (SF 3). TM-PCT052.
Source Panel B: University of Virginia Databook – IAAS (Fall 2004), Virginia Department of Education (Spring 2004).

others. Among the most highly ranked universities, about 14.1 percent of dependent students at MIT come from families with incomes less than $30,000 in the 2000–2001 school year, and of those at Harvard University about 4.4 percent do.[3]

A different (and graphic) indicator of how economic circumstances affect the likelihood of enrollment at a selective school is shown in figure 6.1 for the state of Virginia. The top panel shows the concentration of poverty by school district within the state, with poverty concentrated in the urban areas of Richmond and Norfolk and in the counties on the southern and western borders of the state. Yet, when we turn to enrollment at the University of Virginia, the distribution is reversed, with students drawn disproportionately from the affluent counties in northern Virginia. The simple correlation measure between family income and the attendance measure is 0.34.[4]

That low-income students are underrepresented at selective colleges and universities is not a new phenomenon. Yet the consequences today are magnified by the widening of the family income gap. The question is whether elite colleges and universities unintentionally contribute to the growing inequality by failing to provide enough opportunities for students from low-income families.

Hypotheses Explaining Underrepresentation

It is well established that low-income students are underrepresented in selective higher education. Yet the reasons for this underrepresentation and how public policies can narrow this gap are less clear. The research literature offers no consensus about why low-income students are underrepresented. Among the commonly cited explanations are credit constraints, information constraints, and low academic achievement in the precollege years, and the relative importance of these factors has been much debated. Whatever the answer is in aggregate, it is entirely plausible that barriers to enrollment at the most selective institutions are somewhat different than at the margin of enrollment.[5] We consider evidence related to these explanations before turning to the discussion of recent institutional initiatives designed to increase the participation of low-income students. The success of these initiatives depends in large part on how they are aligned with the causes of underrepresentation.

College Costs

College education is expensive, particularly at the nation's most selective colleges and universities. College tuition, combined with room and board expenses, places the annual sticker price of a college education well above $40,000 at selective private institutions such as Princeton and Brown University (table 6.3). Even with appreciably lower tuition charges for in-state residents, the price of college may approach $20,000 per year at state flagship institutions where on-campus residence is required. High direct college costs support a prima facie case that the most economically disadvantaged students may be squeezed out of collegiate opportunities, particularly at elite schools, by escalating college charges in the face of quite limited mechanisms for financing the full cost of college.

Yet, at the most selective colleges and universities in both the public and private sectors, the net price of college for low-income students is far less than the posted price, owing to the availability of need-based financial aid. The most highly ranked institutions generally maintain policies—by no means universal in higher education—of meeting full

Table 6.3   Cost of Attendance at Selective Public and Private Universities

School	2005–2006 (In-State)	2005–2006 (Out-of-State)
Harvard	$44,350	$44,350
Princeton	$43,385	$43,385
Yale	$43,700	$43,700
Brown	$44,530	$44,530
University of North Carolina–Chapel Hill	$14,294	$28,616
University of Virginia	$16,714	$33,769 to $34,669
University of Maryland	$19,633	$31,957
University of Michigan–Ann Arbor	$19,643	$38,031
Ohio State	$20,283	$31,506
University of Illinois at Urbana-Champaign	$19,240	$33,656

Source: Authors' tabulations.

need, which implies that an admitted student will be offered a package of grants, loans, and work-study to finance the cost of college.[6] Institutions differ markedly in the extent to which they offer financial aid in the form of grants or loans, with the most affluent offering aid packages with a higher fraction of grant aid. To be sure, in many cases, the expected payment from low-income students and families relative to income remains substantial. Catherine Hill, Gordon Winston, and Stephanie Boyd (2004) examine net college prices for students attending selective private institutions. This information replicated in table 6.4. It is clearly the case that, even before the substantial recent changes in the structure of financial aid, low-income students faced tuition charges well below the stated costs, which generally exceeded $33,000 for the 2001–2002 academic year, at private colleges and universities. Across all COFHE schools, the lowest income students, those with less than $24,000 in family income, could expect a direct cost of about $7,500, and those in the next income band, $25,000 to $41,000, could expect charges of about $8,500. At issue is how this burden of college costs affects enrollment and whether reducing the direct costs of college at these schools would substantially increase the representation of low-income students.

The public universities start with much lower tuition charges, but the availability of funds for financial aid is more constrained. Take the case of the University of Virginia, where the total cost of attendance for in-state students was estimated at $16,714 for the 2005–2006 academic year. Of this amount, $7,180 was tuition and fees (State Council on Higher Education in Virginia 2005). Because the maximum Pell Grant is $4,050 and dependent undergraduate students are limited in their borrowing from the federal government to $2,625 in the first year and $3,500 in their sec-

Table 6.4   Prices of Undergraduate Schools, 2001 to 2002

| (Lower Bound) | Lower | | | Upper | | |
	Lowest 0	Middle $24,001	Middle $41,001	Middle $61,379	High $91,701	Sticker Price (Unaided)
Average net price						
COFHE schools	$7,552	$8,547	$11,557	$16,365	$23,690	$33,831
Coed colleges	$5,487	$7,280	$10,374	$15,259	$22,738	$33,403
Women's colleges	$7,863	$9,676	$13,134	$18,297	$25,663	$33,708
Ivy League universities	$8,169	$9,200	$11,893	$16,499	$23,949	$34,508
Non-Ivy universities	$7,495	$7,956	$11,238	$16,249	$23,399	$33,167
Net price/Sticker price						
COFHE schools	22%	25%	34%	48%	70%	
Coed colleges	17%	22%	31%	46%	68%	
Women's colleges	23%	29%	39%	54%	76%	
Ivy League universities	24%	27%	34%	48%	69%	
Non-Ivy universities	22%	24%	34%	49%	70%	

Source: Hill, Winston, Boyd (2005, table 2). Reprinted with permission.

ond year under the Stafford loan program, it is quite plausible that many undergraduate students with high financial need would be constrained from attending in the absence of institutional financial aid and other sources of private credit. Notably, in some states, specifically California and New York, additional means-tested grant aid is available from the state to students attending colleges and universities within the state. The Tuition Assistance Program (TAP) in New York provides up to $5,000 in additional aid and the Cal Grant program offers full tuition at a public institution or stipends over $9,000 at private in-state institutions for students meeting academic requirements. Ronald Ehrenberg (2005) suggests that these state programs may contribute to the relative success of selective institutions in New York and California in recruiting low-income students.

Make no mistake: college costs may be a substantial factor in the underrepresentation of low-income students at the most selective colleges and universities. However, the research evidence on the direct effect of changes in net price on college enrollment or persistence at selective institutions is relatively sparse.[7]

Table 6.5   Distribution of SAT-Test Takers

| | National Test-Taking Population (1 in 10 Sample) | | | | | | |
| | Lower | | | Upper | | | |
(Lower Bound)	Lowest 0	Middle $24,001	Middle $41,001	Middle $61,379	High $91,701	Total	Total Students
1600	0.0%	0.0%	0.0%	0.0%	0.1%	0.0%	30
1520	0.1%	0.2%	0.2%	0.5%	1.3%	0.5%	356
1420	0.5%	0.8%	1.4%	2.1%	4.7%	2.0%	1447
1300	1.8%	3.4%	5.3%	7.5%	11.9%	6.3%	4557
1220	2.6%	5.1%	7.0%	9.1%	12.6%	7.6%	5492
1110	8.1%	12.3%	15.6%	18.5%	21.9%	15.8%	11355
1030	9.0%	13.4%	15.0%	16.1%	14.9%	13.9%	10031
910	20.5%	23.5%	24.1%	22.6%	18.1%	21.7%	15648
830	25.3%	15.4%	14.0%	11.2%	7.9%	12.8%	9200
740	8.8%	13.7%	10.0%	7.6%	4.3%	10.1%	7242
620	15.2%	8.8%	5.4%	3.6%	1.8%	6.5%	4668
500	6.8%	2.9%	1.6%	1.0%	0.5%	2.3%	1681
400	1.4%	0.5%	0.2%	0.1%	0.1%	0.4%	308
Total students	12,117	13,665	14,084	16,000	16,149	72,015	72,015

Source: Hill and Winston (2005, tables 1, A1, and A2).

Achievement Differences

Differences between low-income students and their more affluent peers in measures of achievement start in early grades and widen through the hurdles that lead to enrollment at selective colleges. Low-income students not only are less likely to take college placement tests[8] but also tend to have lower scores on these exams. The gap is particularly marked at the top of the distribution from which elite colleges and universities are likely to draw students.

Considering the distribution of college placement test scores by family income provides a different perspective on the differences in college preparation by family income. Low-income students are dramatically underrepresented at the top tail of SAT scores (see table 6.5), and similar differences by income are apparent in ACT data. Students from families with income below $41,000 make up about 36 percent of all test-takers but only about 13 percent of those with SAT scores greater than 1,300 and only about 10 percent of those with scores over 1,520.

For public universities drawing disproportionately from the pool of state residents, variation across states in the link between test scores and income will have some effect on the pool of potential students. For example, both California and Virginia require the SAT for admission to the

Figure 6.2   Students Scoring 1200 or Better on SAT

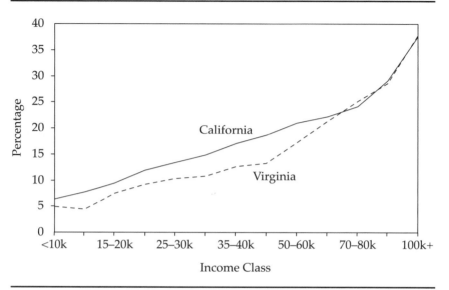

Source: Tebbs and Turner (2005a).
Note: Tabulations from the "Test-Takers Data" covering SAT performance and responses to the Student Descriptive Questionnaire were provided by Jesse Rothstein and are limited to respondents with known race-ethnicity. See Card and Krueger (2004) for additional details about the data.

state flagship institution, but a substantially higher fraction of low-income test-takers in California exceed a score of 1200 (a plausible indicator of preparedness for university study) than their Virginia counterparts do (see figure 6.2). Thus, to some degree, the much higher representation of Pell Grant recipients at University of California institutions relative to the University of Virginia reflects differences in state demographic conditions and inequality in primary-secondary schooling, in addition to the differential effectiveness of the universities in recruiting low-income students.[9] For this reason, we regard the continued use of measures of Pell shares as indicators of how well university policies address the needs of low-income students, such as the recent ranking in the *Chronicle of Higher Education* (Fischer 2006), as misleading and counterproductive (for a detailed assessment of the problems associated with the use of the Pell share measures in policy discussions, see Tebbs and Turner 2005a; Turner 2006).

Given the scarcity of low-income students with relatively high achievement, are there initiatives at the university level that can narrow test-score gaps? What are the prospects for students with modest measured achievement who have overcome substantial economic hurdles at selective institutions? Although university policies can affect test scores only indirectly and over the long run, universities can respond to the observed gaps in the short run. In addition, if traditional measures of achievement are relatively weak indicators of performance for low-income students, universities may benefit from policies that lead to the admission of students with moderate test scores.

Information Constraints

Beyond direct constraints to financing, observers in both local and national markets have suggested that the underrepresentation of low-income students at selective colleges and universities may go beyond the tangible issues of test scores and financial aid. One potential dimension in which low-income students may differ from their more affluent peers is in the information they bring to the college application. One specific information problem is a failure to understand the benefits of college and the extent to which financial aid will reduce the burden of paying for college. Yet, in designing and evaluating an outreach program known as COACH (College Opportunity and Career Help) in the Boston public schools, the economists Tom Kane and Chris Avery found that low-income students' understanding of the benefits and costs of college did not differ systematically from more affluent peers (Avery and Kane 2004).

One question that remains is whether interventions and intensive counseling designed to help students overcome the complexity of the process of applying for college and financial aid would improve outcomes for low-income students. Susan Dynarski and Judith Scott-Clayton (2006) note that the complexity of the needs analysis system poses a substantial challenge for many potential students from low-income families and posit that a radical simplification of the federal student aid application would reduce the barriers for low-income students in understanding aid eligibility. There is, however, little evidence to suggest that existing extracurricular interventions targeted on low-income youth have been systematically effective in increasing college enrollment. For example, Upward Bound, a $250 million federal program designed to motivate and prepare disadvantaged high school students for college was found to have little or no effect on student outcomes. A recent evaluation of the program by Mathematica (Myers et al. 2004) compared Upward Bound applicants who were randomly assigned to either a program or a control group. It found that Upward Bound had no effect on college enrollment, total number of college or high school credits earned, high school grades, or high school graduation in the aggregate. However, the program positively affected some of these outcomes for students who did not expect to earn a bachelor's degree before entering Upward

Bound and may have made its students more likely to enroll in four-year colleges in lieu of two-year colleges.

Another and quite different type of information constraint is associated with perceptions about fit. Students from low-income families are likely to face more uncertainty about what residential college life is about if their parents or acquaintances did not complete a four-year degree.[10] For example, recruiters for Harvard University have faced the challenge of dispelling preconceptions that the university is "a place for all rich white kids" or notions of "people all dressed up in their nice blazers and checkered sweaters" (Marcella Bombardieri, *Boston Globe,* July 16, 2005, p. A1). More generally, Paul Courant, Michael McPherson, and Alexandra Resch (2006) suggest that many students from low-income families simply "never considered the possibility that they could attend, for example, UNC–Chapel Hill or UT-Austin" (307). One question for selective universities is whether well-worn stereotypes are fact or fiction. Are students from moderate means uncomfortable in particular selective university environments? To the extent that preconceptions of low-income students are false, university policy faces an aggressive challenge in reshaping public opinion.

Policy Channels: What Can Universities Do?

To increase the enrollment of low-income students, colleges and universities can have direct effects through recruiting, admissions, financial aid, and on-campus retention efforts. Different institutions may well choose to focus on different channels—and with different policy tools.

Having identified financial constraints, achievement gaps, and information barriers as obstacles to the greater representation of low-income students, the question becomes what universities can do. Potential policy levers include increased financial aid, efforts to increase information and other outreach initiatives, and paying greater attention to family circumstances in the admission process.

New Institutional Initiatives

Over the course of the last several years, many leaders in higher education have spoken out in their determination to improve the representation of students from low-income families in selective higher education. University presidents have gone beyond the public pulpit to committing resources to new policies toward this goal.

Most prominent among these, then Harvard President Lawrence Summers delivered an address at a February 2004 meeting of the American Council on Education in which he described the "manifest inadequacy of higher education's current contribution to equality of opportunity in America" and went on to announce the new Harvard Financial Aid Initiative designed to encourage the enrollment of students from low- and moderate-income families. The announcement that students' families with incomes below $40,000 would no longer make any payments to the cost of attendance was the most visible and transparent change in the Harvard University policies. Others included expanded recruiting, a renewed emphasis on considering family circumstances in the admission process, and new efforts to deepen the pipeline of prospective students considering Harvard University.[11]

Although the Harvard initiative was in some ways the most visible and received a disproportionate amount of press attention, other universities— particularly those in the public sector—had already initiated programs to increase the representation of low-income students. In fact, Princeton was the first university to eliminate loans from the aid packages of low- income students, initially eliminating loans for low-income students in 1998 and then eliminating loans for all aid-eligible students in 2001.

Selective public universities have also launched programs to address the underrepresentation of low-income students in their classes. The Uni- versity of North Carolina introduced the Carolina Covenant program in 2003 and the University of Virginia put forward an aggressive plan known as AccessUVa early in 2004. These initiatives aim to increase pub- lic information, recruiting and need-based financial aid. In the fall of 2004, representatives of the admission office at the University of Virginia engaged in unprecedented efforts to reach low-income students and encourage applications.

Between the fall of 2003 and 2005, at least ten new initiatives aimed at increasing opportunities for low-income students were launched. Tables 6.6 and 6.7 outline the dimension and timing of these initiatives for pri- vate and public universities. Nearly all of the initiatives emphasize trans- parency in the allocation of financial aid. The architects of these programs have been explicit in trying to frame expected college costs in plain lan- guage rather than in the jargon of financial aid administrators with terms like adjusted gross income and expected family contribution. So, Harvard University states its program in terms of covering the entire cost of atten- dance through grants rather than loans for families with incomes less than $40,000, while Princeton guarantees that it will meet 100 percent of need through grants not loans.

Not only do these programs have easily understood financial criteria, but students' eligibility does not depend on merit (conditional on admis- sion). Aside from Ohio State's Land-Grant Opportunity Scholarship, the financial awards are given to any student who is admitted to the univer- sity and meets the financial criteria. This distinguishes these scholarships from older institutional scholarships such as the Longhorn Opportunity Scholarship and the Cal Opportunity Scholarship, for which only the most accomplished disadvantaged students are eligible. It also differentiates

Table 6.6 Programs to Increase Enrollment of Low-Income Students at State Flagship Universities

School	Program Name	Program Description	Date of Announcement	First Class Affected (Date of Entry)	Amount of New Money (Annually) When Fully Implemented
Harvard	None	Harvard covers the entire cost of attendance for students with family incomes below $40,000 through grants and work-study, not loans. In addition, Harvard has greatly reduced the contributions it expects from families with incomes between $40,000 and $60,000.[a]	February 2004	Fall 2004	$2 million
Princeton	None	Princeton meets 100 percent of need for all students through grants and work-study, not loans. Princeton no longer taxes home equity in the financial aid formula and has reduced the rate at which student savings are taxed from 35 to 5 percent, the tax rate on parental savings.	January 2001	Fall 2001[b]	$10.3 million (for one year, in 2003)

Yale	None	Yale covers the entire cost of attendance for students with family incomes below $45,000 through grants and work-study, not loans. In addition, Yale has approximately halved the contributions it expects from families with incomes between $45,000 and $60,000.[c]	March 2005	Fall 2005	$3 million
Brown	Sidney E. Frank Endowed Scholarship Fund	Approximately 128 of Brown's neediest students (typically those with family incomes below $30,000) will have their college costs covered by a combination of expected family contribution, grants, and work-study, not loans. This program is funded by a $100 million gift from alumnus Sidney E. Frank.[d]	September 2004	Fall 2005	$100 million total (not per year)

Source: Authors' compilations based on information available in August 2005.

[a] This is coupled with more active recruitment of low-income students, a summer academy for low-income Boston students to prepare them for college and a consideration of financial difficulty in admissions decisions.

[b] Princeton's initiatives began in 1998 with the elimination of loans for low-income new matriculants.

[c] Yale has also made other recent changes to its financial aid programs including allowing students to take summer school classes on financial aid and paying for a trip for international students to return home each year.

[d] Starting in fall 2002, Brown no longer required freshmen to participate in work-study and starting with the entering class of 2003, Brown's admissions have been need-blind.

Table 6.7   Programs Designed to Increase Enrollment of Low-Income Students at State Flagship Universities

State-School	Program Name	Program Description	Date of Announcement	First Class Affected (Date of Entry)	Amount of New Money (Annually) When Fully Implemented
University of North Carolina	The Carolina Covenant	UNC covers the entire cost of attendance for students with family incomes within 200 percent of the poverty line through grants and work-study, not loans. These students also receive laptops to fulfill UNC's laptop requirement and are offered enrichment opportunities such as faculty mentoring and etiquette dinners.	October 2003	Fall 2004	$13.2 million
University of Virginia	AccessUVa	UVa covers the entire cost of attendance for students with family incomes within 200 percent of the poverty line through grants, not loans or work-study. UVa caps the amount of need-based debt any student is forced to take out at 25 percent of the four-year in-state cost of attendance, providing grants to cover the rest of the student's costs. It also provides financial aid and counseling to admitted students and their families.	February 2004	Fall 2004	Board of Visitors will contribute over $20 million (this number includes some financial aid resources available before program initiation)

University of Maryland	Maryland Pathways	UMd covers the entire cost of attendance for students who have no ability to pay for college as judged by the FASFA (typically those with family incomes below the poverty line) through grants and work-study. UMd caps the amount of need-based debt Maryland resident seniors can accumulate at $15,900 in four years, providing grants to cover the rest of the student's costs. It also provides all students who lose federal Pell aid because they take jobs with grants equal to the Pell Grant they would have received had they not worked.	April 2004	Fall 2004[a] (debt cap implemented in Fall 2005)	$1.6 million[b]
University of Michigan, Ann Arbor	M-Pact	UMich has replaced some loans in the financial aid packages of low and middle-income in-state students with grants. Students who qualify for a full Pell Grant receive $1,500 more in grant assistance in lieu of loans, those who are slightly more affluent receive $1,000 more, and those who barely miss Pell eligibility (typically those with family incomes between $50,000 and $70,000) receive $500 more in grant aid.	February 2005	Fall 2005	$3 million

(Table continues on p. 144)

Table 6.7   Programs Designed to Increase Enrollment of Low-Income Students at State Flagship Universities (*Continued*)

State-School	Program Name	Program Description	Date of Announcement	First Class Affected (Date of Entry)	Amount of New Money (Annually) When Fully Implemented
Ohio State	Land-Grant Opportunity Scholarship	Ohio State covers the entire cost of attendance for one student from each of Ohio's eighty-eight counties through a scholarship and work-study. Within a county, the strongest student whose family income is less than $40,000 a year will be awarded this scholarship. If there are no admitted students from a particular county whose family income is below $40,000, the scholarship will be awarded to a student in another county who qualifies.	January 2005	Fall 2005	$1.5 million
University of Illinois at Urbana-Champaign	Illinois Promise	UIUC covers the entire cost of attendance of in-state students whose family income is at or below the poverty line and whose expected family contribution is zero as determined by the FASFA through grants and work-study.	December 2004	Fall 2005	$280,000 (first year, not including federal and state costs)

Source: Authors' compilations based on information available in fall 2005.
[a] Maryland's online magazine *Outlook Online* says the program's first eligible class entered in Fall 2004 as does *Black Issues in Higher Education*, whereas the financial aid website says the program started in the fall of 2005.
[b] As some of these funds are diverted from other financial aid efforts, this number does not measure the total increase in financial aid funds available.

these programs from statewide financial aid programs such as New York's Higher Education Opportunity Program (1969) and Educational Opportunity Program (1967) and California's Cal Grant (1955) which are also conditioned on ability.[12]

That Harvard, Princeton, Yale, and Brown have adjusted their financial aid packages in similar ways is not a coincidence. Competition pushes these institutions to make very similar offers of financial aid, as they compete for many of the same students. Among these institutions, Yale University is the late entrant to this competition, making its announcement of full grant aid for low-income students in early 2005. Opportunity costs drove the reluctance of Yale to eliminate loans entirely. Speaking on financial aid issues in February 2005, Yale University President Richard Levin notes, "It's a question of how much you can afford to do and what the opportunity cost is of doing it. We have a lot more good ideas around here than we have money." (quoted in Sadeghi 2005)

Beyond changes in financial aid, it is much more difficult to observe how these universities are adjusting recruitment and admissions. Although President Summers was forthright in calling for greater attention to low-income students in the admission process, the characterization of how the disposition of low-income students in the admission process changed must wait for more data. College and university leaders have long promoted the rhetoric of paying special attention to economic circumstances in college admissions, but the data tell a different story.[13] Conditional on measured academic achievement, low-income students are no more likely to be admitted to selective colleges and universities than their high-income peers (Bowen, Kurzweil, and Tobin 2005).

Turning to the initiatives at public universities (table 6.7), one can see a number of parallels with the private programs. Both sets of institutions have aimed to present a clear message with respect to financial aid, but the actual degree of generosity varies by university. Scale, combined with initial endowment, generates a notable difference between the initiatives of public and private universities. The two most generous public university initiatives, the Carolina Covenant and AccessUVa, are similar to the programs at private universities. The Carolina Covenant meets full demonstrated need for students with family incomes within 200 percent of the poverty line, which was $37,700 for a family of four in the 2005–2006 school year, through scholarships, grants, and work study. AccessUVa meets these students' financial needs through grants and scholarships alone.[14] Yet many of the state programs are far less generous. The University of Illinois's Illinois Promise, for example, only eliminates loans for students with family incomes under the poverty line. Public university initiatives show more variation, with programs like M-Pact at Michigan focusing more on increasing the generosity of aid to a range of low-income students rather than eliminating loan burdens entirely.[15]

The total cost of an incremental change in financial aid will inherently have a much larger budgetary impact at institutions like Ohio State or the University of Michigan that have many students and relatively small endowments than at schools with fewer students and larger endowments like Harvard and Princeton. What is more, the number of inframarginal students—those who would choose to attend the university without additional aid—is likely greater at public universities. To illustrate this point, the first-year class at the University of Michigan enrolled 5,961 students in the fall of 2004 and at Harvard enrolled 1,646. Suppose that both institutions plan to use an increase in grant aid of $3,000 per low-income student to increase the enrollment rate of low-income students. The program will be much more expensive at the University of Michigan for several reasons:

- With the same share of low-income students matriculating at Michigan and Harvard, the increase in the aid bill for current students will be more than 3.6 times larger at Michigan than at Harvard. (That is, 7 percent of students aid-eligible at both institutions would imply additional aid commitments of $1,251,810 at Michigan and $345,660 at Harvard.)

- The actual share of aid-eligible students is already higher at Michigan than at Harvard. For example, 7 percent of Harvard undergraduates receive Pell Grants versus 13 percent at Michigan. This would push the increment in the financial aid bills associated with a $3,000 increase in grant aid at Michigan to $2,324,790.

A particularly important point is that spending on inframarginal students—those expected to attend without additional aid—will be higher at the institution with relatively high pre-program enrollment of low-income students. Scale, combined with the status quo representation of low-income students, will have a large effect on the cost of the new initiatives that target the aid margin. Public universities are in general much larger in scale at the undergraduate level than their private counterparts, which increases the cost of any innovation in financial aid. Even among the public universities the disparity in the size of investments is wide, with the University of North Carolina spending over eight times as much as the University of Maryland and Ohio State. The University of Virginia spends even more than the University of North Carolina–Chapel Hill (see table 6.7).

With the exception of the University of Virginia, the public university initiatives are distinguished by a focus on increasing opportunities for in-state low-income students. (Approximately 30 percent of students admitted to the University of Virginia under the AccessUVa banner are from out of state, which is roughly consistent with the overall undergraduate representation of out-of-state students.) The Land Grant Opportunity Scholarship program at Ohio State University takes this further, providing one grant to a resident of each of Ohio's eighty-eight counties based on need and academic achievement.

One potential virtue of the emergence of somewhat different initiatives is that variation in policies and outreach may help sharpen public understanding of how to reduce barriers to collegiate attainment for low-income students.

Assessing the New Access Initiatives

One of the most striking features of the aggressive efforts to increase the representation of low-income students is the extent to which the programs are propelled by strong beliefs about needed change and considerable determination. Several colleges and universities have been aggressive in proclaiming the initial success of their access initiatives in the press, but few have developed long-run strategies for evaluation. Two exceptions appear to be Harvard and Princeton, where independent research teams have requested data and are evaluating the effects of policy changes.[16]

Evidence in the Press

University press offices tend to be unequivocal in their convictions about the success of the new initiatives to increase access. Both Harvard University and the University of Virginia have been aggressive in proclaiming the gains brought about by the new access initiatives, even before the students recruited under these programs started classes.

A July 16, 2005, article in the *Boston Globe* announced that the access initiative introduced by Harvard University had led to an increase of 21 percent in the expected representation of students with incomes less than $60,000 (Marcella Bombardieri, "Elite Colleges Go After Low-Income Recruits," p. A1). New and aggressive recruiting efforts were credited for the change at Harvard, including contacting about 12,000 students identified as potential low-income recruits and expanded outreach by admissions staff.[17]

At the University of Virginia, the lead article in the June 17 internal faculty staff publication *Inside UVA* trumpeted the increase in the expected matriculation of students with family incomes below 200 percent of the poverty line (Dan Heuchert, "The Plan's Working," 2005). There is no question that the basic result holds. The number of students from low-income families accepting offers to matriculate at the University of Virginia increased significantly—by more than 50 percent. Focusing on students from families with incomes less than 200 percent of the poverty line, the change is dramatic. Although only 133 students, a mere 4.3 percent of the first-year class, were in this income range in 2004, 200 first-year students from families with incomes less than 200 percent of the poverty line matriculated in the fall of 2005.[18]

Table 6.8   Changes in Admissions Patterns at the University of Virginia from 2004 to 2005

	Applications	Admit Rate	Matriculation Rate
<200 percent poverty	11%	6%	28%
All other	6%	−3%	2%
Difference in change	5%	9%	26%

Source: Authors' compilations.

What is less clear from the evidence is the mechanism generating this change. Without diminishing the accomplishment of substantial changes in expected matriculation in the first year of these initiatives, evaluation of components of the program is critical to assess the return on marginal dollars. Press accounts and materials describing the program emphasize the role of outreach and increasing the number of applications from low-income students in generating this change at the University of Virginia. Comparing applications and admissions by family income for the fall of 2004 and of 2005 shows that it is at the margin of applications where changes were the smallest relative to admission rates and matriculation conditional on admission.[19] Table 6.8 presents September 2005 data from the University of Virginia Office of Institutional Assessment and the relative changes from the fall of 2004 to the fall of 2005.

At the University of Virginia as well as at the University of North Carolina, the changes in the socioeconomic composition of the recent entering classes following from the AccessUVa and Carolina Covenant initiatives have been impressive. Although such changes are a noteworthy first step, the real effects of selective university admission will only be realized through course completion and graduation, which is too early to assess.

The promotion of personal stories combined with evidence of changes in the admissions profile may serve to encourage low-income potential students in future cohorts to apply to the University of Virginia. Press coverage celebrating the initial accomplishments under AccessUVa can be a powerful agent in spreading the word about the availability of opportunities for low-income students at the University of Virginia. Such coverage may be a very efficient mechanism to diminish informational barriers that inhibit low-income students from applying to and enrolling at the University of Virginia.

Still, measures of initial enrollment available at the early stages of AccessUVa or the Harvard Financial Aid Initiative are incomplete indicators of the extent to which these initiatives will change the longer-term underrepresentation of low-income students among graduates of selective colleges and universities. To evaluate fully the impact of these programs, universities will need to monitor persistence, academic performance, and graduation.[20]

Universities mounting ambitious access programs must separate the objectives of promotion and evaluation. For private and public universities alike, increasing the visibility of aid and outreach programs is one of the objectives. Providing information that the door to selective higher education is open to low-income students is, in fact, an important component of the treatment aspect of these new initiatives. Whether most universities will go beyond "the message" to evaluate these initiatives is an open question. The case for evaluation is compelling because so little is known about how the policies on the table affect outcomes at selective universities. In an environment of scarce resources, universities need to weigh alternatives.

Challenges in Evaluation

Any critique of the absence of comprehensive strategies for the evaluation of the newly initiated college access programs must also acknowledge the magnitude of the challenge. Evaluating these initiatives is inherently difficult because of the complexity of the reform process in many cases. A number of colleges and universities are not simply adjusting one piece of the process but rather simultaneously changing multiple levers affecting collegiate participation, including both recruitment efforts and financial aid policies.[21] Yet the evaluation of these efforts is certainly not impossible and there would seem to be a range of experimental and nonexperimental strategies that colleges and universities could use to gain a clear understanding of which pieces of the initiatives have the highest returns.

A second difficulty is that what economists call partial equilibrium results may differ appreciably from general equilibrium results. The effects of changes in policies at one university—holding policies at other universities essentially constant—are likely to be very different than the results we will observe if all universities change policies. When one college increases the generosity of its aid or makes efforts to increase its reach in underserved areas, its numbers of high achieving low-income students will likely rise appreciably. Yet this is rarely the end of the story—increases in aid by Princeton are likely to be followed by increases in aid from Harvard and Yale, just as those at the University of Virginia induce increases at other selective colleges in Virginia.[22]

That colleges and universities are increasing the level of competition in enrolling high achieving, low-income students certainly benefits this group of students in the short run. An important policy question is whether the overall effects of these initiatives when put in place by a number of colleges and universities will be to reshuffle a fixed pool of students among relatively selective institutions or, instead, will increase the overall representation of low-income students at the nation's most selective colleges and universities. This question cannot be answered empirically yet, but the likely change in the distribution of students among collegiate institutions in response to increases in need-based financial aid at a number of colleges and universities has been explored (Pallais and Turner 2006).

Differences in Outcomes: The Challenge for Public Universities

Selective public universities face some of the toughest challenges in improving outcomes for low-income students. The sources of this challenge are multifold. First, public universities have an obligation to serve their within-state constituency and face considerable pressure from state legislators to recruit a substantial share of students from in state. Second, it is state colleges and universities that may face the greatest competition from selective private institutions as the latter seek to increase opportunities on their own campuses for low-income students. Finally, relative to selective private universities, the challenges faced by state flagship universities are exacerbated by more limited financial aid resources and larger initial cohorts.

Moreover, it is the students now attending state flagship universities who are most likely to be lured to the elite private institutions with more generous aid offers. In discussing the access initiative at Harvard University, Caroline Hoxby notes that "in the short term, we have to face the fact that these kids who get into Harvard would not otherwise be going to a community college, they may be going to the University of Michigan's honors program."[23] Hoxby goes on to suggest the possibility of substantial long-term benefits if the reach of these programs is strong enough to convey the message that "as long as you do well you can go to any school you like" (Marcella Bombardieri, "Elite Colleges Go After Low-Income Recruits," *The Boston Globe*, July 16, 2005, p. A1).

We also need to recognize that public universities are unique in their commitment to serve relatively confined geographic areas. Both benefits and hardships are associated with efforts to increase enrollment and completion of well-qualified low-income students. The benefits are tied to the observation that the returns to outreach and campus contact are likely to be much greater in a confined local area. It is simply much easier for the University of Michigan or the University of Virginia to make direct appeals to students within the state using media and direct outreach than it is for a private university to target a national audience.

Yet, though national scale may be a disadvantage in outreach, it is also an advantage when universities use the margin of admissions decisions to increase advantages for low-income students. Searching within a state, the pool of low-income students across all potential measures of pre-collegiate achievement is smaller than it is in aggregate. Thus, if a national university and a state university, with an expectation of admitting a disproportionate number of in-state students, starting from similar admissions standards, both seek to increase the number of low-income students admitted by the same number, the state university will be required to make much larger changes in admissions criteria than the national university. The intuition follows from the observation that the number of students at any test score in the national distribution is greater than the number of students in the state distributions (for a more detailed example and discussion of this point, see Pallais and Turner 2006). It follows that, to achieve the same increase in the representation of low-income students, the state university will be required to admit students at greater risk of struggling academically.

Conclusion

The tools of program evaluation that economists (and other social scientists) have developed over the last quarter century should be more aggressively employed as selective colleges and universities tackle the vexing challenge of increasing the enrollment and attainment of young people from economically disadvantaged backgrounds. Outreach programs and financial aid initiatives are simply too expensive in both direct costs and the alternative uses of university resources to rely on testimonials and committed beliefs in forming and implementing policies.

For researchers and policy makers, an important objective is to identify programs and strategies that work and hold the potential for replication across institutions. Colleges and universities have the opportunity to increase long-term opportunities for low-income students through multiple channels—recruitment, admission, and financial aid, in addition to strategies promoting persistence within the college years. Universities differ in circumstances, strengths, and weaknesses. Where some private universities lag in the enrollment of low-income students other (often public) universities find challenges at the margin of college completion. There are many opportunities for universities to learn from the successes and setbacks of their peers in improving opportunities for low-income students. At the same time, there should be no one-size-fits-all policy—universities differ in both circumstances and objectives.

Competition among colleges and universities is a powerful force and is surely at work in prompting institutions to devote increased financial aid to low-income students. What merits a watchful eye at this juncture is whether this competition among institutions to increase opportunities for low-income students expands the total range of opportunities. The risk is that institutions will devote more effort to recruiting among the existing pool—essentially a zero sum game among institutions competing for a group of high-achieving students already likely to attend selective schools.[24] Because the returns to many outreach programs and efforts to improve the preparation of high school students are not limited to specific institutions, the social returns to strategies that encourage collective action among universities are likely to be high.

A nagging question in the consideration of the underrepresentation of low-income students at selective colleges and universities concerns how much change can be brought about by college and university policies. There is no doubt that, at current levels of low-income participation, there is room for substantial improvement. Yet the largest challenges persist at the level of preparation, where gaps between low-income students and their more affluent peers in college preparation, as measured by standardized test scores, are both sizable and persistent. University efforts will not close these gaps in the short run; a question for the future is whether the promise of opportunities afforded by current university initiatives will prove powerful enough to contribute to narrowing the achievement gaps between low- and high-income students at the high school level.

Endnotes

1. Note that beyond the equity arguments for increasing the representation of low-income students there are significant efficiency arguments. Universities have a vested interest in promoting the development of extraordinary talent— those potentially capable of breakthroughs and innovations in the sciences or the arts. To the extent that low-income students with high capacity are underrepresented in the traditional application pool, it is in the best interest of colleges and universities to develop alternative strategies to identify and enroll students with substantial expected benefits from college who are from socio-economically disadvantaged circumstances (see Bowen, Kurzweil, and Tobin 2005, 161–62).

2. These are by no means the only policies that help low-income students beyond traditional need-based aid. Several programs giving additional financial aid to disadvantaged students, such as the Longhorn Opportunity Scholarship program at the University of Texas at Austin (1999) and the Cal Grant program in California have been in place for several years. Yet the new programs highlighted in this chapter are a distinct breed. Unlike previous initiatives, they were implemented with the explicit goal of increasing the attendance of low-income students, have eligibility requirements phrased in terms of dollars of family income instead of complex financial aid formulas, and are awarded to all low-income students at the university, not just those judged to be particularly meritorious.

3. Data are assembled by The Institute for College Access and Success (see http://www.economicdiversity.org).

4. Of the 126 districts with more than fifty high school seniors, sixteen had no students represented in the class entering the University of Virginia in the fall of 2004. The ninetieth percentile district sent three times as many students (per 100) as the median school district. An extraordinary outlier is the Thomas Jefferson High School for Science and Technology (TJHSST), a highly selective magnet program located in Northern Virginia. Of the 412 students in the 2005 senior class, 263 (64 percent) applied to the University of Virginia and 226 were admitted. Less than 1 percent of students at this high school are eligible for free and reduced price lunch (Tebbs and Turner 2005b).

5. Moreover, the majority of potential college students are at neither of these extremes. Rather, students in the middle are deliberating between community college enrollment and attendance at modestly selective four-year institutions. The constraints faced by these students may differ appreciably from those faced by students deciding whether to enroll in college at all, and those deciding between a state flagship and an Ivy League university.

6. One survey reported that only about 100 of nearly 1,500 colleges surveyed were able to meet 100 percent of their students' need through the combination of grants, scholarships, loans and work-study awards (Wong 2005). Since many of those institutions able to meet full need are likely to be relatively small private colleges and universities, the proportion of all college students attending institutions where full need is met is likely to be yet smaller.

7. We would expect individual enrollment response to be much greater at the margin of credit constraints (when students are unable to borrow to finance college) than at the margin where the composition of the aid package is shifted from grants to loans. Moreover, we would expect the institution-specific change in enrollment to be much more sensitive than the change measured over a set of institutions with similar, competitive aid policies.

8. Data from the National Educational Longitudinal Study representing eighth graders in 1988 show that 34.2 percent of high school graduates from the bottom quartile of the family income distribution took the SAT relative to about 70.1 percent from the top quartile.

9. Two margins matter in determining the pool of relatively high-achieving low-income students within states. The first measure is the extent to which there are differences in expectations about test scores given economic circumstances (such as the Virginia-California comparison discussed in the text). Concentrations of poverty also differ across states, which may lead to a relatively higher fraction of low-income students. In the comparison of California to Virginia, one difference between the states is that the fraction of people living below the poverty line is higher in California (with an overall poverty rate of 12.9 percent) than it is in Virginia (9.3 percent), with this difference even larger among the college-age population.

10. Writing in the *Chronicle of Higher Education,* Edward Ayers and Nichole Hurd (2005) note: "In many states, however, students and their parents believe that their flagship university is beyond their financial and academic reach. The rhetoric about 'excellence' and 'selectivity' is understood to mean 'exclusivity.' And there is truth to that suspicion. The drive to excellence may be preventing some of our best public institutions from fulfilling their public role" (B12).

11. Christopher Avery and his colleagues (2004) outline Harvard's efforts to increase applications from students from low to moderate income families. Among the tools expanded and added were increased school visits, letters from the admissions office, and outreach from current and former students. In March of 2006 the program was adjusted such that families with incomes between $40,000 and $60,000 would also not be required to contribute to the cost of Harvard attendance beginning the following fall.

12. The Longhorn Opportunity Scholarship and Cal Opportunity Scholarship base eligibility on attendance at high schools classified as disadvantaged, with the California program also requiring individual financial need for eligibility.

13. Quoted in an article in *The Chronicle of Higher Education,* William Bowen notes "College presidents say, 'Yes, we want to give a special boost to the miner's daughter.' I'm sure they believe in good faith that they are giving a boost to the miner's daughter. But, in fact, when you look at the data, as we have, it is simply not true" (Gose 2005, B5)

14. When the Carolina Covenant and AccessUVa were announced, only students within 150 percent of the poverty line were eligible. They both increased their generosity starting with the cohort entering college in 2005.

15. The M-Pact program was shaped by a working group established by the provost to examine the most efficient use of additional financial aid dollars. The group concluded that reducing loan burdens (and net price) was important for low-income students, but that there was little evidence to support a proposition that reducing loan burdens to zero for a small number of students would be a better policy than increased grants for a broader set of low-income students. It should also be noted that at the University of Michigan, administrators are concerned with addressing the somewhat higher attrition rates of low-income students in addition to expanding enrollment opportunities.

16. Administrators at the University of Illinois (Illinois Promise) and the University of Michigan (M-PACT) acknowledge that there is no plan or research design as yet in place to evaluate these programs. Still, there are several researcher-initiated efforts. Chris Avery and Caroline Hoxby are working with data from the admissions, financial aid, and matriculation files at Harvard University. Cecilia Rouse and Jesse Rothstein are pursuing related questions with data from Princeton University.

17. In addition, campus visits for low-income students (approximately 230) were paid for by Harvard and the application fee was waived for more than 2,300 students.

18. However, the number of low-income transfer students matriculating actually decreased somewhat from seventy-nine to sixty-five, out of a total transfer pool of 535 students.

19. One point to note is that these data differ substantially from those based on early (May) tabulations and discussed in Jeffrey Tebbs and Sarah Turner (2005b) with the number of (expected) low-income matriculating students increasing from 172 to 200. Nearly all of the "gain" over the summer occurred on the matriculation margin (the transition from admission offer to enrollment). The numbers presented include out-of-state students as well as in-state students, whereas the analysis in Tebbs and Turner (2005b) focused on in-state prospective students. Among the low-income students enrolling in the fall of 2005, slightly more than 30 percent are from out of state, which is nearly identical to the out-of-state share among students in other income ranges. It is likely that the relative change in low-income students from out of state at the University of Virginia exceeded the change for in-state students in part because the decline in net price with the AccessUVa program would have been the largest for this group.

20. In addition to reducing the net cost of college for low-income students, the Carolina Covenant provides continuing academic and social support for Covenant Scholars while enrolled to help them succeed at UNC and graduate. The program matches students with volunteer faculty mentors and hosts events to help the scholars adjust more comfortably to campus.

21. The University of Michigan appears to be an exception, as the primary parameter changed is the generosity of financial aid. Because the changes in generosity are largely formulaic, several clear tests of the effects of aid on enrollment and persistence present themselves.

22. Most notably, the College of William and Mary in Virginia introduced Gateway William and Mary in August of 2005. As the first major policy initiative of new president Gene Nichol, the program promises a debt free undergraduate education for students from families with incomes less than $40,000. See: www.wm.edu/gateway/. The next month, Virginia Polytechnic Institute unveiled Funds for the Future, its initiative to reduce unmet need for low-income students and protect them against tuition increases (See www.finaid.vt.edu/types_of_aid/grants/FFTF.php).

23. In particular, Catherine Hill and Gordon Winston (2005) find that, conditional on SAT and ACT scores, low-income students are less likely than their higher-income peers to attend selective private universities. If this is because they are more likely to attend elite public institutions, then increases in financial aid at private colleges could potentially induce large substitution effects. Amanda Pallais and Sarah Turner (2006) discuss how much of the initial effect of the programs of private universities can be attributed to these substitution effects.

24. Low-income students are made unambiguously better off by the expansion of financial aid; less certain is whether increasing financial aid increases the total number of low-income students enrolling at selective institutions and improves their completion outcomes.

References

Avery, Christopher, Caroline Hoxby, Clement Jackson, Kaitlin Burek, Glenn Poppe, and Mrindula Raman. 2004. "Cost Should Be No Barrier: An Evaluation of the First Year of Harvard's 2004 Financial Aid Initiative." *NBER* Working Paper 12029. Cambridge, Mass.: National Bureau of Economic Research.

Avery, Christopher, and Thomas J. Kane. 2004. "Student Perceptions of College Opportunities: The Boston COACH Program," in Caroline Hoxby, ed., *College Choices: The Economics of Where to Go, When to Go, and How To Pay for It.* Chicago: University of Chicago Press.

Ayers, Edward A., and Nichole F. Hurd. 2005. "Flagship Universities Must Pursue Excellence and Access." *Chronicle of Higher Education* 51(33, April 22): B12.

Bowen, W. G., Martin Kurzweil, and Eugene Tobin. 2005. *Equity and Excellence in American Higher Education.* Charlottesville: University of Virginia Press.

Card, David, and Alan B. Krueger. 2004. *Would the Elimination of Affirmative Action Affect Highly Qualified Minority Applicants? Evidence from California and Texas.* NBER Working Paper 10366. Cambridge, Mass.: National Bureau of Economic Research.

Courant, Paul N., Michael McPherson, and Alexandra Resch. 2006. "The Public Role in Higher Education." *National Tax Journal.* LIX(2): 291–318.

Dynarski, Susan M., and Judith Scott-Clayton. 2006. "The Cost of Complexity in Federal Student Aid: Lessons from Optimal Tax Theory and Behavioral Economics." *National Tax Journal* LIX(2): 319–56.

Ehrenberg, Ronald G. 2005. "Reducing Inequality in Higher Education: Where Do We Go From Here?" Paper prepared for the Conference on Economic Inequality and Higher Education: Access Persistence and Success. Syracuse University, N.Y. (September 23–24, 2005).

Ellwood, David T., and Thomas J. Kane. 2000. "Who Is Getting a College Education: Family Background and the Growing Gaps in Enrollment." In *Securing the Future,* edited by Sheldon Danziger and Jane Waldfogel. New York: Russell Sage Foundation.

Fischer, Karin. 2006. "Elite Colleges Lag in Serving the Needy." *The Chronicle of Higher Education* 52(36): A1. http://chronicle.com/weekly/v52/i36/36a00101.htm.

Gose, Ben. 2005. "The Chorus Grows Louder for Class-Based Affirmative Action." *The Chronicle of Higher Education* 51(25)(February 25): B5–6.

Hill, Catherine, and Gordon Winston. 2005. *Access to the Most Selective Private Colleges by High Ability, Low-Income Students: Are They Out There.* Discussion Paper 69. Williamstown, Mass.: Williams Project on the Economics of Higher Education.

Hill, Catherine, Gordon Winston, and Stephanie Boyd. 2005. "Affordability: Family Incomes and Net Prices at Highly Selective Private Colleges and Universities." *Journal of Human Resources* 40(4): 769–90.

Myers, David, Robert Olsen, Neil Seftor, Julie Young and Christina Tuttle. 2004. *The Impacts of Regular Upward Bound: Results from the Third Follow-Up Data Collection.* Report 8464-400. Washington, D.C.: Mathematica Policy Research. Available at http://www.ed.gov/rschstat/eval/highered/upward/upward-3rd-report.doc.

Pallais, A., and S. Turner. 2006. "Opportunities for Low-Income Students at Top Colleges and Universities: Policy Initiatives and the Distribution of Students." *National Tax Journal.* LIX(2): 357–88.

Sadeghi, Y. 2005. "Levin States Plan to Alter Financial Aid." *Yale Daily News* (February 23).

State Council on Higher Education in Virginia. 2005. 2005–2006 Tuition and Fees at Virginia's State-Supported Colleges and Universities. Richmond, Va. Available at: http://www.schev.edu/Reportstats/2005-06Tuition&FeesReport.pdf?from.

Summers, Lawrence. 2004. "Higher Education and the American Dream." Speech delivered at the 86th Annual Meeting, American Council on Education. Miami, Fl. (February 29, 2004).

Tebbs, Jeffrey, and Sarah Turner. 2005a. "College Education for Low-income Students: A Caution on the Use of Data on Pell Grant Recipients." *Change* 37(4): 34–43.

———. 2005b. "The Challenge of Improving the Representation of Low-Income Students at Flagship Universities: AccessUVa and the University of Virginia." Paper presented at the Opening Opportunity or Preserving Privilege: The Ambiguous Potential of Higher Education conference. Oak Brook, Ill. (June 2005).

Turner, Sarah E. 2006. "Welcoming Needy Students to the Campus." Letter to the editor. *The Chronicle of Higher Education.* 52(41)(June 16): A47.

U.S. Census Bureau. 2000. *Current Population Survey.* Washington: U.S. Census Bureau. http://www.census.gov/population/www/socdem/school/cps2003.html.

———. 2003. *Current Population Survey.* Washington: U.S. Census Bureau. http://www.census.gov/population/www/socdem/school/cps2003.html.

Wong, Grace. 2005. "How Generous is Your School? Some Schools Show Their Students the Money—and Not Just in Loans and Work-Study." *CNNMoney.com,* June 10, 2005.

Chapter 7

Costs and Implications

AMY ELLEN SCHWARTZ

EW ISSUES ignite the discussion of higher education in America today more consistently and explosively than the escalating cost of attending college. Parents and students, educators, policy makers, and politicians spanning a wide political and socioeconomic spectrum worry about rising tuition. Articles in the popular press regularly decry increasingly outrageous "sticker prices" in higher education fueled by estimates from the consumer price index (CPI) suggesting price increases that outpace overall inflation. Unfortunately, this information about the cost of college is, at best, misleading, in that it overstates significantly the cost that many students will face as they prepare to enroll in college. Most obviously, it ignores financial aid and scholarships, which, for many students, significantly offset tuition and fees. Perhaps equally important, however, the focus is all too often on four-year colleges and the cost of full-time attendance. As an example, a recent article—"Top Ten Priciest Schools . . . and the Cheapest"—included a table showing the listed tuitions for full-time attendance at a set of four-year colleges, beginning with Sarah Lawrence College at over $32,000 and ending with the University of Nevada–Reno at nearly $2,700.[1] Information on the cost of two-year colleges (or community colleges) and of part-time attendance, both of which are particularly important to low-income students, is less widely heralded and less accessible.[2]

It may then, perhaps, not be surprising that students and parents overestimate the cost of attending college (see American Council on Education 1998; Kane 2002). For example, Thomas Kane (2002) reported that Boston-area high school students estimated even the sticker price of Bunker Hill Community College, a local school, to be more than $6,000, substantially more than the true sticker price of $3,140. Even more disturbing, the survey indicates that students from disadvantaged backgrounds have even faultier information about the price of college than their suburban counterparts. Thus, to the extent that good decision making requires an accurate weighing of costs and benefits, it is quite likely that students—and particularly low-income students—are not able to make optimal decisions regarding such things as curriculum, work effort, and persistence in high school and in college. Of course, public officials and policy makers also need high quality and accurate information on the cost of college to make good decisions.

This chapter presents and analyzes trends in the consumer price of both two-year and four-year colleges, distinguishing, where possible, between private and public institutions. The focus is thus on the price paid to attend college, not on the cost of producing and providing higher education services. Understanding and measuring the cost is complicated, however, by the complex nature of the modern college, with its multiple outputs, varied objectives, and diverse financing.

To begin, estimating the price of college requires adjustments for financial aid and scholarships, which is made more difficult by the complex array of programs and eligibility rules. Estimates must be adjusted to account for tax credits, increasingly important with the spread of programs such as the HOPE and Lifetime Learning credits (see Dynarski 2004; Long 2004b).

Further, adjustments must be made to account for the differences in the college "product" necessitated by the heterogeneity in the college market. Whereas some schools are residential, emphasizing campus life and full-time study, others have no dormitories and emphasize no-frills study that can be pursued part-time. Some offer study in a wide range of areas and degrees, others offer only a specialized set of degree programs and study areas. There is a wide range in the size of schools, the splendor of the campuses, the selectivity of admissions, the generosity of the course offerings, the excellence of the faculty, and so on. Furthermore, these characteristics of institutions change over time. It is, then, not surprising that there is also a wide variation in tuition, explained, in part, by differences in the characteristics of colleges (for more on the relationship between prices and the characteristics of colleges, see Schwartz and Scafidi 2004).

Finally, it is important to note the difference between the out-of-pocket costs of college—that is, the price that a student pays for his or her education and attendant activities—and the full economic cost of attending college, which includes the opportunity cost to the student and any disutility of attendance. Opportunity costs are, on the whole, far larger and more important to many students than out-of-pocket costs, particularly for low-income students for whom scholarships and financial aid are significant.[3]

Some Economics of the College Market

Before turning to the evidence on prices, we should note the scope and diversity of postsecondary institutions in the United States. In 2001, for example, the Digest of Education Statistics reported nearly 4,074 degree-granting institutions and nearly 16 million enrolled students (U.S. Department of Education 2003, table 217).[4] Of these, 260 granted doctoral degrees, 637 degrees through the master's level, 636 only bachelor's degrees, and 771 degrees primarily in single fields of study such as medicine, business, fine arts, theology, and engineering.[5] The largest group—1,770—offer only the associate of arts degree (that is, two-year colleges). Schools vary widely in size, some (474) serving fewer than 200 students and a handful (43) enrolling more than 30,000. Public institutions are disproportionately large. Although more than half (2,386) are private, roughly three-quarters of those enrolled attended public institutions. Perhaps most interesting, however, is the importance of the public two-year colleges, which enrolled roughly 95 percent of all of the two-year college students (more than 6 million). As discussed in greater depth in chapter 5, the importance of two-year colleges is both substantial and increasing.

Beyond the degrees offered and public versus private control, colleges of course also differ widely in other characteristics. Postsecondary institutions are, in many ways, best viewed as multiproduct firms, producing a range of goods beyond the education that is their hallmark (Schwartz and Scafidi 2001; see also McPherson, Schapiro, and Winston 1993; Clotfelter 1999;Winston 1999; Kane and Rouse 1999).[6] They provide food services, accommodations, and amusements; minor league professional athletics (that is, amateur spectator sports where the athletes are compensated with scholarships); investment management (that is, management of their endowment and other financial resources); and an array of pecuniary and nonpecuniary benefits that accrue to others. In some instances, for example, colleges are seen as a tool for local economic development, yielding benefits quite separate from the benefits accruing to the students, or even the benefits the students themselves subsequently offer the community as graduates (see Verry and Davies 1976).

Clearly, some of those products are more important to some colleges, and some college students, than others. Research, for example, though clearly integral to the mission of research universities, is typically less of a priority for two-year colleges. Similarly, dormitories and campus life are critical for residential colleges—some of which even require dorm residence for some period—but less relevant for the large group of schools educating commuter students. The characteristics of the student body are clearly important and both prospective students and college administrators pay a great deal of attention to the composition and character of the student body.[7] In addition to the specific characteristics that students pay for, it is a widely held view (by college admissions officers, among others) that students pay for the school "reputation" or "brand." Interestingly, though the consensus that brand matters for four-year colleges is strong, among two-year colleges, brand may be relatively unimportant and convenience and proximity more important (see, for example, Kane and Rouse 1999).[8]

Not all of the services provided are paid for by students, nor are all those offered necessarily provided to them. What, then, do students pay for and what do they get? For our purposes, college students purchase educational services with their tuition dollars, and, when attending residential colleges and living on campus, to pay room and board charges as well. Additionally, evidence that student decisions about college are influenced by tuition and aid is ample (see Schwartz and Scafidi 2004; Turner 2004; Manski and Wise 1983; Kane 1999). Other things equal, students are less likely to attend college, choose a particular college, and stay in college if the price is higher. Further, the cost of room and board matters, though the evidence on this is somewhat thinner. Interestingly, there is surprisingly little research examining the way in which perceived costs shape decisions and, particularly, the difference in responses to perceived rather than actual prices. As noted earlier, the evidence is mounting that the quality of cost information is particularly poor among low-income families without college backgrounds and that this translates into less college-going among their children. To take one example, David Post (1990) finds that children of Spanish speakers had the highest and most unrealistic estimates of college tuition and that college plans were sensitive to cost estimates.

Of course, colleges derive only part of their revenues from tuition. Much of the financing comes from private donors (including the income from endowments from past donors) and government sources—including both federal and state governments. Understanding the pricing behavior of colleges and universities is complicated by the competing objectives and needs of the different constituents. Of particular concern, however, is the possibility that increases in government financial aid—through tax credits, grants, or scholarships—will be captured by colleges in rising tuition. The so-called Bennett hypothesis (after Former Secretary of Education William Bennett) argued that "increases in financial aid in recent years have enabled colleges and universities blithely to raise their tuitions" ("Our Greedy Colleges," *New York Times*, February 18, 1987, p. A31). Michael McPherson and Morton Schapiro (1993), on the other hand, argued that tuition prices might fall as a result of increased federal financial aid to students. Colleges competing with one another for low-income, high achieving students might find that higher sticker prices, ceteris paribus, make them less able to attract these students. Or, to the extent that increases in government aid draw more low-income students to campus, other forms of aid may increase to address the greater needs of these students. Finally, even if sticker prices do rise, the rise may be offset by increases in college quality, depending on the uses to which the colleges put the additional resources. Rises even in net prices may be consistent with constant or even falling quality adjusted prices.[9]

Two recent studies have attempted to provide some empirical evidence on the relationship between financial aid and sticker prices by examining the impact on tuition of Georgia's 1993 merit-based HOPE scholarship program. The results are somewhat contradictory. Bridget Long (2004a) finds evidence that sticker prices rose in response to HOPE, yet Benjamin Scafidi and his colleagues (2001) find little evidence for significant "capture" of the scholarship in higher prices. In this chapter, we examine price trends, taking the levels of aid and tuition as given, ignoring any behavioral relationships between these.

The Sticker Price of College and Room and Board

The consumer price index for college tuition and fees tracks the sticker prices of four-year colleges (tuition and fees) with no adjustment for scholarships given or other discounts or of changes in quality.[10] That said, it carefully tracks a consistent "basket" of colleges, facilitating comparability over time and with overall prices. As shown in table 7.1, rises in the consumer price index for college tuition and fees have consistently outpaced rises in the overall price level. Between 1999 and 2004, prices rose overall by about 13 percent and the CPI-college tuition and fees more than 38 percent. Further, the rise was not the result of a singular event—a price shock in one year amid years of moderate growth. Instead, costs rose faster than inflation every year (as it had in previous periods) and the divergence seems to be speeding up.

Although CPI estimates do not distinguish between different types of institutions, information on tuition and fees is available from the College Board's *Trends in College Pricing, 2004*, which is based on data from their Annual Survey of Colleges. The survey asks "institutions to provide tuition and fee data based on charges to first-year full-time students based on a nine-month academic year of thirty semester hours or forty-five quarter hours" (22). As shown in table 7.2, these statistics reveal considerable differences in tuition inflation between public and private institutions and between two-year and four-year institutions. The left columns show the current dollar figures for tuition and fees for private four-year institutions, public four-year institutions, and public two-year institutions. Both levels and percentage changes are shown, as is, in column 5, the ratio of tuition in four-year public institutions to four-year private institutions. Column 8 shows the ratio of tuition in public two-year institutions to four-year institutions. The pattern is clear. Again, the price of college tuition and fees rose for all types of institutions (columns 1, 3, and 6) and rose faster than inflation (columns 10, 12, and 14).

Prices are rising faster in public institutions than private and, within the public sector, faster at the four-year institutions. To be specific, in the

Table 7.1   Consumer Price Indices

	CPI[1]	CPI[1]
	All Items (Percent Increases)	College Tuition and Fees (Percent Increases)
1999	166.6	318.7
2000	172.2 (3.4%)	331.9 (4.1%)
2001	177.1 (2.8%)	348.8 (5.1%)
2002	179.9 (1.6%)	372.6 (6.8%)
2003	184.0 (2.3%)	403.9 (8.4%)
2004	188.9 (2.7%)	442.1 (9.5%)

[1] Consumer Price Index for all urban consumers: U.S. city annual average (1982–84=100)
Sources: Author's compilations; U.S. Bureau of Labor Statistics (2001, 2002, 2003, 2004, 2005).
Source: http://www.bls.gov/cpi/cpid01av.pdf, http://www.bls.gov/cpi/cpid02av.pdf, http://www.bls.gov/cpi/cpid03av.pdf, http://www.bls.gov/cpi/cpid04av.pdf, http://www.bls.gov/cpi/cpid0506.pdf

1980–1981 school year, two-year public colleges cost about half as much (49 percent) as four-year schools and tuition at public four-year institutions was about a quarter (22 percent) that at private institutions. These relative prices were the same five years later, in the 1985–1986 school year, and somewhat lower in 1990, but began shifting in the 1990s. By academic year 2004–2005, two-year college costs were 40 percent of public four-year colleges, and public colleges about 26 percent of private colleges. Adjusting for inflation, as in the right hand columns, shows a similar pattern.[11] Thus, not only is tuition becoming more expensive overall, but the relative price of institutions that serve the middle and lower income groups—public institutions—is also becoming relatively more expensive than that of private colleges.

Table 7.3 presents the full cost of attendance, which adds room and board charges to tuition and fees for four-year institutions. Costs for two-year colleges, which are significantly residential, are not shown. Again, prices are rising, both in current and constant dollars, and, since the 1990s, in public institutions relative to private institutions.

Note that these statistics are enrollment weighted, reflecting the costs paid by the average student. While weighted statistics are appealing in a market such as this one in which there is a large range in the size of institutions, to some extent, changes in prices may reflect changes in the distribution of enrollment, rather than in the actual prices charged. To examine this, we show unweighted statistics in table 7.4 for comparison purposes; tuition and fees are shown separately from the room and board charges. Here, the overall pattern is the same, although it is worth noting that tuition is rising faster than room and board.

Table 7.2 Average Published Tuition and Fee Charges

| | Tuition and Fees (Current Dollars) | | | | | | | | Tuition and Fees (Constant 2004 Dollars) | | | | | |
| | (1) | (2) | (3) | (4) | (5) | (6) | (7) | (8) | (9) | (10) | (11) | (12) | (13) | (14) |
Academic Year	Private Four-Year	Percent Change	Public Four-Year	Percent Change	Public-Private	Public Two-Year	Percent Change	Two Year/ Four Year	Private Four-Year	Percent Change	Public Four-Year	Percent Change	Public Two-Year	Percent Change
1980–1981	$3,617		$804		0.22	$391		0.49	$7,910		$1,758		$855	
1985–1986	$6,121	69.2%	$1,318	63.9%	0.22	$641	63.9%	0.49	$10,657	34.7%	$2,295	30.5%	$1,116	30.5%
1990–1991	$9,340	52.6%	$1,908	44.8%	0.20	$906	41.3%	0.47	$13,213	24.0%	$2,699	17.6%	$1,282	14.9%
1995–1996	$12,216	30.8%	$2,811	47.3%	0.23	$1,330	46.8%	0.47	$14,979	13.4%	$3,447	27.7%	$1,631	27.2%
2000–2001	$16,072	31.6%	$3,508	24.8%	0.22	$1,642	23.5%	0.47	$17,390	16.1%	$3,796	10.1%	$1,777	9.0%
2001–2002	$17,377	8.1%	$3,766	7.4%	0.22	$1,608	-2.1%	0.43	$18,475	6.2%	$4,004	5.5%	$1,710	-3.8%
2002–2003	$18,060	3.9%	$4,098	8.8%	0.23	$1,674	4.1%	0.41	$18,788	1.7%	$4,263	6.5%	$1,710	0.0%
2003–2004	$18,950	4.9%	$4,645	13.3%	0.25	$1,909	14.0%	0.41	$19,292	2.7%	$4,729	10.9%	$1,943	13.6%
2004–2005	$20,082	6.0%	$5,132	10.5%	0.26	$2,076	8.7%	0.40	$20,082	4.1%	$5,132	8.5%	$2,076	6.8%
1990/2001– 2004/2005		115.0%		169.0%			129.1%			52.0%		90.1%		61.9%

Source: The College Board (2004, table 4a); author's calculations
Note: Enrollment weighted

Table 7.3   Average Published Tuition, Fee, Room and Board (TFRB) Charges at Four-Year Institutions, Enrollment Weighted

Academic Year	Total Charges (Current Dollars)					Total Charges (Constant 2004 Dollars)			
	Private Four-Year	Percent Change	Public Four-Year	Percent Change	Public/Private	Private Four-Year	Percent Change	Public Four-Year	Percent Change
1980–1981	$5,594		$2,551		0.46	$12,234		$5,579	
1985–1986	$8,902	59	$3,791	49	0.43	$15,498	27	$6,600	18
1990–1991	$13,476	51	$5,074	34	0.38	$19,064	23	$7,178	9
1995–1996	$17,382	29	$6,743	33	0.39	$21,314	12	$8,628	20
2000–2001	$22,240	28	$8,439	25	0.38	$24,064	13	$9,131	6
2001–2002	$23,856	7	$9,032	7	0.38	$25,363	5	$9,603	5
2002–2003	$24,867	4	$9,672	7	0.39	$25,870	2	$10,062	5
2003–2004	$26,057	5	$10,530	9	0.40	$26,527	3	$10,720	7
2004–2005	$27,516	6	$11,354	8	0.41	$27,516	4	$11,354	6
		24		35			14		24

Source: Author's calculations; The College Board (2004).

Table 7.4   **Average Annual Published Costs for Undergraduates, by Institution Type, in Current Dollars, Unweighted**

Sector	Tuition and Fees			
	1994–1995	1995–1996	2000–2001	2004–2005
Two-year Public	$1,267	$1,399	$1,703	$2,247
Percent change		10.4%	21.7%	31.9%
Four-year Public	$2,585	$2,741	$3,380	$4,843
Percent change		6.0%	23.3%	43.3%
Two-year/Four-year	0.49	0.51	0.50	0.46
Four-year Private	$9,993	$10,528	$13,772	$17,270
Percent change		5.4%	30.8%	25.4%
Public/Private	0.26	0.26	0.25	0.28
	Room and Board			
Two-year Public	—	—	—	—
Four-year Public	$3,708	$3,847	$4,669	$5,816
Percent change		3.7%	21.4%	24.6%
Four-year Private	$4,385	$4,536	$5,445	$6,606
Percent change		3.4%	20.0%	21.3%
Public/Private	0.85	0.85	0.86	0.88

Source: The College Board (2004, table 7A); author's calculations.
Note: All data are unweighted averages, intended to reflect the average prices set by institutions.

Finally, it is worth noting that there is significant regional variation in the sticker price of college. In the 2005 *Trends in College Pricing*, the College Board examines regional differences in tuition and fees and finds that the average published tuition and fees at private, four-year colleges was nearly twice as high in the New England region, at more than $27,000, as in the Southwest, at less than $17,000. The range in the sticker price of public colleges is narrower. Tuition and fees in four-year public colleges in New England averaged nearly $7,300, considerably higher than those in the West and South, which were roughly $4,400. Public two-year institutions in the West posted tuition and fees that averaged roughly $1,300, almost $2,000 less than the prices in New England.

Interestingly, the geographic pattern of room and board expenses is somewhat different than that of tuition and fees. As an example, higher costs for room and board make the cost of attending college in the West exceed the cost in the Southwest. Notice that the geographic distribution of the prices is important. Although many students attend college in jurisdictions outside of their home towns, proximity is clearly important to college decisions. The desire to live close to parents and friends, greater awareness of local opportunities, and avoiding additional costs for room and board, for example, undoubtedly means that for many students the cost of college will be the cost of attending a college nearby—in the same region or state, if not the same county. That a college thousands of miles from home is less expensive than a local college is not likely to appreciably affect attendance at the local college. The geographic distribution of prices are thus critical to determining the affordability of college for low-income students and the extent to which college serves as a pathway to the middle class for poorer students.

Net Prices and Quality Adjustments

Increases in the sticker price of colleges are not in and of themselves evidence that college is less affordable. Perhaps education policy makers heeded the advice of economists arguing for a high tuition–high aid strategy in the hopes of realizing efficiency gains simultaneously with equity gains. As is well known in the economics literature, higher prices create more room for price discrimination. Higher sticker prices may in fact be a sign of more equity in higher education, rather than less. Financial aid has also increased significantly. According to The College Board, financial aid for undergraduates and graduate students totaled more than $122 billion, in 2003 and 2004, an 11 percent real increase from the previous year (2004). Taking a longer perspective, aid has increased 122 percent in real terms over the previous decade. To some extent, this increase reflects increases in enrollments, but even when measured in terms of full-time equivalent students, aid has increased significantly.[12] Whether—or the extent to which—it does, depends on how that aid is distributed. If it is targeted at low-income students, the impact may be ameliorated or the overall trend reversed. If not, rising prices may well exacerbate inequities in access.

Assessing the impact of the rising sticker prices and aid on net prices would be best performed using individual level data on the amount of aid received, tuition paid, college attended, and income, and importantly, the amount of tax credits and private scholarships received. Unfortunately, such data are unavailable on a broad enough scale to allow an industry-wide analysis of net prices.[13] Three recent studies have, however, examined the trends in net prices using institutional level data. Amy Ellen Schwartz and Benjamin Scafidi (2004) used data from the Annual Survey of Colleges and Integrated Postsecondary Educational Data System from the National Center for Education Statistics to estimate net prices for four-year colleges. They used the same data to examine net prices for two-year colleges in a 2003 study. The College Board's *Trends in College Pricing* for 2004 estimates net prices for both markets, for the ten years between 1993 and 2003.[14]

In all cases, the analyses show that net prices are on average significantly lower than sticker prices (see figure 7.1). In every sector and every

Figure 7.1 Net Price: Published Tuition and Fees and Tuition and Fees
After Average Grant and Education Tax Benefits per Student
by Institution Type, in Constant (2003) Dollars, 1993–1994

The net prices reported in these graphs are estimated averages for the sector. Students pay different prices depending on their circumstances. Not apparent in the average prices illustrated below is the reality that the changing distribution of state and institutional grant aid, combined with the introduction of education tax credits in 1998 and the tuition and fee deduction in 2002, has reduced net price for middle- and upper-income students relative to net price for lower-income students.

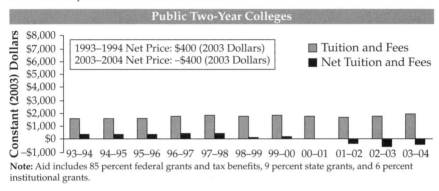

Public Two-Year Colleges

1993–1994 Net Price: $400 (2003 Dollars)
2003–2004 Net Price: –$400 (2003 Dollars)

■ Tuition and Fees
■ Net Tuition and Fees

Note: Aid includes 85 percent federal grants and tax benefits, 9 percent state grants, and 6 percent institutional grants.

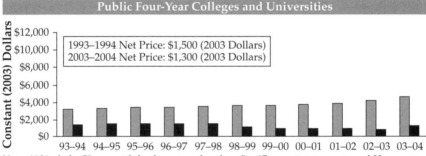

Public Four-Year Colleges and Universities

1993–1994 Net Price: $1,500 (2003 Dollars)
2003–2004 Net Price: $1,300 (2003 Dollars)

Note: Aid includes 59 percent federal grants and tax benefits, 17 percent state grants, and 23 percent institutional grants.

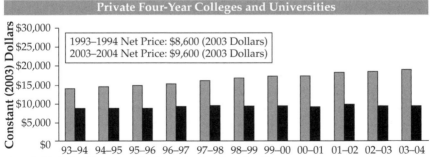

Private Four-Year Colleges and Universities

1993–1994 Net Price: $8,600 (2003 Dollars)
2003–2004 Net Price: $9,600 (2003 Dollars)

Note: Aid includes 24 percent federal grants and tax benefits, 12 percent state grants, and 65 percent institutional grants.

Source: The College Board (2004).

year, financial aid offsets the cost of tuition plus fees by a substantial amount. The results are perhaps most stark for two-year colleges. According to the College Board estimates, the net price of two-year college has on average declined continuously over the decade. By the 2000–2001 school year, the average net price per student at a public two-year college was virtually zero and in subsequent years was negative. This is an important phenomenon. At the same time that college tuition rose in this market segment, increases in financial aid have been so large that the average student receives more in financial aid than the cost of tuition and fees. Although the magnitude of the net subsidy is relatively small—about $400—and, in particular, not large enough to significantly offset opportunity costs or living expenses, the implication for income inequality and policy making is important. Despite rising tuition, college is, in some measure, more affordable now than ten years ago. Of course, the average net price undoubtedly masks significant variation even within this sector—both within and between institutions—and there is no accounting here for changes or variations in the quality of the education provided. If the quality of the education provided by two-year colleges is declining, due, say, to greater demands on the physical plant, then students attending two-year colleges may not enjoy the economic returns to education that earlier cohorts enjoyed. Thus the impact on income inequality is unclear. I will return to this point shortly.

Turning to four-year colleges, the College Board estimates again find that net prices are significantly lower than sticker prices. The trends in the public and private sector, however, diverge. In the public sector, net price increased between 1993 and 1997, falling thereafter. (Federal education tax credits were introduced in 1998.) By the end of the decade, net prices were lower at $1,300 (in 2003 dollars) than the $1,500 average net price in 1993. In the private sector, on the other hand, net prices rose, reaching a high of $9,600 by 2003. Notice that the sticker price of four-year public colleges had risen relative to that of four-year private colleges. Net prices, however, show a different pattern. In 1993, the net price of a four-year public college was, on average, roughly 17 percent of the price of a private college. By 2003, that figure had dropped to 13 percent. Whether this reflects a move by the public sector toward a high tuition–high aid policy, or any of the myriad other possible explanations, is worthy of further study.

The two Schwartz and Scafidi studies focus explicitly on estimating price indices for college, using regression analyses of hedonic equations to adjust for differences in quality.[15] Due to data limitations, the sample is somewhat dated; the most recent data is for 1995. The analyses are interesting nonetheless, for two reasons in particular. First is the exploration of the role of quality in driving price differentials and changes over time. Second is the analysis of the distribution of net prices.

Schwartz and Scafidi (2004) estimate a hedonic model of the price of four-year colleges that links the net price of college to a set of variables capturing the characteristics of colleges, a set of college fixed effects, and a set of year dummies. In principle, the set of characteristics should include measures of all of the characteristics of the college bundle valued by consumers—undoubtedly a long and varied list including features of the campus, the faculty, the student body, the resources, and so on. In practice, the list is limited, significantly, by the availability of data. Schwartz and Scafidi make use of publicly available data provided to students choosing colleges—presumably because these are characteristics they care about—and includes the pupil-teacher ratio, average student SAT scores, NCAA membership, among others (see table 7.5 for means). In addition, college fixed effects capture any "brand" or reputation effects as well as those of any time-invariant characteristics, including variables that are unmeasured and others (such as location) that cannot be included simultaneously with the fixed effects.

More specifically, the hedonic model they estimate follows:

(1) $P_{jt} = \alpha + \beta_X X_{jt} + \beta_S S_{jt} + \rho_t I_t + C_j + \varepsilon_{jt};$ $j = 1,\ldots., J; t = 1,\ldots,T$

where:

X_{jt} = time varying characteristics of college j at time t,
S_{jt} = time varying characteristics of the student body at college j in time t,
I_t = year dummies
C_j = a college fixed (or brand) effect, and P_{jt} is the natural logarithm of net price.

Table 7.5 shows the variables used and descriptive statistics by year.

Table 7.6 shows the hedonic results. In this model, an index of the price of colleges can be constructed based on the estimated parameters on the year dummies, ρ_t. To be clear, the resulting price indices are adjusted both for changes in the quality measures used and purge the impact of any time-invariant characteristics such as location or a brand or prestige effect.[16]

Like those of the College Board, the Scafidi and Schwartz (2003) analyses indicate significant differences in the trends in net prices and sticker prices in the first half of the 1990s (see tables 7.7 and 7.8). Sticker prices for both the public and private four-year colleges rose during this period, exceeding inflation only for the public colleges.

Like Scafidi and Schwartz (2003), sticker prices also rose for two-year colleges, again, more quickly for the public schools. The trend for net prices is somewhat different, however. Net prices rose but did not keep up with inflation, suggesting declines in prices in real terms and, for two-year schools, declines in both nominal and real prices.

Table 7.5   Means by Year

Variable	1991	1992	1993	1994	1995
Tuition + fees	5,480	5,971	6,406	6,810	7,220
Aid per student	1,600	1,791	1,998	2,399	2,619
Tuition + fees—					
aid per student	3,880	4,179	4,407	4,412	4,601
Pupil-teacher ratio	20.64	20.71	20.57	20.27	20.37
Faculty with PhD	0.81	0.75	0.76	0.77	0.79
Part-time faculty	0.27	0.26	0.26	0.27	0.27
Full-time students	8,507	8,498	8,311	8,147	8,154
Part-time students	1,828	1,834	1,805	1,827	1,743
PhD granting					
institution	0.47	0.46	0.48	0.48	0.48
NCAA member	0.87	0.88	0.90	0.90	0.91
Fraternities and/					
or sororities	0.84	0.84	0.84	0.84	0.85
Verbal SAT score 75th					
percentile*	611	609	609	612	611
Reports SAT score	0.67	0.69	0.70	0.70	0.74
Requires SATs for					
admission	0.94	0.95	0.94	0.95	0.94
Average age of entering					
freshmen	18.63	18.58	18.59	18.53	18.58
Minority students	0.15	0.15	0.16	0.17	0.18
Living in dorms	0.42	0.42	0.42	0.42	0.42
N	534	534	534	534	534

Source: Schwartz and Scafidi (2004), table 3.
All variables weighted by FTE in the 1990–1991 school year.
*Colleges who did not report an SAT score received a value of 0, and are not included in the mean and standard deviation reported.

Of particular interest, however, is the analysis of the distribution of net prices within the set of two-year colleges. As shown in table 7.9, many of the schools in the sample charge prices that, on average, are less than the amount of aid the student receives. Over time, the number of the net subsidy schools increased, as did the share of students in the market attending those schools, presaging the College Board findings in later years. That said, it seems likely that the average negative net price shown in the College Board estimates reflects a combination of both net cost and net subsidy schools. How these net subsidy schools are distributed around the country is critical to how affordable college is for low-income students.

We turn, finally, to the impact of quality adjustments. Table 7.10 presents the quality adjusted net price indices from Schwartz and Scafidi (2004). Figure 7.2 presents the same information graphically. Introducing quality-adjustments yields significant changes in the estimated price

Table 7.6   Hedonic Equations*

	Full Sample		Public		Private	
	Estimate	SE	Estimate	SE	Estimate	SE
p92	0.106	0.014	0.134	0.021	0.062	0.013
p93	0.168	0.013	0.200	0.020	0.112	0.014
p94	0.177	0.014	0.209	0.024	0.116	0.013
p95	0.226	0.018	0.258	0.032	0.155	0.014
Pupil-teacher ratio	−0.0002	0.003	0.002	0.007	−0.002	0.001
Faculty with PhD	0.007	0.011	0.012	0.013	−0.045	0.045
Part-time faculty	−0.080	0.092	−0.087	0.141	0.005	0.095
LN full-time students	0.236	0.075	0.134	0.122	0.373	0.060
LN part-time students	0.012	0.007	0.015	0.009	0.010	0.005
PhD granting institution	0.017	0.033	−0.001	0.049	0.039	0.027
NCAA member	−0.001	0.052	0.011	0.083	−0.017	0.021
Fraternities and/or sororities	−0.016	0.046	0.139	0.215	−0.048	0.020
Verbal SAT score 75th percentile	0.0004	0.000	0.0019	0.0010	−0.00014	0.0002
Reports SAT score	−0.235	0.227	−1.104	0.580	0.088	0.101
Requires SATs for admission	−0.074	0.027	−0.104	0.037	−0.024	0.037
Average age of entering freshmen	−0.026	0.012	−0.033	0.018	0.0000	0.004
Minority students	1.027	0.526	1.731	0.833	−0.382	0.222
Live in dorms	0.105	0.049	0.054	0.066	0.110	0.053
Constant	6.210	0.688	6.312	1.176	6.065	0.455
N	2,670		740		1,930	
R**2	0.976		0.931		0.958	

Source: Schwartz and Scafidi (2004), table 6.
*Dependent variable equals LN(Net_price). Weighted by the number of FTE undergraduates in 1990–1991. Each regression is estimated via fixed effects.

indices. The quality adjusted index for all colleges indicates a price increase of 25.4 percent (column 3) between 1991 and 1995, compared to a 28.6 percent increase in the unadjusted net price index—suggesting increases in the quality of college services provided. Quality adjustment also leads to substantial decreases in the net price increase for public colleges but slight increases for private colleges. The differential between the adjusted and unadjusted prices suggests that quality has increased in public institutions, but decreased (slightly) in private institutions.[17] Nonetheless, net

Table 7.7   Comparison of CPI and Unadjusted Real Price Indices, Public Colleges

Year	(1) CPI-U	(2) CPI: College Tuition and Fees	(3) Four-Year Public Tuition+Fees*	(4) Two-Year Public Tuition+Fees*	(5) Four-Year Public Net Price*	(6) Two-Year Public Net Price*
1990	100.0	100.0	100.0	100.0	100.0	100.0
1991	103.0	105.7	106.8	107.6	101.7	93.6
1992	106.1	117.1	120.3	114.9	118.2	91.1
1993	108.8	128.0	130.9	122.3	128.6	98.7
1994	111.9	137.0	140.2	123.9	131.4	96.0

Source: Scafidi and Schwartz (2003).
*These real price indices were created using estimates from weighted fixed effects regressions of the sticker or net price of college on year dummy variables. All regression coefficients are significant at the 1 percent level.

Table 7.8   Comparison of CPI and Unadjusted Real Price Indices, Private Colleges

Year	(1) CPI-U	(2) CPI: College Tuition and Fees	(3) Four-Year Public Tuition+Fees*	(4) Two-Year Public Tuition+Fees*	(5) Four-Year Public Net Price*	(6) Two-Year Public Net Price*
1990	100.0	100.0	100.0	100.0	100.0	100.0
1991	103.0	105.7	109.1	102.2	108.0	94.8
1992	106.1	117.1	117.8	106.0	114.3	91.8
1993	108.8	128.0	125.7	109.8	119.4	91.5
1994	111.9	137.0	133.3	114.0	119.8	92.1

Source: Scafidi and Schwartz (2003).
*These real price indices were created using estimates from weighted fixed effects regressions of the sticker or net price of college on year dummy variables. All regression coefficients are significant at the 1 percent level.

Table 7.9   Colleges with Negative Net Prices

Year	# Schools Positive	# Schools Negative	% Schools Negative
1990	720	159	18
1991	697	182	21
1992	682	197	22
1993	692	187	21
1994	679	200	23
	# Students Attending Positive Net Price Colleges	# Students Attending Negative Net Price Colleges	% Students Attending Negative Net Price Colleges
1990	2,124,276	391,661	16
1991	2,084,086	473,594	19
1992	1,998,879	523,320	21
1993	2,031,167	465,397	19
1994	1,917,423	543,122	22

Source: Scafidi and Schwartz (2003).

prices rose far more rapidly in public colleges than private colleges. Looking within these sectors, we see significant differences in net price increases between doctoral, comprehensive, and liberal arts institutions. Whereas prices in public comprehensive and liberal arts colleges increased by 36 percent and 31 percent, respectively, in the first half of the 1990s, prices of private comprehensive and liberal arts colleges increased only 16.6 percent and 14.6 percent, respectively, in that same period. Again, quality adjustment generally suggests quality improvements in the public schools that offset price rises, along with a mild suggestion of quality decline in the private colleges. It is worth noting, however, that changes in the mean values of the college characteristics are relatively small over time—there are no large and dramatic changes that seem to be driving price changes.

Discussion

Evidence shows that sticker prices are rising, but increases in financial aid have been significantly offsetting. For two-year colleges, most of which are public, the trend in net prices has been downward and current net prices are, on average, negative. Among four-year institutions, the net price of public colleges declined in the last decade, with some modest increases in the last few years offsetting larger decreases in the 1990s. The trend for four-year private colleges, however, has been unambiguously positive. Net prices are significantly higher than a decade ago.

Table 7.10   Quality-Adjusted Net Price Indices*

Year	(1) CPI-U	(2) CPI: College Tuition and Fees	(3) All Colleges	(4) All Public Colleges	(5) All Private Colleges	(6) Public PHD	(7) Private PHD
1991	100.0	100.0	100.0	100.0	100.0	100.0	100.0
1992	103.0	110.7	111.2	114.3	106.4	107.3	113.3
1993	106.1	121.1	118.3	122.2	111.8	114.9	114.3
1994	108.8	129.6	119.3	123.3	112.3	116.5	113.3
1995	111.9	137.3	125.4	129.5	116.8	125.0	121.1

Year	(8) Public Comprehensive	(9) Private Comprehensive	(10) Public Liberal Arts	(11) Private Liberal Arts
1991	100.0	100.0	100.0	100.0
1992	121.8	104.4	112.8	105.4
1993	130.7	111.0	116.1	111.4
1994	131.7	112.3	112.8	111.6
1995	135.8	116.6	130.9	114.6

Source: Schwartz and Scafidi (2004).
*Price indices in columns 3 through 11 are created using regression coefficients reported in tables 7.7 and 7.8.
Price indices for four-year colleges only.

Figure 7.2   Quality-Adjusted Net Price Indices by Market Segment

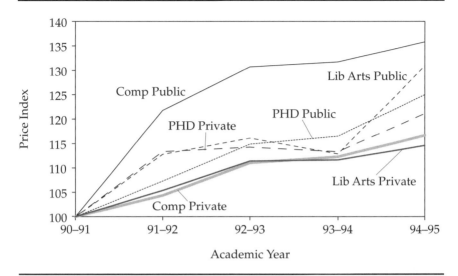

Source: Schwartz and Scafidi (2004, figure 7).

The trends in relative prices are also important. Over time, two-year colleges are becoming more affordable relative to both public and private four-year colleges. And, among four-year colleges, private colleges are growing more unaffordable, even while the sticker price of four-year public colleges has risen, relative to the sticker price of four-year private colleges. Put differently, incentives are shifting—the relative price of public education is dropping and, within that sector, the price of two-year colleges is dropping relative to the price of four-year colleges.

Interestingly, the implication is that, even if the level of scholarships has been increasing at the private institutions and even if those increases significantly offset tuition increases, students who are most price sensitive (that is, of course, lower-income students) face increasing prices at these institutions relative to public institutions and may, then, be more inclined to choose public institutions. And, because the relative price of two-year colleges is falling even more, low-income students may be more inclined to choose two-year institutions over four-year. Thus, greater economic sorting may emerge and the role of two-year colleges in providing access to higher education for low-income students is likely to continue to expand.

If the quality of the education provided at these institutions is equivalent or, more important here, if the economic returns to the education are equivalent, there may be no cause for concern, even if more sorting does occur. If, however, quality differences are significant, then the changing prices may lead to greater inequality than might be predicted by rising enrollments.

Turning, then, to quality, although current estimates of quality adjusted price changes are unavailable, evidence from the 1990s indicates that, to some extent, changes in quality are important in understanding price movements. If the lower cost of public education reflects falling quality, then caution is warranted in heralding the change as a boon for affordability. If low-income students buy lower quality education at a lower net price, then college education may fail to deliver the promised economic opportunities and reduction in income inequality.

This raises the larger set of questions that need to be answered for policy making. What should the price of college be? What sort of price differentials would be optimal overall? For different institutions? For different individuals? Answering these questions is difficult because it requires addressing more fundamental questions about the role of college—the efficient provision of college—education in the United States today, which in turn requires strong evidence on the benefits and costs of college attendance, and behavioral responses of individuals and institutions to changing prices and policies. This evidence is building but much work needs to be done (for a seminal introduction, see Manski and Wise 1983; for a sense of current research, see Hoxby 2004; Bowen, Kurzweil, and Tobin 2005). Although a fully satisfying answer is, perhaps, unattainable, we can, at least, provide a productive beginning.

In economists' terms, the rationale for government intervention in the market for college rests primarily on the notion that individual decisions about college going, attendance, and graduation may be inefficient for several reasons, among them individuals' liquidity constraints that prevent them from investing in their own human capital, the existence of externalities from an individual's education, or incompleteness of information that may hinder an individual from making optimal decisions. There are, of course, other arguments. One that is particularly interesting here is that college provides an increasingly important pathway to economic success including both access to middle-class life and to the leadership positions occupied by those attending elite institutions. Additionally, government intervention may be warranted to guarantee that these benefits are fairly distributed in succeeding generations.

How well is the market working now? As Sarah Turner (2004) shows, enrollment in college has been steadily increasing, though college completion has not. That is, more and more students are going to college but a smaller share of them are graduating, moderating the impact on the overall completion rate. At the same time, two-year colleges are serving a larger share of the students, and the public comprehensive institutions a smaller share. Further, a growing body of empirical research indicates that decisions about whether to attend college, which school to attend, and how long to stay are in some measure sensitive to prices.

Interestingly, there is some evidence that the college attendance decision may be less price sensitive than other decisions. As an example, Susan Dynarski (2004) and Bridget Long (2004b) find that recently implemented merit aid programs—such as HOPE—have had little impact on attendance, but may have significantly influenced students to "upgrade" from two-year to four-year colleges. This is, perhaps, to be expected, predicted by the low tuition prices, high levels of financial aid, and net negative prices found among two-year institutions. In the end, the presence of these very low- or no-cost colleges suggests that college is very affordable, such that it seems likely that the majority of students qualified to attend college should not be prevented from doing so by out-of-pocket costs.

Of course, out-of-pocket costs do not reflect opportunity costs. Attending college imposes a set of costs considerably higher than out-of-pocket expenses. The opportunity costs—forgone wages or leisure and the disutility of attending school—are likely to be large. Residential colleges, of course, carry the additional costs associated with living away from home. It seems therefore likely that increasing college attendance—let alone completion—will not easily be accomplished by influencing price. Students who are not now attending college are quite likely handicapped by inadequate high school preparation for college work, either inadequate or incorrect information about college, or facing significant demands to join the labor force and earn what income they can (see chapter 3). Decreases in the earnings of high school graduates may therefore lead to increases in college attendance as the opportunity cost of attendance declines.

Notice, however, that the increasing affordability of college may have unintended—and disturbing—consequences for income inequality. In particular, as attending some sort of college becomes (or has become) truly affordable for the vast majority of high school graduates, the earnings penalty for those not pursuing postsecondary education may, perversely, increase. The reason is that as the cost drops, more of the high-ability high school graduates will likely opt for at least some college, reducing the average ability level of the remaining pool of workers. This can lead to a reduction in the average level of earnings among the high school–only group if the high ability students now going to college had been earning higher than average wages within the high school–only group. It can also lead to a reduction in average earnings in the high school–only group through an entirely different mechanism—signaling. College education may be increasingly regarded as a signal of ability and those without college education increasingly treated as low ability by the labor market.

Where, then, do we go from here? There are, of course, many different forms of government intervention and it is interesting that, though intervention in the primary and secondary education market is motivated by many of the same concerns that motivate intervention at the college level, the tack taken there is somewhat different. Learning from that experience may be useful. Elementary and secondary education is characterized by heavy reliance on direct provision, tax based financing with essentially zero marginal tuition costs (that is, given residence) and compulsory attendance through adulthood or high school completion.[18] Of course, relying on local taxes to finance K–12 education means that, though every student can attend some school, enrollment at better schools typically costs more, albeit in taxes. Interestingly, the public policy debate over the financing and cost of K–12 education, which had focused on equity for some time (too often defined narrowly as equality in resources) has, increasingly, shifted to an emphasis on adequacy and accountability. Although it may not be possible for every student to attend a school with the quality and characteristics of the schools in affluent suburbs such as Scarsdale in New York or Shaker Heights in Ohio, the notion is that every school should be good enough. Defining adequacy and designing funding mechanisms to provide it is the challenge that legislatures and school districts around the country now face. At the same time, state and federal policy makers are acting to increase accountability by schools and districts—through measures such as those provided in the federal No Child Left Behind legislation—intending to improve performance, given resources. Finally, though enthusiasm for providing vouchers to subsidize private school attendance continues, the momentum seems to be waning. Charter schools—which are, fundamentally, public schools—and other forms of public school choice seem to be gaining traction.

It may be that a similar focus at the college level would be useful and effective. The vast majority of low-income college students will be educated at—or, for those who do not attend, will consider enrolling at—one of the nation's public two-year colleges or one of the many non-elite four-year colleges. It is, perhaps, surprising that so little attention is paid them, to their role in providing opportunity and access to the middle-class lifestyles, particularly when viewed in comparison to the voluminous literature on elite institutions.

A tremendous amount of attention is paid to the very high priced and selective institutions. Recent books such as *The Source of the River* (Bowen and Bok 2003), which followed intellectually from *The Shape of the River* (Massey 2000), garner tremendous public interest and policy attention. Additionally, these are useful for understanding the ways in which low-income students can gain entry into the highest economic strata and positions of leadership (or not). That said, we give comparatively short shrift to the pathways through which low-income students can gain the education needed to be nurses and teachers and insurance brokers and lawyers among other middle-class occupations. It may be that, after all, policy and public resources should be refocused on institutions that provide an adequate if no frills education to the large group of low-income students for whom Sarah Lawrence is out of reach. The ballyhooed "arms race" among elite institutions competing for students with increasingly luxurious campuses, swimming pools, dorms, and so on may make this shift in focus even more important as escalating costs at the high end make it impossible for public scholarship money to offset those rises.

Where and how should public funding for higher education be spent? The research base on which to build answers is woefully thin. We need to understand the impact of additional dollars spent at different types of institutions and in different ways and on the myriad products of institutions of higher education. What characterizes an adequate education at the postsecondary level? How much breadth in course offerings is good enough and what depth? What role does residential life play in the production of economically successful graduates? Can we get more bang for our buck by reducing public support at the high end of the market and allocating to the low end? Notice, however, that care must be taken in designing these responses. Reducing spending at the very top may well have little impact on economic outcomes, but the public sector has little influence in that piece of the market. Instead, the temptation may be to reduce resources at the good state schools and increase financing at the low end. My sense is that this would not be a productive response. Providing good college opportunities to middle-class students with good high school grades and good SAT scores seems to me to be an appropriate role for state universities, both because of the impact on the students who attend and because it may well lead to greater support for public higher education overall. This, in the end, may also help to expand opportunities to lower-income students as well.

Finally, focusing more attention on high school and the transition from high school to college seems warranted. If we hope to help low-income students acquire the best college education they can, then we need to reach them while they are still in high school to make sure that they have the necessary academic preparation and information—including information on financial aid and scholarships.

In the end, the news about college costs is not all bad. The availability of low-cost college options seems to be expanding. Recent evidence also shows that the net price of attending two-year colleges is, on average, negative. Thus it seems likely that few students are truly unable to attend some type of postsecondary institution because of prohibitive out-of-pocket costs. That said, out-of-pocket costs are not the full price of attending college. Room and board and opportunity costs are critical and large. And, the low-cost college option may not be a good quality option. Put simply, it is unclear whether the economic returns sought will be delivered by the education provided at these low-cost colleges. Further, the trend toward decreasing cost of public institutions, relative to private institutions, and, within the public colleges, the decreasing cost of two-year colleges relative to four-year colleges, create a stronger and stronger incentive to attend two-year colleges. It is likely that low-income students will be most responsive to these changing incentives. Thus, whether college education serves to reduce income inequality in the coming years will depend increasingly on the success of the two-year colleges.

Endnotes

1. To be specific, the article reported figures based on "tuition and required fees charged to first-time, full-time undergraduates at four-year colleges and universities, based on a nine-month academic year of thirty semester hours or forty-five quarter hours. The numbers represent 2004–2005 costs gathered by the College Board. Prices for public colleges and universities are for in-state residents." In fairness, the text of the article notes the availability of financial aid in various forms. "Top 10 priciest colleges . . . and the cheapest." By Erin Peterson. Bankrate.com, posted on August 11, 2005. Available at: http://bankrate.com/brn/news/cfguide/top-ten1.asp.

2. I will use the term two-year college to include both community colleges and junior colleges; some provide an academic program that prepares students to enter four-year colleges, others focus on remediation, vocational, or professional training.

3. To be clear, even if opportunity costs are at the same level for both high- and low-income students (driven, say, by the earnings potential of a job with only a high school degree), low-income students may still find that opportunity costs are a higher share of the full economic cost because scholarships and financial aid translate into lower net prices for low-income students than for their higher income peers.

4. Note that these numbers include private for profit institutions, which enrolled roughly one half million students across the country (see U.S. Department of Education 2003, table 199).

5. Also, includes some institutions that have four-year programs, but have not reported enough data to identify program category.

6. See also the winter 1999 issue of *Journal of Economic Perspectives* for more information.

7. The literature on peer effects in higher education is growing with attempts to address endogeneity and the reflection problem (for more on peers, see Winston 1999; Stinebrickner and Stinebrickner 2002; Rothschild and White 1996).

8. Amy Schwartz and Benjamin Scafidi (2004) and Scafidi and Schwartz (2003) have explored brand effects in a hedonic analysis of the price of four-year and two-year colleges, respectively. Although evidence points to the importance of college fixed effects, they were unable to disentangle brand effects from other time invariant characteristics of colleges such as location.

9. The literature examining costs in higher education and the factors driving cost increases is extensive (see, in particular, Bowen 1980; McPherson and Schapiro 1993; Clotfelter 1996; Ehrenberg 2000).

10. The tuition and other school fees index, which includes college tuition and fees, elementary and high school tuition and fees, childcare and nursery school and technical school and business school fees, had a relative importance of 2.544 percent in the CPI-U (the CPI for All Urban Consumers) in 1999, with college tuition and fixed fees accounting for about 47 percent of the weight of this index (BLS 2001).

11. Adjusting for inflation should not, by construction, change relative prices unless different measures of inflation are used for the different types of colleges. This might be appropriate if, for example, location-specific inflation measures are used and different types of colleges are distributed differently across locations. To be concrete, if a regional price deflator is used and there are differences in the price level between, say, the Northeast and Midwest, then inflation-adjusted prices will differ if, in addition, public colleges are disproportionately located in the Midwest than the Northeast, compared to private colleges.

12. The term financial aid includes a broad range of scholarships, grants, loans, tax credits, and subsidies that students receive to finance the cost of college. In this discussion, I refer only to the aggregate amount. However, it is important to note that the composition of aid is changing. As an example, although earlier aid policies were aimed at low-income students (for example, Pell Grants), more recently, several programs are designed to reward merit (for example, HOPE scholarships) or are targeted at middle-income taxpayers. The implications for affordability and for college attendance are important (see Dynarski 2004; Long 2004b).

13. Note that such data can sometimes be obtained for selected subsets of students— say, students attending elite colleges, or four-year colleges only—and the National Postsecondary Student Aid Study (NPSAS), which includes information on tuition and aid for a large sample of students and schools, is particularly useful. Perhaps most important is the recently released report by Lutz Berkner and Christina Wei (2006), which uses NPSAS to examine the net price of attendance including the federal tax benefits.

14. The net price calculation was introduced in *Trends in College Pricing* in 2003. The 2004 calculation included information on federal tax benefits, which was not included in the Schwartz and Scafidi studies or the 2003 College Board statistics.

15. The hedonic model treats products as collections of constituent characteristics, each of which is valued by the consumer. The implication is that differences in observed prices of heterogeneous products will reflect, in part, differences in characteristic bundles, apart from differences in firm cost structures or inefficiencies and the like. Hedonic regressions, then, link prices to measures of the relevant characteristics and are used to isolate quality-adjusted price changes from price changes due to changes in characteristics or quality. Hedonic price analyses have been applied widely to create quality adjusted price indices and in real estate economics, in particular, to disentangle changes in prices from changes in the quality or characteristics of houses sold.

16. Although the coefficients in hedonic models can often be interpreted as estimates of the shadow values of the characteristics, that interpretation may not be appropriate here, because of complex and imperfectly competitive nature of the college market. That said, the estimated prices indices can be interpreted as usual.
17. The logic here is straightforward. Changes in prices can be separated into changes in quality-constant prices and quality changes. Adjusted prices that differ from unadjusted prices suggest that quality changes drove some of the change in the unadjusted prices. Adjusted prices that exceed unadjusted prices suggest quality decline. Adjusted prices that are lower than unadjusted prices suggest quality improvement.
18. In the elementary-secondary market, another important rationale stems from a student's inability to choose and the parents' not choosing well for the student.

References

American Council on Education. 1998. *Too Little Knowledge Is a Dangerous Thing: What the Public Knows and Thinks It Knows about Paying for College.* Washington, D.C.: American Council on Education.

Berkner, Lutz, and Christina Chang Wei. 2006. *Student Financing of Undergraduate Education: 2003–04, With a Special Analysis of the Net Price of Attendance and Federal Education Tax Benefits.* NCES 2006-186. Washington, D.C.: National Center for Education Statistics.

Bowen, Howard R. 1980. *The Costs of Higher Education.* San Francisco: Jossey-Bass.

Bowen, William G., and Derek Bok. 2000. *The Shape of the River.* Princeton, N.J.: Princeton University Press.

Bowen, William G., Martin A. Kurzweil, and Eugene M. Tobin. 2005. *Equity and Excellence in American Higher Education.* Charlottesville: University of Virginia Press.

Clotfelter, Charles T. 1996. *Buying the Best: Cost Escalation in Elite Higher Education.* Princeton, N.J.: Princeton University Press.

———. 1999. "The Familiar but Curious Economics of Higher Education: Introduction to a Symposium." *Journal of Economic Perspectives* 13(1)(Winter): 3–12.

Dynarski, Susan M. 2000. "Hope for Whom? Financial Aid for the Middle Class and Its Impact on College Attendance." *National Tax Journal* 53(3): 629–62.

———. 2004. "The New Merit Aid." In *College Choices, The Economics of Which College, When College, and How to Pay for It*, edited by Caroline Hoxby. Chicago: University of Chicago Press.

Ehrenberg, Ronald G. 2000. *Tuition Rising: Why College Costs So Much.* Cambridge, Mass.: Harvard University Press.

Hoxby, Caroline. 2004. *College Choices: The Economics of Where to Go, When to Go and How to Pay for It.* Chicago: University of Chicago Press.

Kane, Thomas. 1999. *The Price of Admission: Rethinking How Americans Pay for College.* Washington, D.C.: Brookings Institution Press.

Kane, Thomas. 2002. "Student Perceptions of College Opportunities." Unpublished manuscript. University of California, Los Angeles.

Kane, Thomas J., and Cecilia E. Rouse. 1999. "The Community College: Educating Students at the Margin between College and Work." *Journal of Economic Perspectives* 13(1): 63–84.

Long, Bridget Terry. 2004a. "How Do Financial Aid Policies Affect Colleges? The Institutional Impact of the Georgia HOPE." *Journal of Human Resources* 39 (4): 1045–66.

———. 2004b. "Does the Format of a Financial Aid Program Matter? The Effect of State In-Kind Tuition Subsidies." *The Review of Economics and Statistics* 86(3): 767–82.

Manski, Charles F., and David A. Wise. 1983. *College Choice in America*. Cambridge, Mass.: Harvard University Press.

Massey, Douglas S., Camille Z. Charles, Garvey F. Lundy, Mary J. Fischer. 2003. *The Source of the River: The Social Origins of Freshmen at America's Selective Colleges and Universities*. Princeton, N.J.: Princeton University Press.

McPherson, Michael S., and Morton O. Schapiro. 1993. "The Effect of Government Financing on the Behavior of Colleges and Universities." In *Paying the Piper: Productivity, Incentives and Financing in U.S. Higher Education*, edited by Michael McPherson, Morton Schapiro, and Gordon Winston. Ann Arbor: University of Michigan Press.

———. 1998. *The Student Aid Game: Meeting Need and Rewarding Talent in American Higher Education*. Princeton, N.J.: Princeton University Press.

McPherson, Michael S., Morton O. Schapiro, and Gordon C. Winston, eds. 1993. *Paying the Piper: Productivity, Incentives and Financing in U.S. Higher Education*. Ann Arbor: University of Michigan Press.

Post, David. 1990. "College-Going Decisions by Chicanos: The Politics of Misinformation" *Educational Evaluation and Policy Analysis* 12(2)(Summer): 174–87.

Rothschild, Michael, and Lawrence White. 1996. "The Analytics of the Pricing of Higher Education and Other Services in Which Customers Are Inputs." *Journal of Political Economy* 104(3)(June): 573–86. Available at: http://www.nber.org/vitae/vita441.htm.

Scafidi, Benjamin, Ross Rubenstein, Amy Ellen Schwartz, and Gary Henry. 2001. "Merit-Based Financial Aid And College Tuition: The Case Of Georgia's Hope Scholarships." Unpublished paper.

Scafidi, Benjamin, and Amy Ellen Schwartz. 2003. "What's Up With the Price of Two-Year Colleges?" Paper prepared for the Cornell Higher Education Research Institute conference. Ithaca, N.Y. (May 21–22, 2003). Available at: http://www.ilr.cornell.edu/cheri/conf/chericonf2003-may.htm.

Schwartz, Amy Ellen, and Benjamin Scafidi. 2001. "Quality Adjusted Net Price Indices for Four year Colleges" *Bureau of Labor Statistics* Working Paper WP-337. Washington: U.S. Bureau of Labor Statistics. http://www.bls.gov/ore/abstract/ec/ec010050.htm.

———. 2004. "What's Happened to the Price of College? Quality-Adjusted Net Price Indices for Four-year Colleges." *Journal of Human Resources* 39(3): 723–45.

Stinebrickner, Todd R., and Ralph Stinebrickner. 2002. "Peer Effects Among Students from Disadvantaged Backgrounds." University of Western Ontario Working Paper. London, Ont.: University of Western Ontario and Berea College. Available at: http://econpapers.repec.org/paper/uwohcuwoc/20013.htm.

The College Board. 2004. *Trends in College Pricing 2004*. Trends in Higher Education Series. New York: The College Board.

The College Board. 2005. *Trends in College Pricing 2005*. New York: The College Board.

Turner, Sarah E. 2004. "Going to College and Finishing College: Explaining Different Educational Outcomes." In *College Choices: The Economics of Where to Go, When to Go and How to Pay for It*, edited by Caroline Hoxby. Chicago: University of Chicago Press.

U.S. Bureau of Labor Statistics. 2000. "Consumer Price Index Statistics." Washington: U.S. Bureau of Labor Statistics. http://www.bls.gov/cpi/cpifacct.htm.

———. 2001. "How BLS Measures Price Change for College Tuition." Washington: Government Printing Office. http://www.bls.gov/cpi/cpifacct.htm.

U.S. Department of Education. 2003. *Digest of Education Statistics, 2003*. National Center for Education Statistics, Integrated Postsecondary Education Data System (IPEDS). Washington: Government Printing Office.

Verry, Donald, and Bleddyn Davies. 1976. *University Costs and Outputs*. New York: Elsevier.

Winston, Gordon C. 1999. "Subsidies, Hierarchy and Peers: The Awkward Economics of Higher Education." *Journal of Economic Perspectives* 13(1)(Winter): 13–36. Available at: http://links.jstor.org/sici?sici=0895-3309(199924)13%3A1%3C13%3ASHAPTA%3E2.0.CO;2-I.

= Part III =

Looking to the Future

Chapter 8

Reducing Inequality in Higher Education

Ronald G. Ehrenberg

As Robert Haveman and Kathryn Wilson point out in chapter 2, differences in college enrollment rates across students from families of different socioeconomic levels have only marginally narrowed since the early 1970s (Baum and Payea 2004, figure 21). Moreover, students from lower-income families are much more likely to start higher education in two-year public colleges and public four-year institutions than are their higher-income counterparts (figure 21). Among students who initially enter four-year institutions, six-year graduation rates of students from families with incomes of less than $50,000 are substantially less than the rates of students from families with incomes of more than $75,000 (figure 24). Finally, at a set of our nation's most selective private colleges and universities, the proportion of students coming from families whose family incomes are in the lowest two-fifths of the distribution of family income average only about 10 percent in recent years (Hill, Winston, and Boyd 2005).

I begin this final chapter by discussing some of the forces influencing public and private higher education in the United States in recent years that have worked against improving access and persistence of students from the lower tail of the family income distribution. Where students go to college may be as important as whether they go to college. A considerable body of research shows that, other factors held constant, students who attend better-funded more selective colleges earn more after graduation, an effect most pronounced among students from lower-income families.[1] I therefore also discuss why it became increasingly difficult for students from lower-income families to enroll at top public and private institutions during the period under study.

Spurred by public attention that has been drawn to the underrepresentation of students from lower-income families, both selective public and private universities have begun to institute policies to improve their access to talented students from lower-income families (Hill, Winston, and Boyd 2005; Kahlenberg 2004; Bowen, Kurzweil, and Tobin 2005). In this chapter, I discuss a number of these strategies and provide preliminary estimates for some of their success to date. Efforts have also been made to enhance college preparedness of lower-income high school students and to provide them with improved information about college costs, the availability of financial aid, and prerequisites needed to succeed in college. I also address a few issues related to these efforts and, in conclusion, speculate about directions that future institutional and public policies might take.

Pessimistic Forces

A host of forces have both influenced public and private higher education during the last thirty years and have served to reduce progress at improving access in general and to our nation's most selective academic institutions.[2] First, following the Reagan revolution and federal income tax cuts in the 1980s, which reduced the value of the state income tax deductions on federal income tax returns, taxpayers clamored for state income tax cuts. Increased state funding needs for Medicaid, for elementary and secondary education, and for the criminal justice system since then have increased pressure on state tax revenues and the structural deficits that have appeared in many state budgets. Revenues to fund public higher education generously have proved inadequate and dramatic reductions in the share of state budgets devoted to higher education have therefore taken place (Rizzo 2006). Enrollments in public higher education grew by more than 50 percent between 1974 and 2000 and state support per full-time equivalent student at public higher education institutions remained roughly flat, in terms of the higher education price index, during the period.[3]

Traditionally, public higher education has been viewed as a social good that yields benefits to the nation as a whole. However, because the earnings differences between highly educated and less educated individuals widened and the private return to higher education grew, policy makers focused much more on the private return to public higher education. Any increase in real expenditures per student at the publics had to come from tuition increases and from students and their families paying a greater share of their higher educational costs.

On average, private higher education institutions increased their tuition levels by more than 3 percent a year above the rate of inflation during the last thirty years. Faced with no real increases in state appropriation per student, in an effort to generate resources as a way to remain competitive with their private counterparts, public colleges and universities raised their tuitions at roughly the same rate during the period. However, because the publics started off with much lower levels of tuition, the dollar increases in tuition they generated from these increases were much smaller than those of their private counterparts. As a result, expenditures per student in public higher education fell substantially relative to expenditures per student in private higher education. This was reflected in declining relative salaries of faculty at public institutions, growing student-faculty ratios at the publics relative to the privates, and more rapid increases in usage of part-time and full-time nontenure track faculty at the publics than at the privates (Ehrenberg 2003; Kane and Orszag 2003; Ehrenberg and Zhang 2005a). Research suggests that, other factors held constant, increased use of these types of contingent faculty is associated with reductions in five-year graduation rates at colleges and universities (Ehrenberg and Zhang 2005b).

As public tuition levels have increased, states and the federal government have responded to political pressure from the middle class by shifting financial aid away from need-based financial aid. At the state level, aid is increasingly merit, rather than need-based; one study calculated that between 1983 and 2003, the percentage of total state aid that is not based on need grew from about 9 to 26 percent (The College Board 2005, 19). This occurred because thirteen states, most of which were southern, had introduced broad-based merit scholarship programs modeled along the lines of Georgia's Hope Scholarship Program, which had been designed to encourage high school graduates to attend in-state institutions. Susan Dynarski has calculated that in many of these states the 30 percent or more of high school students who qualify for these awards are disproportionately white and come from middle- or upper-income families (2004). Hence the growth of these programs can be understood as policy makers responding to large voting blocs concerned with rising college tuition, rather than as an effort to increase access.

At the federal level, the major growth in financial aid has been in loans and tax credits for college attendance, not in increases in the real level of the maximum Pell grant award per recipient. Given evidence that students from lower-income families are not inclined to take on large loan burdens, these policies have also not stimulated access. Increasingly, financial aid to guarantee access at both public and private academic institutions will have to come from institutional, rather than state or federal funds.[4]

Data on the share of Pell grant recipients among the undergraduate student bodies at our nation's major public universities (a crude estimate of the share of their student bodies coming from the lowest two-fifths of the distribution of family incomes) indicate that a number of these institutions currently enroll relatively few students from these groups (some flagships, such as the University of California campuses, are notable exceptions). For example, Don Heller has estimated that in the 2001–2002 school year, Pell grant recipients were 19 percent of the undergraduate student bodies at our nation's most selective public universities, whereas by my calculations they were about 27 percent of the undergraduate student bodies nationally at all public four-year institutions that year (Heller 2004).

The flagship publics are the ones most likely to privatize and raise their tuitions substantially in the years ahead (Ehrenberg 2006). This is likely to lead to even greater stratification of public higher education, with upper and upper middle income students studying at relatively well-funded public flagships and lower-and lower-middle income students studying at other public four-year and two-year institutions, unless the flagships also devote significant resources to need-based financial aid as well. Large expenditure per student differentials already exist across these institutional categories; for example, in the 2000–2001 school year, instructional expenditures per full-time student averaged $9,673 at public flagship (doctoral-extensive campuses), $4,903 at public comprehensive institutions and $3,979 at public two-year colleges (Snyder 2005, table 345). As I have already indicated, these differences make a real difference in students' lives; students attending better funded institutions are more likely to graduate and to achieve higher earnings after graduation.

What about the privates? Donald Heller (2004) as well as Catherine Hill and her colleagues (2005) show that the share of students coming from lower-and lower-middle income families at many of our nation's most selective and best funded private colleges and universities is quite small. In part this arises from these institutions being involved in an arms race to achieve prestige; the prestige of an institution is heavily determined by the test scores of its entering students, and students from lower-income families are underrepresented in the high test score student population (Winston and Hill 2005, table 1). Fueled partially by the *U.S. News & World Report* rankings, which started in 1983 and quickly became the gold standard of the rankings business, partially by the consent degree between the Ivy League institutions and the U.S. Department of Justice in 1991 that prohibited these institutions from colluding on financial aid offers, and partially by the growing use of preferential packaging (giving different levels of grant aid to students with the same levels of financial need based on their perceived "attractiveness to the institution"), both public and private academic institutions have increasingly competed for top test score students using merit aid (McPherson and Schapiro 2005).

As noted, test scores are correlated with family income levels. It is therefore not surprising that recent research I conducted with colleagues showed that as institutions increase the share of their first-year students who receive institutionally financed national merit scholarships, the share of Pell grant recipients falls (Ehrenberg, Zhang, and Levin 2006). Given limited resources, increased use of institutional merit aid more generally threatens to crowd out need-based financial aid, which would further stratify private higher education, with students from lower-income families who are less likely to be high test score students increasingly likely not to make it to the best funded selective private institutions.

Financial Policies

The leaders of the flagship campuses at a number of our nation's public universities understand the importance of increasing their accessibility to students from lower-income families and other underrepresented groups. Examples of public flagships that have undertaken such efforts are the University of North Carolina–Chapel Hill with its Carolina Covenant and the University of Virginia with its AccessUVa programs.[5] Both programs guarantee students with incomes of less than twice the federal poverty level that they can attend the institutions without incurring any debt. Both include comprehensive efforts by the universities to recruit more students from low income families and, in the case of Virginia, a promise to report to the state each year on the socioeconomic distribution of its student body.

Increased enrollment of students from low income families at these institutions can come one of three ways. First, the programs may succeed in increasing the flow of applicants from lower-income families. Second, once admission officers are aware that increasing enrollments from these groups is a university goal, they are likely to take it into consideration in the admissions process. Third, the improved financial packages being offered to accepted applicants from these groups may increase the likelihood that they accept the university's offer of admission. A careful study of the first year's experience of AccessUVa found that the program did increase enrollments of students from lower-income families, with much of the impact coming from admissions officers putting in William Bowen, Martin Kurzweil, and Eugene Tobin's words (2005) "a thumb on the scale" for these students (Tebbs and Turner 2005). Although their initial evaluation suggested that the increase was due primarily to the increasing probabilities of these students' being admitted, not to an increase in a number of applications from students in the group, chapter 6 of this volume suggests that at least part of the increase was due to an increasing flow of applicants from lower-income families. It is likely that it will take a number of years before application behavior will increase substantially because lower-income students enrolled in high schools that are not traditional feeder schools to UVa will need time both to realize that attending UVa is now a real option and to take the courses that will make them eligible for admission.

A similar program is the University of Texas Longhorn Opportunity Scholarship, which provides scholarships to students from high schools located in census tracts with average family incomes of less than $35,000 whose students were historically underrepresented at the University of Texas. The program also provides coordinated focused mentorship opportunities designed to provide substantial assistance to students in their first year of enrollment (see http://www.utexas.edu/student/connexus/scholars). This program was originally designed, along with the top 10 percent rule, to help counter the effect of the Hopwood decision, which prohibited racial preferences in admissions in Texas and other states in the appeals court region.

A number of states have need-based financial aid programs for in-state high school graduates attending in-state institutions. Two notable examples are New York State's Tuition Assistance Program and California's Cal Grant program. A careful evaluation of the latter suggested that it substantially increases college enrollment rates for students from lower-income families (Kane 2003). Still another innovative program is the D.C. Tuition Assistance Grant Program that allows residents of the District of Columbia to attend public institutions in other states, but pay only the tuition charged to residents of that state. The program led to an increase in college enrollment rates of District high school graduates. Although this program is not need-based, given the socioeconomic distribution of high school graduates in the District, it is not surprising that the increases in college enrollments it induced were largely among students eligible for Pell grants (Kane 2004).

As noted, our nation's richest and most selective private higher educational institutions have also begun to realize their social obligation to enhance their enrollments of top students from lower-income families.[6] Princeton took the first step in 1998 when it eliminated all loans from its financial aid packages. Researchers found that the program increased the enrollment rates of accepted low income applicants by about 3 percentage points and of accepted low income minority applicants by about 8 to 10 percentage points, but only the latter increase was statistically significant (Linsenmeier, Rosen, and Rouse 2006).

Not to be outdone, Harvard quickly matched this program and went even further when it announced in the spring of 2004 that parents of students from families earning less than $40,000 a year would not be required to pay anything toward their students' education. Students would still, however, be expected to contribute through academic and summer job earnings, and families earning between $40,000 and $60,000 would be expected to pay a small amount. The program also included increased recruitment efforts, labeling the applications of students from lower-income families so that they might receive special consideration in admissions and establishing summer programs for talented disadvantaged high school students in the Boston area to enhance their preparation for selective four-year institutions (Basinger and Smallwood 2004). In April 2005, it was reported that the Harvard class starting in the fall of 2005 would have 22 percent more students from families with family incomes of less than $60,000 than the previous year's class (Kahlenberg 2005). A formal evaluation suggested that Harvard's growth in enrollment of students from lower- and lower-middle-income families was due to an increase in the number of applications it received from students from these groups, not because of any change in admission decisions (Avery et al. 2006). Evidence that Harvard's policy was beginning to work led Yale, not to be outdone, to adopt a similar no parental contribution policy for families with family incomes of less than $45,000 in March of 2006 (Pacia and Sadeghi 2005).

Other Policies to Improve Access and Persistence

Financial aid and college costs, which Amy Schwartz discusses extensively in chapter 7, are not the only barriers preventing access to, and persistence in, higher education for students from lower-income families. Other chapters have discussed the role of inequalities in elementary and secondary school preparation and linkages between secondary schools and colleges (Michael Kirst in chapter 3), the increasingly important role that community colleges play (Dan Goldhaber and Gretchen K. Peri in chapter 5) and the role of remediation (Eric Bettinger and Bridget Long in chapter 4). My remarks here will be brief.

First, concern has been expressed that high school students from lower-income families have less information about the expected returns from attending college than their higher-income counterparts, and that they are discouraged from applying to college by the complexity of the financial aid application and admissions process. Research by Christopher Avery and Thomas Kane as part of the Boston COACH (College Opportunity and Career Help) program suggests that the first concern is probably incorrect, but that the second is very important in restricting college entrance for students from high schools that enroll primarily lower-income students (Avery and Kane 2005). The COACH program includes mentoring inner-city Boston high school students by Harvard graduate students on the college applications and admissions process and it will be interesting to learn how the program impacts upon college-going behavior.

Second, removing all financial barriers to attending college does not guarantee success for talented students from lower-income families. Berea College in Kentucky has been ranked as the top regional college in the South by *U.S. News & World Report,* in large part because of its high endowment per student and the high test scores of its entering student body. It restricts its enrollment to students from families with lower- and lower middle-class incomes; in 1997, virtually all of its undergraduates came from families with incomes of less than $50,000. It provides all of its students with free tuition and grants that cover most of their living costs. All students are required to work for approximately ten hours a week in a mandatory work study program and are not permitted to work longer hours.

In spite of Berea's efforts, research suggests that even after controlling for test scores, distance from home to the college, family size, race and gender, persistence is positively related to family income at Berea (Stinebrickner and Stinebrickner 2003). This research did not permit the authors to isolate the factors responsible for the relationship; plausible candidates relate to parental background differences, pre-college schooling quality differences (though this does not appear to be an important variable), the types of peers that students from different income levels had while in high school, or the difficulty students from very low income families have adjusting to an environment in which they are surrounded by wealthier classmates. It does suggest that though the net cost of attending college influences persistence, it is clearly not the only thing that matters for students from lower-income families.

Third, access to higher education includes access to two-year colleges and persistence in higher education includes the ability to transfer from two-year to four-year colleges. As tuition levels at four-year institutions rise, increasingly two-year colleges are becoming the entry point to higher education for students from lower-income families.[7] The ability of students enrolled in academic programs at two-year colleges to transfer to four-year institutions is likely to play an increasingly important role in the future in terms of persistence (to four-year degree) of students from lower-income families.

States differ widely in how easy it is for students to transfer from two-year to four-year colleges within their public higher education systems. Some states have common course numbering systems for all public institutions in the state, which makes requirements for transfer and for the four-year institutions to grant credit for classes taken at the two-year institutions more transparent. In other states, articulation agreements between individual two-year and four-year colleges often lay out terms for transfer. Such arrangements, however, often guarantee only admission to a four-year institution if certain conditions are met, not to a specific major at the institution.

Research suggests that the probability that graduates of two-year colleges who transfer to four-year colleges receive four-year degrees within three years of the time they transfer varies widely across institutions that are members of the same state system (Ehrenberg and Smith 2004). Moreover, the success rate of two-year college students at the four-year institutions appears to be related to the share of these students in the student body; institutions that depend heavily on transfer students for enrollment management purposes appear to devote more attention to helping transfer students to succeed. If we are serious about enhancing the persistence of students from lower-income families to four-year degrees, much more attention must be directed to facilitating transfers and enhancing success once transfer students reach those colleges.[8]

Finally, federal and state governments, foundations, and higher education institutions have been devoting resources to help students from low income families to better prepare for access to higher education. The federal interventions began with the TRIO program in the 1960s, which today as Upward Bound provides services to eligible students between the ages of thirteen and nineteen to enhance the skills and motivation necessary for them to enroll and succeed in postsecondary education.

Two recently completed analyses of many of these programs, including a meta evaluation of existing evaluations, suggested that early interventions are particularly important and that the most effective programs are those in which services continue from middle school through high school (Perna 2005; Jager-Hyman 2004). Given the inequities between the quality of elementary and secondary school educations that students from different family incomes receive in the United States, if one truly wants to substantially reduce differences, the numbers of students are likely to be very large and thus the costs of the interventions very large. Inevitably, therefore, a tradeoff between the numbers of students from low-income families these programs can serve and the comprehensiveness of the programs that can be provided to them is likely.

Looking to the Future

Will our nation succeed in substantially reducing the inequities in college access and persistence that currently exist between students from lower-income and other families? Economists, especially this economist, are notoriously bad at making predictions, but some speculations are in order.

Our nation's public higher education institutions, in which 80 percent of all college students and 65 percent of all four-year college students are educated, will continue to face enormous pressures. Achieving the twin goals of improving (or at least maintaining) both access and quality is unlikely to be an easy task for them. Given the structural deficits present in so many state budgets, public higher education is likely to be increasingly viewed as a private investment and financed primarily by increases in tuition rather than in state appropriations. The increases in tuition are likely to be the largest at the flagship public research universities, where the demand for undergraduate positions is the greatest.

Many of these institutions do not have the large flow of annual giving and the large endowments that the University of Virginia or the University of North Carolina at Chapel Hill have. It will thus be more difficult for them to develop the resources necessary to support programs such as AccessUVa or the Carolina Covenant. If these flagship institutions are successful in diversifying their student bodies along racial-ethnic and socioeconomic lines, they run the risk of alienating the traditional supporters of their institutions—the upper- and middle-class families whose children attend the high schools that have long been large feeder schools. This may translate into either political pressure to reverse policies that led to the diversification, or a further loss of financial support for the public institutions. Certainly the pressure that has been building in Texas to modify the top 10 percent policy is an example of how quickly such pressures can arise (Elliott 2005).

Further cutbacks in state support are likely to be very damaging to the public comprehensives and two-year colleges. Efforts by them to replace state support with tuition increases are likely to be more problematic, because these are the institutions in which enrollment demand is likely to be most sensitive to price and which are most likely to have only limited capacity to raise funds for increased institutional need-based financial aid. Inasmuch as they already are the public institutions with the highest proportion of students from low income families, cutbacks in their state support would likely have an adverse effect on the goals of increasing access and persistence.

What about state support for need-based financial aid? The trend here has been in the opposite direction, with the share of state funding for grant aid based not on need but on merit aid increasing. To the extent that merit aid programs disadvantage students from lower-income families, which they appear to have done in the past, they are unlikely to expand access or persistence in the future.

The very richest selective private colleges and universities have the resources to continue their efforts to expand enrollments of talented students from lower-income families. This is a good thing. However, unless they expand their overall enrollments (which Princeton is doing), they will be forced to make hard choices about who these students will displace.

As one moves down the prestige pecking order in private higher education, resources rapidly fall off. Institutions increasingly use financial aid to help them craft classes that make them look more selective and to increase their net tuition revenue rather than to promote access. As long as prestige is the currency of the day that enables private colleges and universities to attract higher test score students, better faculty and more resources, and resources are tight, this is unlikely to change. The vast majority of private colleges and universities are already heavily involved in tuition discounting; preliminary results from the 2004 annual National Association of College and University Officers (NACUBO) Tuition Discounting study suggests that freshman tuition discount rates averaged 38.6 percent at private colleges and universities in the United States (Shedd and Redmont Daulton n.d.). Given tuition discount rates of this magnitude, which increasingly reflect merit rather than need-based financial aid, the net effect of the policies of the most selective richest privates might be to shift increasing numbers of talented lower-income students from less selective to more selective private institutions. Although this may be socially desirable, it will not lead to an increase in the overall enrollment of lower-income students in selective private higher education.

What then can be done to improve access and persistence for students from lower-income families? Actions will have to come from academic institutions themselves and reflect the important social value that they place on doing so. However, given the competition for status that all institutions find themselves in, such actions are unlikely to occur unless incentives exist for all institutions to take the actions. Put simply, higher education needs to redefine the metric by which it judges success.

Given the impact that the annual *U.S. News & World Report* (USNWR) rankings have on the behavior of academic institutions, I have argued elsewhere that the rankings methodology could be modified in several ways to provide incentives for our nation's four-year colleges and universities to direct more efforts to increasing access and persistence of students from low income families (Ehrenberg 2005). First, information on the share of Pell grant recipients in each institution's first-year class could be added as an additional data element in the rankings formula, with positive weight being assigned to this variable. If institutions' USNWR rankings improved when they enrolled more Pell grant recipients, they would most certainly devote more efforts to doing so. Although some might argue that it would be inappropriate for private higher education institutions to be judged by this standard, at the very least public institutions should be.[9]

Second, given that more and more students from lower-income families are finding that attendance at two-year public institutions is the only way that they can begin their college careers, four-year institutions could be required to provide information on transfer student success (for example, the three-year graduation rate of students transferring after completing two-year college degrees) that is analogous to the six-year graduation rate data for freshmen that now appear in the USNWR formula. If institutions' USNWR rankings were based on the success rates of their transfer students, colleges would have an incentive to devote more efforts to ensuring that their transfer students graduate.

Federal and state governments could also play a role by providing financial incentives for public and private four-year colleges to enroll, and see through to graduation, students from lower-income families. One way to do this would be to provide payments to the institutions for each Pell grant recipient that received a degree from them. Such payments would also encourage four-year colleges to expand their enrollment of transfer students from two-year colleges, because the institutions would receive full payments for graduating these students, but only bear the costs of educating them during part of their college careers.[10] The federal government could also make the HOPE and Lifetime tax credits that it offers "refundable" to lower-income families. Currently these credits can only be used to offset income tax obligations, which effectively excludes many potential students from lower-income families from gaining access to them.

Endnotes

1. Even Stacy Dale and Alan Kruger (2002), who dispute the "college selectivity matters" finding of other researchers, such as Dominic Brewer, Eric Eide, and Ronald Ehrenberg (1999), find that expenditure per student is related to subsequent earnings, with the effect being largest for students from lower-income families, other factors held constant.
2. Much of the material in this section draws on Ehrenberg (2006)
3. Relative to the CPI, state support did grow slightly in real terms, but at a much lower rate than tuition was increasing in private higher education institutions.
4. See Caliber Associates (2003) for evidence suggesting that educational choices of students from lower-income families are limited by their families' aversions to take out loans.
5. For details of these programs, see www.unc.edu/carolinacovenant and www.virginia.edu/accessuva. Amanda Pallais and Sarah Turner discuss these programs in much more detail in chapter 6.
6. My own institution, Cornell, has long had a policy of eliminating loans from the financial aid packages of students coming from families with incomes of less than $35,000 a year and not surprisingly this has led it to be among the selective private institutions that have the highest share of Pell grant recipients in their student bodies (see Heller 2004).
7. Andrew Nutting (2005) shows that as the tuition levels at four-year public colleges and universities in New York State rise relative to the tuition levels at two-year public colleges in the state, enrollments in academic programs at the two-year college rise.
8. In April 2005, several foundations announced an initiative to enhance the flow of community college graduates to our nation's most selective colleges and universities (see Jack Kent Cooke Foundation 2005)
9. USNWR now includes data on the share of Pell grant recipients in the undergraduate student body at many institutions in its rankings issue, but these data are not used by it in its computation of the rankings.
10. This proposal is modeled after the Bundy Aid program in New York State that provides a grant of $1,500 to private colleges in the state for each New York State resident who receives a bachelor's degree from them. This program has provided an extra incentive for private colleges in the state to enroll transfer students from the public 2-year colleges in the state, in addition to their desire to do so for enrollment management purposes. Recently, the *Report of the Governor's Task Force on Higher Education* (2004) in New Mexico suggested that state funding to public higher education institutions in the state should be tied

to the number of students graduated, as well as to the number of students enrolled as it currently is. More generally, John Cheslock (2005) discusses transfer students in the context of enrollment management decisions and shows that when the benefits to enrolling transfer students increases, institutions enroll more transfer students.

References

Avery, Christopher, and Thomas J. Kane. 2005. "Student Perceptions of College Opportunities: The Boston Coach Program." In *College Choice: The Economics of Where to Go, When to Go, and How to Pay for It*, edited by Caroline Hoxby. Chicago: University of Chicago Press.

Avery, Christopher, Caroline Hoxby, Clement Jackson, Kaitlin Burek, Glenn Pope and Mridula Raman. 2006. "Costs Should Be No Barrier: An Evaluation of the First Year of Harvard's Financial Aid Initiative." *NBER* Working Paper 12029. Cambridge, Mass: National Bureau of Economic Research.

Basinger, Julianne, and Scott Smallwood. 2004. "Harvard Gives a Break to Parents Who Earn Less Than $40,000 a Year." *Chronicle of Higher Education* 50(27) (March 12): A35.

Baum, Sandra, and Kathleen Payea. 2004. *Education Pays 2004*. New York: College Board Publications.

Bowen, William G., Martin A. Kurzweil, and Eugene M. Tobin. 2005. *Equity and Excellence in American Higher Education*. Charlottesville: University of Virginia Press.

Brewer, Dominic J., Eric R. Eide, and Ronald G. Ehrenberg. 1999. "Does it Pay to Attend an Elite Private College? Cross-Cohort Evidence on the Effects of College Type on Earnings." *Journal of Human Resources* 34(1): 104–23.

Caliber Associates. 2003. *Cultural Barriers to Incurring Debt: An Exploration of Borrowing and Impact on Access to Postsecondary Education*. Santa Fe, New Mex.: ECMC Group Foundation.

Cheslock, John. 2005. "Differences Between Public and Private Institutions of Higher Education in the Enrollment of Transfer Students." *Economics of Education Review* 24(June): 263–74.

Dale, Stacy B., and Alan B. Krueger. 2002. "Estimating the Payoff to Attending a More Selective College: An Application of Selection on Observables and Unobservables." *Quarterly Journal of Economics* 117(4): 1491–1527.

Dynarski, Susan M. 2004. "The New Merit Aid." In *College Choices: The Economics of Where to Go, When to Go, and How to Pay for It*, edited by Caroline Hoxby. Chicago: University of Chicago Press.

Ehrenberg, Ronald G. 2003. "Studying Ourselves: The Academic Labor Market." *Journal of Labor Economics* 21(April): 267–87.

———. 2005. "Method or Madness? Inside the *USNWR* College Rankings." *Journal of College Admissions* 189(Fall): 29–35.

———. 2006. "The Perfect Storm and the Privatization of Public Higher Education." *Change* 38(January/February): 46–53.

Ehrenberg, Ronald G., and Christopher L, Smith. 2004. "Analyzing the Success of Student Transitions from 2-Year to 4-Year Institutions Within a State." *Economics of Education Review* 23(February): 11–28.

Ehrenberg, Ronald G., and Liang Zhang. 2005a. "The Changing Nature of Faculty Employment." In *Recruitment, Retention and Retirement in Higher Education: Building and Maintaining the Faculty of the Future,* edited by Robert Clark and Jennifer Ma. Northampton, Mass.: Edward Elgar.

———. 2005b. "Do Tenured and Tenure Track Faculty Matter?" *Journal of Human Resources* 40(Summer): 647–59.

Ehrenberg, Ronald G., Liang Zhang, and Jared M. Levin. 2006. "Crafting a Class: The Trade-off Between Merit Scholarships and Enrolling Lower-Income Students." *Review of Higher Education* 29(Winter): 195–211.

Elliott, Janet. 2005. "College Admissions Unlikely to be Changed: Lawmakers Bids to Alter 10 Percent Rule are Dying Off." *Houston Chronicle,* May 22, 2005. http://www.chron.com/disp/story.mpl/special/05/legislature/3192821.html.

Governor's Task Force. 2004. *Report of the Governor's Task Force on Higher Education in New Mexico.*

Heller, Donald E. 2004. "Pell Grant Recipients in Selected Colleges and Universities." In *America's Untapped Resource: Low-Income Students in Higher Education,* edited by Richard Kahlenberg. New York: Century Foundation Press.

Hill, Catherine, Gordon Winston, and Stephanie Boyd. 2005. "Affordability: Family Incomes and Net Prices at Highly Selective Private Colleges and Universities." *Journal of Human Resources* 40(Fall): 769–90.

Jack Kent Cooke Foundation. 2005. "Foundations Begin $7 Million Dollar Initiative to Give Community College Students New Opportunities at America's Best Colleges and Universities." News Release, April 13, 2005. Lansdowne, Va.: Jack Kent Cooke Foundation.

Jager-Hyman, Joie. 2004. "Pre-College Outreach Programs for Low-Income Students: A Literature Review." Paper prepared for the Advisory Committee on Student Financial Assistance. Boston Mass. (July 2004).

Kahlenberg, Richard D., ed. 2004. *America's Untapped Resource: Low-Income Students in Higher Education.* New York: Century Foundation Press.

———. 2005. "Springtime for Summers." News and Opinion Release, April 12, 2005. New York: Century Foundation.

Kane, Thomas J. 2003. A Quasi-Experimental Estimate of the Impact of Financial Aid on College-Going. *NBER* Working Paper 9703. Cambridge Mass.: National Bureau of Economic Research.

———. 2004. "Evaluating the Impact of the D.C. Tuition Assistance Grant Program." *NBER* Working Paper 10658. Cambridge, Mass.: National Bureau of Economic Research.

Kane, Thomas J., and Peter R. Orszag. 2003. "Funding Restrictions at Public Universities: Effects and Policy Implications." Working Paper. Washington, D.C.: Brookings Institution Press.

Linsenmeier, David M., Harvey S. Rosen, and Cecilia E. Rouse. 2006. "Financial Aid Packages and College Enrollment Decisions: An Econometric Case Study," *Review of Economics and Statistics* 88(February): 126–45.

McPherson, Michael S., and Morton O. Schapiro. 2005. "Watch What We Do (and Not What We Say): How Student Aid Awards Vary With Financial Need and Academic Merit." Paper presented at the Opening Opportunity or Preserving Privilege: The Ambiguous Potential of Higher Education conference. Chicago. (June 2005).

Nutting, Andrew. 2005. "Relative Tuition Levels and the Educational Focus of First-Time Full Time Community College Students." *Cornell Higher Education Research Institute* Working Paper 81. Cornell, N.Y.: Cornell University. http://www.ilr.cornell.edu/cheri.

Pacia, Raymond, and Yassmin Sadeghi. 2005. "Yale Reforms Financial Aid Policy." *Yale Daily News* (March 4, 2005).

Perna, Laura. 2005. "Intervening Early and Successfully." Paper presented at the Access and Persistence Symposium. Washington, D.C. (September 8, 2005).

Rizzo, Michael J. 2006. "State Preferences for Higher Education Spending: A Panel Data Analysis, 1977–2001." In *What's Happening to Public Higher Education,* edited by Ronald Ehrenberg. Westport Conn.: ACE Prager Series on Higher Education.

Shedd, Jessica, and Christina Redmont Daulton. n.d. "A Current Look at Tuition Discounting." Available to NACUBO members at: www.nacubo.org/x99.xml.

Snyder, Thomas D. 2005. *Digest of Education Statistics, 2004.* Washington: U.S. Department of Education.

Stinebrickner, Ralph, and Todd R. Stinebrickner. 2003. "Understanding Educational Outcomes of Students from Low-Income Families: Evidence from a Liberal Arts College with a Full Tuition Subsidy Program." *Journal of Human Resources* 38(Summer): 591–616.

Tebbs, Jerry, and Sarah Turner. 2005. "The Challenge of Improving the Representation of Low-Income Students at Flagship Universities: AccessUVa and the University of Virginia." Paper presented at the Opening Opportunity or Preserving Privilege: The Ambiguous Potential of Higher Education conference. Chicago, Ill. (June 2005).

The College Board, 2005. *Trends in Student Aid 2005.* New York: College Board Publications.

Winston, Gordon C., and Catherine B. Hill. 2005. "Access to the Most Selective Private Colleges for High-Ability Low-Income Students: Are They Out There?" *Williams Project on the Economics of Higher Education* Working Paper DP-69. Williamstown, Mass.: Williams College.

Index

Boldface numbers refer to figures and tables.